CROSSINGS

CROSSINGS

Africa, the Americas
and the
Atlantic Slave Trade

JAMES WALVIN

REAKTION BOOKS

Published by
REAKTION BOOKS LTD
33 Great Sutton Street
London EC1V 0DX, UK

www.reaktionbooks.co.uk

Printed and bound in Great Britain
by TJ International, Padstow, Cornwall

A catalogue record for this book is available
from the British Library

ISBN 978 1 78023 194 5

Contents

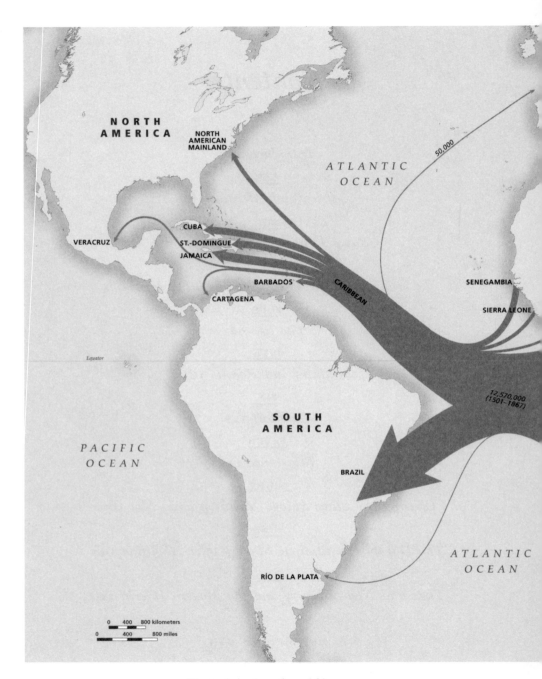

The trade in slaves from Africa, 1501–1900.

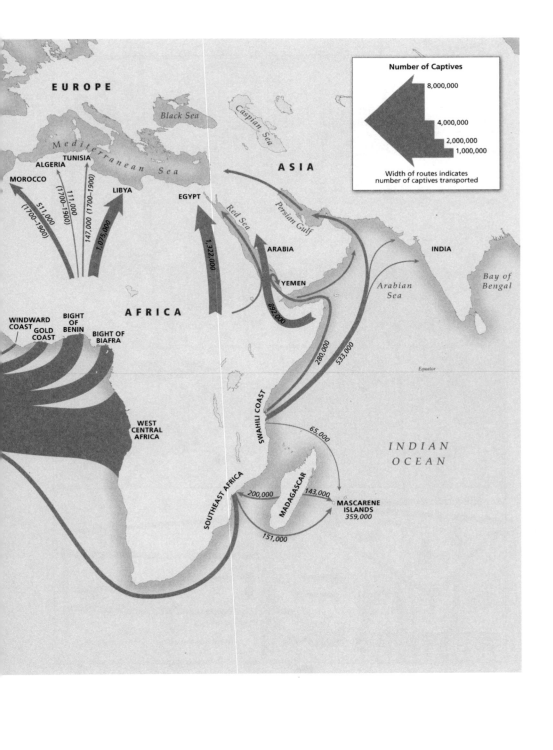

Pl. 1.

Indigoterie, Travail du terrein pour planter l'Indigo et pour le recolter. 35

The backbreaking daily work of a slave; indigo farming and harvesting.

Introduction:
A Different Perspective

Today, the story of slavery in the Americas is a subject of enormous scholarly and popular curiosity on both sides of the Atlantic, generating an astonishing wealth of writing and media attention. The different slave systems which evolved across the Americas were all made possible by the enforced transportation of millions of Africans in an armada of Atlantic slave ships, and in conditions of pestilential horror, to populate and to work key areas of the colonial Americas. The numbers involved are astonishing: 12 million plus loaded onto the slave ships; 11 million plus surviving to landfall. Until the 1820s the number of Africans who had crossed the Atlantic greatly exceeded the emigrant Europeans settling in the Americas. The results of that enslaved labour – more especially the tobacco, rice, sugar, cotton and other crops that it produced – substantially transformed the habits and the economies of the Western world. The consequences for Africa, however, were altogether more ruinous.

All the major European maritime nations were involved in Atlantic slavery. So too were the emergent new powers and states in the Americas, notably the British North American colonies, later the USA, and Brazil. Together they created a system which prevailed from the sixteenth century and went effectively unchallenged for three centuries. Then, in the course of the nineteenth century, there was a dramatic change of heart. The British ended their slave trade in 1807, the Americans in 1808. Thereafter the scene was set for a fluctuating struggle to free the slaves. It was to take fifty years, from full British emancipation in 1838 to the final act of emancipation in Brazil in 1888. Thus, long after the British and the Americans had abolished their oceanic trade in African slaves, slavery remained a profitable, but deeply troubling, presence in the Americas, notably in the USA and Brazil.

In the space of a century, the nations which had perfected both the Atlantic slave trade, and the various American slave systems, turned their back on both. What had once been considered economically vital and morally neutral was, by 1888, universally damned as uneconomic and morally repugnant. Yet why was slavery such an anathema in 1888 but not in 1788 (or 1588)?

Throughout this shift – slow-moving and often hesitant – the British were major (and often the dominant) players, first as slave traders, then as abolitionists. Indeed perhaps the most perplexing issue of all in this story is how Britain, the great slave-trading power of the eighteenth century, became the pre-eminent force for abolition in the nineteenth century.

What follows is an attempt to explain the rise and fall of this slave system. Throughout, I have been at pains to stress the role of the Africans themselves, too often viewed merely as victims, with little role or agency in the entire story of enslavement and freedom. Africans were central in ways that are not often considered. First, it has been esti-mated that about 90 per cent of the people entering the Atlantic slave ships had been acquired through commercial transactions with African traders. Moreover, the story that followed, on the Atlantic ships and especially in the colonial settlements of the Americas, was shaped not simply by what slave traders and slave owners *wanted*, but by how the African victims reacted to their enslaved conditions. The story of slavery in the Americas is the story of Africans and their descendants coping with and resisting the enslavement that trapped them.

It is an astonishing story, and it becomes more remarkable the more we learn about it. But this was not always apparent, even to pro-fessional historians. It is really only in the past forty years that Atlantic slavery has become a subject of widespread academic and popular interest: a major topic in undergraduate and graduate history teaching and a subject which regularly appears in the media and public debate.[1] In large part, this is because we now know so much more about slav-ery and the slave trade. Indeed, the sheer volume of information about the topic is sometimes overwhelming, though hardly surprising since it concerns the peoples and economies of three continents – Europe, Africa and the Americas – drawn together in a complex trad-ing and human nexus over a period of four centuries. The slave trade helped to transform the face of all three continents. The millions of people removed from Africa toiled to tap the fruitful environment of the tropical and semi-tropical Americas, and all for the economic betterment of Europe. Many key features of the modern world which we now take for granted (the human face of the Americas, the food-ways of the world, the questions of lingering poverty across swathes of sub-Saharan Africa – all these and many more) have historical roots which take us back to the story of slavery and the Atlantic slave trade. It is a story which we can now discuss with great precision, thanks largely to the extraordinary *Trans-Atlantic Slave Trade Database*. This dusty-sounding title is in fact a dazzling piece of historical research and reconstruction (and is itself an example of some of the major trans-formations in the study of history at large in recent years). Along with all other scholars in the field, I am greatly indebted to the historians behind that project, and this book has emerged in large part via the evidence embedded in that database.

The commemorations of the bicentenary of the abolition of the British slave trade in 2007 left a number of serious historical questions unanswered. First, and most complex, why did Britain, the nation which had come to dominate the North Atlantic slave trade by, say 1783, turn its back on that trade within a mere generation? Even more puzzling perhaps is the fact, which has become clearer with subsequent scholar-ship, that the Atlantic slave trade did *not* end in 1807. The last Africans stepped ashore from a slave ship (in Cuba) in 1866. What was so im-portant about the British abolition of the slave trade in 1807, and the American in 1808, if, by other means, Africans *continued* to be ferried across the Atlantic? Moreover, slavery itself thrived long *after* 1807. The British ended colonial slavery in 1838, American slavery survived until the Civil War, and slavery in Cuba lasted until 1886, in Brazil until 1888. Why, then, the great fuss about 1807? What was so virtuous about the abolition of 1807 when it left millions of people mired in slavery across the Americas?

The following discussion about slavery and the slave trade is con-cerned solely with slavery in the Atlantic world: the history of Africans carried into the Americas. There were other forms of slavery which tend to go unnoticed in the shadow of Atlantic slavery. We know, for example, that Europeans initially enslaved native peoples in the Americas. Indeed, it was rising concern about the Spanish enslavement of Native American peoples in the sixteenth century that helped to persuade Spanish settlers and officials to turn to African slaves as an alternative. Equally, a large quantity of Europeans travelled to the Americas as unfree people: prisoners of war, indentured servants and others tied to the land or to owners for some years. Yet all this was overshadowed – dwarfed, really – by the sheer scale of African slavery.

The number of Africans who became American slaves was enormous, and in the process Africans, and their local-born descendants, became so ubiquitous in the colonial Americas that the assumption developed that to be black was to be a slave. Yet there were large and growing numbers of black and mixed race freed people. The consequential mix – more striking in some regions than others (more notable in Brazil, for example, than in North America) – does not diminish the critical point that slavery in the New World became ethnically defined. To be a slave was to be black; and to be black, it was assumed, meant being a slave. The converse was also true. To be white was to be free.

There were other parts of the world, however, where such associations did not apply – or rather did not apply in the same way. Slavery in sub-Saharan Africa, obviously, could not be defined in the same way. Similarly, there were parts of North Africa where slavery was the lot of white people, seized by Barbary pirates roaming in the eastern Mediterranean, and out into the Atlantic. Slavery under Islam had not traditionally been demarcated by ethnicity, though a flourishing Islamic slave trade developed in moving black Africans to the slave merchants on the west and the east coast of Africa. The simple and obvious point here is that slavery took many different forms, and this was true in all kinds of historical epoch. It was true in the classical world of Greece and Rome and in the story of medieval European serfdom and slavery, not to mention the myriad forms of slavery to be found in other continents (including among the aboriginal peoples of the Americas and of Africa before the European incursions). In any number of different societies, people found themselves consigned to bondage for a host of reasons, often after considerable journeys from their place of enslavement, and bequeathing that bondage to their children. Slavery was unexceptional and commonplace long before the first African slaves were shipped to the Americas.

Nonetheless, what emerged on the plantations of the Americas was very unusual indeed. Only in the Americas did slavery come to be defined by colour. Roman and Greek slaves were generally indistinguishable from their owners, but no one could mistake an eighteenth-century Jamaican planter for one of his slaves. Nor would a Jamaican slave be confused with the master. Each had their own defining ethnic characteristics – and those characteristics were what made American slavery different.

There is another feature of slavery in the Americas that distinguishes it from other forms of slavery. Every single one of the eleven million people who entered the Americas as a slave had endured a prolonged oceanic crossing of undreamt-of terror. There were, it is true, other peoples shipped into bondage, in the Indian Ocean and in Asia. But the scale of the Atlantic slave trade, the length of the voyages, the prolonged periods spent on board a ship *even before* the vessel cast off for the Americas, all created a hellish experience. The levels of sickness and death en route, in dirty stable-like conditions, were compounded by a brutal shipboard regime. For months on end, this had been the toxic experience of every single African who landed in the Americas.

The traumatic experience at sea was an apprenticeship served by all the Africans involved for bondage in the Americas. In the age of sail, long-distance oceanic travel was normally a terrifying experience, but little came close to the Atlantic slave ships for the scale and intensity of suffering they imposed on their African prisoners. Quite apart from the impersonal terrors, and the filth of a crowded slave ship, the experience was made worse by the poisonous relations between African captives and sailors. With a few exceptions, it was a relationship defined by fear and loathing, one side for the other, and always lubricated by violence. It set the pattern for what was to follow in the Americas.

Africans greatly outnumbered the crew on the slave ships. Africans and their children (with some notable exceptions) also outnumbered their masters and employers on the plantations. Herein lies another of slavery's great paradoxes. How could a small handful of sailors maintain control over a ship full of resentful Africans at sea? And how did small bands of white men and their managers control gangs of slaves in the fields? Was violence and fear the only, or the dominant, means by which slavery functioned? If so, how could it possibly be efficient?

There are, then, certain critical questions which need to be explored for a fuller understanding of Atlantic slavery, and this book has emerged from a variety of questions which have continued to puzzle historians. The more we know about slavery, the more troublesome and unclear many of those questions appear to be. What follows is thus an attempt to explore some of the major issues lurking behind the remarkable story of slavery and the slave trade in the Atlantic world. I begin from an assumption which, when I first worked on slavery forty years ago, seemed unclear, but which today seems glaringly obvious: that slavery is a topic of extraordinary historical importance, which has a resonance clean around the Atlantic littoral and which continues to exercise a troubling influence right down to the present day. How did that come about?

ONE

Africa and Africans

On 19 July 1545, the *Mary Rose*, pride of Henry VIII's navy, set sail from Portsmouth to confront a large French invasion fleet. Transformed by a costly refit, the vessel now boasted the addition of heavy canons among her total of 96 guns. But within minutes, and before the monarch's own eyes, the *Mary Rose* keeled over and sank in the Solent, suddenly and without any obvious warning or cause, taking 500 men to their deaths. An abundance of valuable ordnance settled under 6 fathoms (11 m) of water, and though initial salvage efforts yielded some rigging, the valuable guns lay deep and apparently irretrievable. A year later, the Admiralty engaged a Venetian salvage expert, Piero Paolo Corsi, and his team of divers to locate and retrieve the guns, giving them a broad remit to explore other wrecks in the area. A specialist diver, Jacques Francis, was brought in by his Venetian master specifically to lead the salvage of the *Mary Rose*, and he and his fellow divers managed to raise a large number of sunken valuables to the surface. Disputes soon arose, however, about the ownership and value of some of the items raised from the seabed.

These arguments found their way in February 1548 before the High Court of Admiralty in London. A key witness was the head diver, Jacques Francis, but his evidence was instantly challenged: he was an African, 'an infidel borne and so ys commonlye reputyd and taken of all men knowing hym'. He 'was not christenyd. And therefore . . . no credite nor faithe ought to be geven to his Sayenges'. How could an African pagan give honest testimony in an English, Christian court? The Court of Admiralty dismissed these objections however, determining to listen to Francis's word as it would any other witness.[1] Jacques Francis's evidence, translated from an Africanized form of Portuguese, revealed that he was a slave, and that he had been born, about twenty years earlier, on the 'Insula de Gynney' – Arguin Island – off the African coast of Mauritania. This was the very spot where a century before, in 1445, the Portuguese had set up their first African trading post.

This small and apparently insignificant event raises a number of puzzling questions. What was a Portuguese-speaking African doing, living and working in Europe in the first place? Was it significant that his owner was Italian? And was it not odd that an English court had to decide whether to accept the evidence of a non-Christian – an African 'pagan'? The questions prompted by Jacques Francis in 1548 begin to make sense when we understand what had unfolded on the Atlantic coast of Africa over the previous century.

Long before they set foot on the West African coast, Europeans had distinct ideas about Africa, many of them fanciful. Equally, African people and African goods – gold, incense and myrrh, for example – had for centuries found their way to Europe along tortuous overland routes. But it was the mythologies as much as the realities of Africa which continued to maintain a powerful grip on the European imagination. What precisely *did* Europeans know or think about Africa – and its inhabitants?

From the tenth century onwards, information about sub-Saharan Africa had spasmodically filtered into Europe via Arabs travelling those routes. In the same period, on a more intellectual level, there was a steady accumulation of knowledge by the great traditions of Arab geographical studies. Most notably, the first Arabic account of the Western Sudan (the vast savannah land lying between the forest and the Sahara) had been brought to Europe as early as the tenth century. Thereafter scholars accumulated ever more Arab scholarship about Africa. Though much remained untranslated, occasional Arabic accounts were translated and became available in educated and courtly circles in southern Europe. The most famous account was *Description of Africa* by Leo Africanus, a Maghribi whose extensive travels in Africa ended abruptly when he was enslaved by Christians in the Mediterranean. His real identity – and his real story – have proved of continuing fascination to scholars, but his word, in various languages and forms, became hugely influential from the mid-sixteenth century in shaping images of Africa in the educated European mind. Available in Italian in 1550, editions were available in Latin, French and English fifty years later. Much later it appeared in German. It was a book, claims Natalie Zemon

Davis, which 'continued to shape European visions of Africa, all the more strongly because it came from someone who had lived and travelled in those parts'.[2] By 1600, other Arabic descriptions of Africa had begun to appear in European centres of learning.[3] But such accounts were, in the sixteenth century, complemented by reports of a different kind: eyewitness accounts by European sailors and merchants (led by the Portuguese) edging their way along the coast of West Africa.

The European exploration of the West African coastline was pioneered by the expansive Portuguese in the early fifteenth century, inspired by commercial speculation, by an urge to explore, and fuelled by a religious enthusiasm for outflanking the dominance of Islam in the eastern Mediterranean. The Portuguese were aware of the vastness of the continent they were seeking to circumnavigate and knew that their maritime ventures were risky. Encouraged by Prince Henry the Navigator, successive voyages brought under Portuguese control a number of Atlantic islands and opened up ever more distant locations on the African coast.

Although that coastline remained a vast, dangerous and largely uncharted expanse, and the African interior a region of unimaginable size and variety, Europeans had long been familiar with the concept of Africa. They had also been accustomed to the sight of Africans – in Europe. Long before Africans arrived in large numbers in the ports and major cities of Europe, they had dotted the human, graphic and literary landscape of the Western world.

The story of Europe's involvement with West Africa began as one aspect of the remarkable age of European (largely Portuguese) exploration in the fifteenth century, much of it made possible by innovations which evolved from *existing* systems of shipping and also from much older navigational principles. All of this was absorbed into new knowledge and into the experience acquired by simple trial and error in distant waters.[4] The transformation in ship design and construction, for example, had been prompted largely by the growth of maritime commerce between the Mediterranean and the Atlantic. New types of ships evolved which were suited both to long-distance oceanic sailing and to complicated coastal navigation. Spanish and Portuguese shipbuilders adapted older types of vessels, constructing ships capable of carrying bulky cargoes, yet which had greater manoeuvrability. As the early voyagers to Africa accumulated experience of the Atlantic's currents and wind systems, this new type of ship, the lateen-rigged caravel, capable of sailing close to the wind, proved its value. Experienced sailors came to regard these ships as perhaps the most seaworthy and versatile vessel available.[5] But the major problems facing voyagers to and along the African coast was not so much the nature of the ship, as the difficulties of navigation. Finding the way at sea posed the greatest of all problems.

The Portuguese exploration and settlement of the Atlantic islands – Madeira, the Azores, the Canaries and the Cape Verde islands – provided invaluable experience of sailing in the Atlantic. But sailing south of Cape Bojador posed serious navigational difficulties. An inhospitable coastline was compounded by the sailors' great fear of not being able to return. Winds and currents which had assisted the early ships' movement south had to be battled against on any return leg. Otherwise, ships had to sail well out to sea, hundreds of kilometres into the Atlantic, to catch a westerly wind for home. And then, with luck, they would find their way back to the Atlantic islands for provisions and recovery before the final leg back to Europe. Though smaller ships made the initial ventures, it was the newer, sturdier caravels that were to make West African exploration safer.[6]

Along with changes in ship construction, the pioneering sailors to West Africa benefited from improvements in navigational techniques. Again, the initial improvements began in the Mediterranean. Most important of all was the magnetic compass (which had been used in the Mediterranean for centuries), enabling ships to sail out of sight of land. Allied to simple measurements of time, made by observing the position of the sun and stars, plus the use of the sandglass to measure hours and half hours, navigators could make manageable approximations of their position. The data acquired was then computed by simple mathematics. Later, printed navigational tables made the task easier.

The development of marine charts – again in the Mediterranean – provided another vital navigational tool. These originated in notes kept by individual pilots, which were widely disseminated, and later issued in printed form, covering the entire Mediterranean. Navigators in the Atlantic, unlike those in the Mediterranean, also needed to know the details of local tides: high and low tides and the flow of tidal streams. Much of this was gleaned initially by reference to the changing cycle of the moon. Sailing in the Atlantic (and northern Europe where – in contrast to the Mediterranean – the coastal shelves and waters changed quickly and dramatically) required mariners to take frequent soundings.

Trailing lead on long lines was vital in waters which were not visually clear and whose depth changed suddenly and unexpectedly. The lead weights were also designed to retrieve samples from the ocean bed. From the fifteenth century onwards Atlantic sailors edged along the shoreline, effectively 'with one foot on the bottom'.[7]

The acquisition of information and experience in strange waters was passed on to subsequent voyagers by word of mouth, through commercial discussion and, eventually, in print. New maps and charts, new or refined instruments, printed accounts of voyages, navigational almanacs – all and more provided an increasingly accessible corpus of knowledge and experience for sailors and merchants about to set out for the African coast. All this, especially the necessary instrumentation, took time to develop and evolved in response to the systematic pursuit of sailing routes along, and eventually around, Africa. The modification of the quadrant and astrolabe for use in the Atlantic was an obvious example of adaption to new circumstances. Successive navigators began to mark the position of the Polar star when they reached particular African capes, rivers or islands, and that evidence was added to new navigational aids made or drafted for later voyages. By 1473, the Portuguese had a table of coastal latitudes as far south as the equator. Successive voyages brought a growing understanding of the entire coast of West Africa and by 1500, the Portuguese had also developed proficient nautical charts for the entire African coast north of the Congo.[8]

Literate pilots throughout Europe had long kept notes about their work: about the necessary features of the sea, the shore and prevailing conditions. Known as 'rutters' (*roteiros* in Portuguese), they became an invaluable aid for all sailors – especially after the widespread introduction of printed versions in the late fifteenth century.[9] From one voyage to another the Portuguese had developed these *roteiros*, which were effectively books of sailing directions outlining sailing routines, obstacles and dangers. Despite the initial secrecy surrounding these books, they were soon copied by the Dutch and by the English and helped to provide a basis for the cartography of the coastal waters of Africa, the very area which was to become the slave routes along the Atlantic coast of Africa. The *roteiros* contained not only incredibly detailed navigational (and human) information about the African coast, but also specified what remained *unknown*. One such, written between 1505 and 1508, remarked of a river in modern-day Ivory Coast that it has a small mouth, but as we are not accustomed to enter it and have no practical knowledge of it, we will therefore not write about that which is unknown to us.

The *roteiros* described in very great detail what a ship could expect to see and encounter: distances between specific locations; the positions of hills and villages; clusters of trees; streams running to the ocean; the depths of river estuaries; the size and colour of cliffs; the shallowness of coastal waters ('the depth near the shore is thirty or forty fathoms, but it is less than two leagues out at sea'). The bay at the town of Samaa (today's Shama in Ghana) 'is full of shallows and a ship should anchor in ten or twelve fathoms on a clean sandy bottom a league from the shore and not go further in'.[10]

On top of this growing abundance of navigational advice and information, experienced navigators continued to use traditional methods of seafaring: looking out for 'the colour and run of the sea, the kinds of fish and seabirds . . . the varieties of seaweed which they encountered, and so forth'.[11] Captains regularly entered into their logs fresh sightings of birds – an augury that they were approaching land. It was then that the ship's eyes needed to be alert, with men sent aloft, and others positioned in the bow, to scan the waters and horizon for any sign of breakers – and inevitable shoals.[12] When he approached the African shore in 1750, John Newton took regular soundings from the seabed, writing to his wife that: 'The passage from England has not been the shortest, but remarkably pleasant, *and free from disaster*.'[13] Like every Atlantic sailor, from the days of the Portuguese pioneers to the mid-nineteenth century, Newton knew that whatever their skills and good fortunes, disaster was always close at hand even for the most knowledgeable and experienced of mariners. And nowhere was this more evident than along the Atlantic coast of Africa, with its natural hazards on land and at sea.

Little by little, the Portuguese moved along the West African coast, south of Mauritania, past Senegal and Gambia until, at the southern edge of present-day Liberia, the coast swings east, along today's Ivory Coast and the Gold Coast. Here the European ships entered what was to be known as the Slave Coast – the Bight of Benin – thence on to the massive Niger delta, before sailing south again as the African coast curves ever further south, along a line that drops past Cameroon, Gabon, onward past the mighty delta of the Congo River and on to

Angola. The distances are immense: some 8,000 km along the African coast, measured as a straight, uninterrupted or uneventful line. But no sailing voyage following that line could ever hope to be uneventful. There were contrary currents, offshore winds, Atlantic breakers, hidden shoals and reefs – all these and more pushing and tugging the tiny sailing ships against their masters' instructions. Battling against the elements was, of course, the commonplace of oceanic sailing everywhere. But for pioneers, it all took place in a climate of unknowing and of learning something new, day by day, voyage by voyage. Gradually, with the accumulation of experience, know-how, good seamanship and good luck, the Europeans learned how to nose their way along the entire African coast. By 1460, the Portuguese were trading in Sierra Leone, and twenty years later they had entered the Congo. By 1488, Bartholomew Diaz had rounded the Cape. At the end of the century, Vasco da Gama had both rounded the Cape and sailed north along the East African coast, and thus made contact with the existing trade routes of the Indian Ocean, with their links to India and even beyond to China.

There was, however, more than enough to occupy the Portuguese on the Atlantic coast, and their presence there initiated a wider European drive towards trade and dominion in the area. Soon a complexity of European national and commercial groups hurried to explore and exploit the African coastline. Some voyages were dispatched with Spanish backing, some with Italian money and others with papal blessing. The aim was profitable trade, and among the commercial items acquired they all bought African slaves, and no one showed any sense that here was a business which posed ethical problems. In the 1450s, the Venetian Ca'da Mosto recorded that he had acquired ten to fifteen slaves in return for one horse.[14] If contemporaries had doubts about their involvement (admittedly very modest in extent) with African slaves, they rarely mentioned them. This early, small-scale European engagement with African slavery on the coast was made easy, 'normal' even, by the fact that African slavery was ubiquitous and went largely unchallenged.

To strengthen their commercial and territorial ambitions, the Portuguese had embarked on their African adventures armed with papal approval. A papal bull of 1442 had granted Portugal a monopoly on any discoveries in Africa. Ten years later, Pope Nicholas v, alarmed at the threat from an expansive Islam, granted Portugal the bull *Dum Diversas* (Until Different) of 1452, authorizing them to secure infidels and 'other unbelievers who were inimical to Christ' and 'to reduce their persons to perpetual slavery'. Scholars have argued about the full meaning of the bull, but there seems little doubt it was aimed at sub-Saharan Africans. Three years later, it was followed by the *Romanus Pontifex* (From the Roman Bishop), now widely accepted as 'the charter of Portuguese imperialism'.[15] It proved to be what was effectively a blank cheque for Portugal's dealings with non-Christian peoples. As if to compound papal support, there was ample financial and commercial assistance from Italy for Portuguese expansion. The fall of Constantinople had cut off the great Genoese financiers from their investments in the eastern Mediterranean, and henceforth they looked westwards, to the Atlantic islands and, later, to the even greater speculative prospects on the far side of the Atlantic. Thus Portugal developed its African trade equipped with both papal support and Genoese money.

On the African coast itself, Europeans encountered local Africans, who, like the ocean and the coastline, were depicted by generations of outside visitors as strange objects to be studied and approached with great caution. Generations of sailors, merchants and military men wrote at length about Africans in all their physical and 'exotic varieties' as they saw it: their nakedness or their clothing, their commerce and products, their beliefs (or apparent lack of them), their imagined virtues and vices. But one fact remained central to all subsequent dealings with Africans. It quickly became clear that Europeans could not expect easily to cow or overawe the people fringing the Atlantic coast, even when those seaborne strangers possessed overwhelming firepower and weaponry.

Information about the African coast, and about the people living there, increased enormously as trade to and from the coast expanded. Sailing to and along the African coastline, navigating the inshore waters, dealing with African merchants and traders – all became well-honed routines among thousands of European merchants and sailors. This growing merchant marine went about its business in a highly efficient fashion, captains and crew armed with the latest equipment, guides and assistance for the waters, currents, winds and peoples of West Africa. Europeans familiarized themselves with the slaving coast, acquiring experience and know-how: what to do and what not to do, how best to stay alive and to thrive commercially in what was, almost invariably, a hostile physical and social world. They quickly learned that the African societies they faced and traded with varied enormously. From the first, the Europeans, on board ship or those growing numbers who lived on the shore, most notably in the great forts which they built, had to remain alert. If they survived the dangers of the sea, they faced the ubiquitous dangers posed by African disease – and by hostile Africans. As if all that were not enough, they were threatened by dangers posed by other Europeans, especially during those long periods when Europeans were at war with each other and sought to gain military advantage over their enemies in all corners of the colonial world.

One indirect result of the increased Portuguese presence on the African coast was the number of Africans taken back to Portugal itself. Indeed, in the century after 1441, Africans could be found scattered across Portugal, sometimes working at menial tasks, but often, too, deployed as exotic and decorative items in the homes of the wealthy and influential. African servants, dressed in suitably eye-catching attire, signified their owners' position and status. The rich, and ruling elites, had traditionally asserted their positions by lavish displays, and by the early sixteenth century there was nothing more eye-catching or exotic than a liveried African. The Portuguese court quickly absorbed imported Africans into their various palaces and courtly routines. Africans worked as domestics and court jesters, as pages and as servants 'in the royal apothecaries, kitchens, gardens and stables'. They were deployed as musicians, dancers and cooks. (King João III presented his new Queen Catherine with a black pastry chef in 1526.) The same Queen also gave black slaves as gifts to her favourites and to relatives. This black presence at the Portuguese court was not simply a display of lavish wealth and royal standing, for it also served to remind observers that the monarch ruled far beyond Portugal and was master/mistress of distant dominions and trading posts, however tenuous control of those places might be in reality.[16]

The vogue for employing Africans and their descendants as domestics, as fashionable acquisitions and as status symbols for the rich and powerful, spread across Europe in the sixteenth century. Most, initially at least, were slaves, and worked and jested at royal courts from Lisbon to London. And although it is true that many were used in menial labouring tasks, it was the African as an eye-catching exotic social artefact that is best remembered – largely of course because, as possessions of the wealthy and ruling elite, they entered the documentation and the iconography of the period. Yet the role of Africans as items of luxurious display and adornment also tells us something more profound, namely that African slaves were not vital or important as labouring people in Europe. There was no fundamental demand for African labour – free or enslaved – in mainland Europe, and there was no pressing reason to import Africans to Europe merely to labour. There were, it is true, some exceptions to this rule, notably in the back-breaking efforts required to drain the Algarve in Portugal. But this was an unusual case on a continent where labour was, by and large, cheap and plentiful. African labour was not required in Europe.

One stretch of African coastline which was very well known to Europeans – the North African shore of the Mediterranean – had been integral to European history, trade and commerce for centuries. The Mediterranean Sea had long served to incorporate Africa into the life and economies of Europe. The history of sub-Saharan Africa was, however, so different from that of North Africa that the two have often been portrayed as distinct and discrete entities. The Mediterranean coast of Africa was doubly important, for it not only linked Africa to southern Europe, but its interior trade and overland migration routes linked the Mediterranean to black Africa (that is, sub-Saharan Africa). For centuries a series of arduous overland routes had seen peoples and goods from the south of Africa traverse the vastness of the Sahara (and along the Nile) to the cities and markets of the Mediterranean, thence onwards to Europe – and even further afield. Long before the rise of the Greek and Roman empires, with their own distinct engagement with North Africa, Egypt had spawned a series of civilizations whose cultural legacies influenced Europe.[17]

Even so, when Europeans embarked on their pioneering voyages into the Atlantic, North Africa was both alien and threatening. Clean along the North African coast (and much further south, deep into Africa itself) lay the realm of Islam. In the four centuries after the death of the prophet Muhammad (632 CE), Arab power and Islam had established themselves, hand in hand, across North Africa. Islam also spread south into Africa (in East Africa it spread more easily along the maritime trade routes of the Indian Ocean).

The rise of Islam in Africa had helped to integrate sub-Saharan Africa more closely into the affairs of the north, and thence into the wider world.[18] As Islam crossed the Sahara, it forged links not merely with the people of West Africa but it also opened rich commercial

Cristóvão de Morais, *Juana of Austria with her Black Slave Girl*, 1555, oil on canvas.

potential by engaging with local and regional trading systems. Products from West Africa – especially West African gold – were prized by the world at large. Gold coins, for example, began to usurp silver in Italian states in the mid-thirteenth century, and in northern Europe a century later. The resulting increase in demand for African gold was to be a critical factor in shifting state systems, and power, across large swathes of West Africa.

African gold had long been vital to Europe. From about 1000 – perhaps earlier – gold from the Sudan had provided a vital element in trade and prosperity across North Africa and even into Muslim Spain. It was largely responsible for North Africa, notably the Maghreb, becoming a major economic driving force in the Mediterranean. Inevitably, gold lured Christian and Jewish merchants and traders to the major North African urban centres of trade, from Tunis in the east to Ceuta and Tangier in the west. From there, they had relatively easy access to the ports of Catalonia, Marseilles, Sicily, Venice and Genoa, and to their onwards markets.[19] Those North African-based merchants could also dispatch their own goods south, along existing African trade routes, across the desert, to the edge of sub-Saharan Africa. European goods for sale in North Africa were thus sold into black Africa. It has been claimed that five commodities dominated these routes: gold, black slaves, copper, salt and textiles. The first two – gold and slaves – travelled north; the others moved south. And en route, at towns and oases which were stopping points along the overland trade routes, exotic commodities entered the local market. Leo Africanus himself told how Venetian cloth fetched exorbitant prices at Timbuktu in 1515.[20] People on both edges of this trade – Africans south of the Sahara and Europeans on the northern termini – wanted, and secured, goods and products which originated in societies about which they had no real knowledge.

Above all, Europeans wanted African gold. At the time the Portuguese began their first tentative explorations of the African Atlantic, the need for gold had become a pressing concern for Europe. The ancient sources of gold *within* Europe itself had effectively dried up, and bullion was being exhausted to pay for the expansion of long-distance trade. Perhaps the problem of bullion could be solved by oceanic exploration in the Atlantic?

In the gradual exploration of the African coast, the Atlantic islands off the northwest coast of the continent were to prove vital, both in themselves and in the subsequent history of West African navigation and trade. Even here, the question of African gold was an incentive. The Canaries, for example, had been visited, explored and settled by a range of European powers in the late Middle Ages. The Catalan kingdom of Majorca, the Crown of Aragon, later still the French, all laid claim to the islands. Though each wanted to convert local people to Christianity, each also had an eye on the mythical 'River of Gold' which, legend had it, would lead explorers to the heart of the African gold fields. The Canaries were, then, seen as a route towards African gold – and all this took place long before the better-known Portuguese efforts in the fifteenth century.[21]

When the Portuguese took Ceuta in 1415, they learned a great deal about the city's commercial networks, and about the lands of the Upper Niger and Senegal rivers where gold originated. Prince Henry himself talked openly about acquiring information regarding gold from Moorish prisoners in Ceuta, and how that gold might be accessed by sea. Here was more encouragement for further explorations along the African coast. Of course Portuguese motives for each successive voyage were varied, but the desire to develop access and trade to African gold by sea routes, and thus circumvent the protracted (and Islamic-dominated) trans-Saharan trade routes, was important. Gradually, the Portuguese efforts yielded results.

By 1442, Portuguese traders to West Africa had acquired gold dust on the Mauritanian coast. Although we do not know the volumes involved, by 1457 enough gold had become available for the Lisbon mint to issue the *Cruzade*, a new coin of almost pure gold.[22] As the Portuguese edged ever further along the coast, they encountered a host of new commercial possibilities, but most tantalizing of all were the ubiquitous rumours of gold. They bartered for it with the Tuareg on the Mauritania coast, found it traded on the Senegal and Gambia rivers, and finally, and more abundantly, they discovered that gold from the interior Akan gold fields was to be had in the Gulf of Guinea. Although in every case the gold originated far inland, the Portuguese had made a pioneering breakthrough: they were now trading for gold on the Atlantic coast. Henceforth, African gold began to enter Europe directly, in growing volumes, by sea. Between 1500 and 1520, the Portuguese shipped perhaps 700 kg of gold annually. There were inevitable dips and recessions, and later competition from the discoveries of precious metals in the Americas, but African gold inevitably attracted many other Europeans to the African coast. (This thriving trade in Atlantic gold did not, however, curtail the traditional movement of gold across the Sahara.) The most valuable stretch of coastline was (inevitably perhaps) named the Gold Coast, roughly modern Ghana, and England's new gold coin took the name 'Guinea' when it was first struck in 1663. Eventually, the export value of gold from West Africa was to be surpassed he value of transported slaves, yet African slaves hardly figured he initial commercial ambitions of the early voyagers along the ican coast.

By the mid-fifteenth century, the Portuguese had secured a firm nmercial base at key points on the African coast. They had almost mpleted the construction of their castle at Arguin, a tiny island 80 1 off the coast of Mauritania – ideally located, despite dangerous efs, as a way-station for ships trading further south and east along the ast. In time Arguin was to become a prototype of the fortresses built y most of the European maritime nations at vital locations along stretches of the slaving coast. In its early days Arguin facilitated trade between neighbouring Arabs and seaborne Europeans. The Venetian Cadamosto, working in the service of Prince Henry, paid two visits to Arguin, in 1455 and 1456, noting that, whereas only a few years before, piratical raiders of African villages had seized African slaves to be shipped back to Portugal, such raids had now ended, and 'for some Time past, Peace and Commerce has been restored to them all'. Slaving continued, however, though in an orderly, regulated manner, with Arab traders acting as middlemen. In return for woollen goods, silver, tapestry and grain, the Arabs offered slaves and gold to the European merchant ships.[23] The Portuguese had quickly learned that barter and trade were the means of acquiring slaves (even though those enslaved peoples might have been acquired in Africa via earlier raids or warfare). Jao Fernandez, instructed by Prince Henry to stay behind and trade on Arguin, made himself familiar with Ahude Meymam, a local trader, and 'learned that he had black slaves who he wished to sell'.[24] From such small beginnings the practice grew of buying Africans from local merchants and middlemen. Jacques Francis, the African diver working on the wreck of the *Mary Rose*, must have been born on Arguin, or brought there from the mainland, at much the same time as the early Portuguese efforts to settle and develop the island. He, too, as we have seen, was a slave; one of a growing number of Africans traded to ship-based Europeans and normally sold by an African middleman, in many cases initially by Arabs. It was already apparent that the best way of obtaining slaves was through trade – not by raiding or fighting but by exchanging imported goods wanted by a local trader. However, someone else – out of sight within Africa – had to do the fighting and the slave raiding. The Portuguese had encountered Muslim merchants offering slaves who had been captured in warfare and slave raids. The Tuareg, for example, had long been known as slave raiders, attacking societies to the south and traditionally selling their captives into the northern trans-Saharan slave routes. Henceforth, many of those victims were to find themselves sold into the hands of Europeans on the African coast.

The general principle was established: that whatever Europeans needed from Africa, they required the help of Africans. This acquisition of African slaves was an early and simple form of trade and inevitably saw a movement of goods the other way. European goods, and even items from the wider world, entered the local African economy. In the process, a blueprint was established which was to last for centuries. A form of trade and barter evolved between two parties striking a commercial deal. One of the items of trade was the African slave.

Europeans were not surprised to encounter slaves on the African coast. When European explorers and merchants made contact with coastal African peoples, they already knew that slaves were to be had in Africa. Enslaved Africans had found their way to Europe via ancient Saharan slave routes. For centuries, Africans had been bought and sold along the complexity of trading routes which criss-crossed the Sahara before ending up in the Arab slave markets of North Africa. The overland routes proved an amazingly durable slaving system, lasting more than a millennium and ensnaring more than 3.5 million people.[25]

The desert caravans, so linked in the popular mind with images of the Sahara, were the means of transporting goods across immense stretches of desert, connecting black Africa to the Mediterranean. African slaves were generally used, en route, as porters to transport other goods in the caravan: they were, at once, both porters and slaves heading to market. The inhospitable terrain was criss-crossed by well-established overland routes threading their way between oases and small settlements which permitted rest and refreshment from the rigours of a desert crossing. Caravan routes crossed Africa in various directions. They linked ancient African kingdoms in the west (Ghana, *c.* 1000 CE, Mali, *c.* 1300 CE and Sudan in the sixteenth century) to the

Red Sea in the east. The more familiar routes traced north–south axes, between the Mediterranean and the southern edge of the Sahara. Both in the south and the north, caravans made contact with other markets and merchants, with links onwards to other societies. Some of these overland African links were ancient. A pastoral people living around the north of Lake Chad were, for a millennium, the main suppliers of slaves from West Africa to the Islamic world of the north. In return, they acquired horses, which they used on slave raids. The ancient kingdom of Ghana also had large-scale slave-trading systems which fed the victims onwards to northern Islamic traders. There were major towns and cities (Gao, for example, at the junction of modern Mali and Niger) which became trading posts for the departure of slave caravans heading north to cross the Sahara.

These ancient overland trade routes were, however, more complex than they might seem at first sight. The caravan journeys and the commerce they carried were broken up into different legs or sectors, with goods and slaves being traded to a new group of traders, who then set out on the next part of the journey. African slaves thus passed through various hands, and were sold and exchanged a number of times, long before they found themselves offered for sale at the major slave markets in the Mediterranean. This pattern was to characterize slave trading in the era of the Atlantic slave trade, with Africans passing from hand to hand – within Africa, on the coast, on the ships, and then in the Americas. Even there, at landfall in the Americas, African slaves were resold to new owners.

These traditional African slave-trading routes may seem very different from the later Atlantic trade. Yet both had features in common. Both were dangerous and costly of life. Equally, trans-Saharan slaves, and those crossing the Atlantic, underwent excruciating uncertainty. In the protracted business of enslavement and of being moved (often huge distances), African slaves did not know, from one day to another, what was happening to them, who owned them, who might be their master tomorrow – or even where they were or where they were going. From the first moment of enslavement, they lived in a climate of great insecurity. Nor was this dispelled when they settled into their 'final' workplace because, even then, slaves remained the material possession of their owners. Slaves might be shuffled around in the latest turn of their owner's commercial or family fortunes: sold, bequeathed, inherited – and removed once again. A slave who might seem to be

'Turks taking the English' and 'Selling Slaves in Algiers', from W. Okeley,
Eben-ezer, or, A Small Monument of Great Mercy (1675).

enjoying security – when rooted in a position for years, with family, partners and children close by – could never be certain how long that good fortune might last. The life of a slave – at enslavement, during transportation by land or water and at work in a settled location – was *always* subject to capricious change and upheaval beyond their control. Theirs was, from beginning to end, a life overshadowed and threatened by insecurity.

Though the evidence for the pre-modern Saharan trade is difficult to assess accurately, it is clear enough that the slaves' suffering and mortality on desert crossings were enormous. Before the tenth century, the evidence is largely archaeological; in the following four centuries it is provided by North African Arabic sources. Thereafter, there is data from European sources on the Atlantic coast.[26] But whichever evidence we turn to, one point is abundantly clear: slavery and slave trading were widespread south of the Sahara long before the Europeans appeared on the coast in the fifteenth century. One eminent historian of African slavery has claimed that anything between 30 and 60 per cent of Africa's population were slaves, though such extraordinarily high figures are impossible to verify.[27] It is also clear that, while slavery was commonplace in Africa, it took many different forms, ranging from being one feature of kinship at one extreme, through to chattel slavery at the other. Similarly, people *became* slaves by a number of routes. A desperate family – and great areas were prone to natural disasters and consequent hunger – might hand over children in return for money or food, in an arrangement which might be temporary (a pawn) or permanent: a slave.

More familiar, however, were the violent means of enslavement: raids, attacks, warfare, inter-village raiding parties (sometimes using mercenaries for the task) – all yielding prisoners who then became slaves to be sold on for profit to other societies in need of labour. Here was a system which, later, was ideally suited to provide slaves to European traders on the coast. Through all this complexity of African enslavement patterns, and the great variety of slave systems, it becomes impossible to generalize about 'African slavery'. Slaves were to be found as part of a massive slave holding – upwards of 1,000 strong among traders on the edge of the Sahara – or in the form of individual children, temporarily housed as pawns in a more prosperous household. There was, quite simply, no single or simple African system of slavery, and nor was there a particular kind of slave work. Slaves worked at a range of tasks. Females were often used as domestic workers or as concubines; men were put to strenuous labouring tasks, in fields and in salt mines, and used as soldiers. Some slave-holding African societies, like classical Rome, also employed slaves as major administrators and officials. But whatever their work, and however small or large their grouping, slaves and slave holding went unchallenged across large tracts of the continent. There was nothing unusual or surprising, then, when African slaves were offered to the early European sailors and traders at a number of locations on the Atlantic coast. The Portuguese found plenty of Africans willing to sell slaves as part of their everyday trade.

Slaves brought to Arguin were supplied by Moors already active in the Saharan slave trade. Further south, on the Senegal River, the Portuguese encountered a local ruler, supporting himself by slave raids, who was keen to exchange slaves for horses. Local Wolofs paid the Portuguese upwards of fourteen slaves for a single horse. When the Portuguese reached the Gold Coast in 1471, they found both gold and slaves. This initial Portuguese involvement in slave trading was, however, largely coastal – shipping and selling Africans from one part of coastal Africa to another. For instance, the Portuguese sold Africans from Benin, from the Niger delta, and from Igbo country, to the Akan people of the Gold Coast, who, in turn, paid with gold. Further south, after 1483, the Portuguese established trading relations with the king of Kongo (roughly modern nothern Angola and the Cayo republic), whose own power base was founded on slavery. By 1526, they were acquiring upwards of 3,000 Africans a year, and shipping them from Kongo to work on new sugar plantations established by Portuguese settlers on the island of São Tomé in the Gulf of Guinea.[28]

Thus, from the 1440s onwards, small numbers of Africans found themselves on board European vessels and shipped out of their African homelands, some heading to other coastal regions of Africa, others to the Portuguese islands in the Atlantic and even to Portugal itself. And through most of these transactions between outsiders and Africans, and indeed throughout much of the later history of the Atlantic slave trade, there is little evidence that contemporaries felt that the slave trading was wrong, or frowned upon.

Africans transported to the Atlantic islands provide the link to what was to follow in the Americas. Europeans had settled the Azores, Madeira, the Canaries, the Cape Verde islands and then, and most crucially for this story, São Tomé and Príncipe in the Gulf of Guinea. There, in the pioneering days of exploration and settlement, Africans were imported to undertake the harsh labour required to bring the new lands into manageable settlement and productive cultivation. The need for labour was accentuated by the introduction of one particular crop – sugar cane – transplanted into some of those islands. Wherever sugar cane was introduced, it created a local demand for a strong and durable labour force. Though no one could have foreseen the enormity of what was to follow, the pattern was quickly established: the cultivation of sugar cane and African slave labour seemed ideally suited to each other.

In 1486, the Portuguese settled São Tomé in the Gulf of Guinea. Along with the neighbouring island of Príncipe, São Tomé was a suitable stopping place for ships, en route south along the African coast to Kongo and Angola. In addition, the island had fresh water and a luxuriant environment. It had rich potential in itself, and was ideally located for the provisioning of vessels trading up and down the African coast. Later, São Tomé was to be vital for slave ships making their last port of call before heading west to the Americas. Sugar cane proved an ideal crop for São Tomé, but it was a crop which required a plentiful supply of cheap, manageable labour – and one which could be replenished easily. Lying only 320 km off the African coast, the answer was obvious. The last piece in the jigsaw was slotted into place in the form of African slaves.

The story of sugar and slavery is closely linked to changing patterns of material consumption in Europe, though sugar was more than a culinary ingredient, having long been part of Western pharmacology and an ingredient in a range of medicines, as it had been in Arab medicines. Europeans had first acquired a taste for cane sugar via the Crusades, when sugar had been brought back from Palestine. But it was Islam, not Christianity, which drove sugar westward, on the back of the Arab expansion, with sugar cultivation developing around the Mediterranean, notably in the Maghreb and in southern Spain. Cane sugar also reached Western Europe along traditional trading routes, from India and Persia, for instance, but sugar from all these sources was costly and well beyond the reach of all but the rich. Nonetheless, these exotic centres of sugar production had established a European taste for sweetness: for adding sugar as an ingredient to a range of drinks and foodstuffs.[29]

The technology of sugar cultivation and production was well known by the time the Europeans moved out into the western Atlantic, though producing cane sugar was unusual in that it was part agricultural (growing sugar cane in the fields) and part industrial (processing that sugar cane into sugar). The process had been perfected on plantations, but they, in turn, were labour-intensive. It was back-breaking work which stretched out over a yearly cycle. The clearing of land, then planting fields with regular lines of sugar cane, the systematic tending and manuring of the plants and then, hardest of all, the harvesting of the tall sugar cane by gangs working with machetes, the cane then collected and trundled to the sugar factory.

In the Mediterranean the labour problem had been solved by using a mix of free and unfree labour. Sugar plantations were also costly to establish: they needed capital investment and that was available in a number of Italian and Spanish cities, where enterprising merchants and financiers were keen to find new outlets for their money and initiatives. To complete this complex international process, the raw sugar, shipped from its various distant locations to Western Europe, was refined in European port cities – initially in Antwerp, later in the great ports which dominated both the slave trade and the import of sugar into Europe: Bristol, Bordeaux, Liverpool and London. Around this one simple commodity – sugar – there evolved a complex international network. The production, financing and transportation of cane sugar spawned an international industry and forged links between widely separated and apparently unconnected parts of the world. Initially the links were between the Mediterranean and Western Europe; later they were between Europe, Africa and the Americas. Beneath these obvious patterns of trade there lay a much more complex structure of finance and banking: a commercial underpinning of international trade and industry which brought substantial (though often unseen) material rewards to Western Europe.

Small-scale sugar production was, then, a familiar and traditional process at key locations around the Mediterranean, and sugar refinement had found a home in Europe itself. All had been made possible by European financiers whose expertise and money encouraged and increased Europe's appetite for sweetness in all things. The development of the Atlantic islands by Spain and Portugal now offered new locations for sugar cultivation. At first Madeira and the Canaries began to help satisfy the expanding appetite for sugar among European elites, but it was the new Portuguese sugar industry in São Tomé which made the critical leap – by turning to Africa for labour. There, just 320 km away on the African coast, supplies of slaves were on offer in return for the goods imported by European merchants. While the importation of African slaves to São Tomé filled the labour vacuum, it also created a host of new and entirely undreamt-of difficulties: of control, management, housing, feeding and disciplining a hostile and alien labour force. Unlike free labour, slaves had to be maintained throughout the year: they could not be laid off out of season or when work slackened. For all that, São Tomé had the incalculable advantage of having slave labour available more or less on the doorstep.

São Tomé proved an important new stage in the emergence of slavery in the Atlantic world. It was a good locale for sugar cultivation, with sugar experience provided by sugar planters from Madeira and an apparently plentiful supply of slaves from Africa close by. Moreover, the island had already been accustomed to the arrival of African slaves, in transit from Kongo and Old Calabar (in southeastern Nigeria) to the slave markets of the Gold Coast to the north. Throughout the sixteenth century – a time of booming demand for sugar in Europe – São Tomé thrived as a producer of slave-grown sugar. At its height as a sugar producer, its landscape was dotted with 200 sugar mills, and the island's population rose to more than 100,000, 3,000 of them Portuguese.[30] But all this was to end, by mid-century, when competitors in the new settlements in Brazil were able to produce better, and ultimately

35

cheaper, sugar. Unable to compete, many planters from São Tomé undertook the transatlantic move to Brazil, taking their slaves with them. As the island's sugar industry declined, sugar even had to be imported from Brazil, and by 1700 the São Tomé sugar industry had virtually vanished.

From its early days of Portuguese settlement, São Tomé had been an entrepôt, a trans-shipping point, where Africans were gathered and moved onwards to other locations along the African coast. Africans were brought to São Tomé from Kongo and Old Calabar before onward sale on the Gold Coast, where they were exchanged for gold. Here was an early, embryonic, oceanic slave trade, not across the Atlantic, but along the African coast. The numbers of Africans involved in this early European slave trading system along the African coast were relatively small. By 1500, for example, fewer than 2,000 a year had been shipped to Europe or to the Atlantic islands. By the 1520s, a similar number were being landed in São Tomé, but these figures were tiny compared to what was to follow the European settlement of the tropical Americas.[31]

These early days of European slave trading on the Atlantic coast might appear minor, insignificant even (though clearly not for the victims involved). Their importance, however, lay in the foundations which were laid for a distinct kind of slave economy between Europeans and the African societies on the Atlantic cloast. Those ranged from the simplest of agreements with a single African trader – one individual trying to strike a good deal using the handful of slaves in his possession – right through to mighty kings and potentates with powerful armies and commercial systems at their disposal for large-scale enslavement and slave trading. Moreover, most of these transactions for buying and selling slaves, between Africans and the Europeans, looked little different from other forms of slavery with which Europeans had long been familiar closer to home. Europeans knew of slavery in a variety of forms: European domestic slavery in Italian city states, galley slaves in the Mediterranean, Christians enslaved by the Barbary pirates, slaving raids on European ports or on the extremities of the Europe landmass by Mediterranean slavers, and the sentencing of prisoners (especially prisoners of war) to lifetime bondage.

The early European involvement with African slavery had begun and thrived *before* Columbus had crossed the Atlantic, long before the first Africans had been shipped to the Americas to work as slaves. Even so, a pattern had been established. An early Atlantic trade in African slaves had developed, but it was geographically limited, with Africans shipped from one African coastal region to another, to the newly settled Atlantic islands, and to Spain and Portugal. It was, at heart, a *trade*, a commercial deal struck between traders. The first Africans to find themselves on European ships in the Atlantic were items of trade: bought, sold, bartered and exchanged in return for other commodities. Moreover, with the exception of those handfuls of Africans seized as slaves by the earliest explorers and traders, the Africans who passed into European hands were not enslaved initially by the Europeans but by Africans.

These early European encounters with slavery on the African coast were part of a process which enabled Europeans to develop new forms of trade along a huge stretch of coastline. They had found direct access to the vital supplies of African gold, had developed successful sugar production in the Atlantic islands and were even able to flatter the pretensions of fashionable European society by providing them with African slaves to adorn their social world. In the long term, however, these encounters were perhaps more important for laying the basis for everything else that followed: the massive expansion of Atlantic slave trading, and the transformation of African slavery from a small-scale business between coastal Africans and transient Europeans, into a massive, brutal industry with global consequences.

TWO

Slave Trading on the Coast

In the course of the fifteenth century, Europeans greatly expanded their understanding and knowledge of the wider world, of its geography and potential, and of its varied peoples. That growing European understanding derived in large measure from the maritime explorations which were driven forward by events in Europe itself. Maritime Europeans looked to the wider world when their traditional dealings with the East were curbed by the rise and power of Islam in the eastern Mediterranean. A determination – indeed a need – emerged to secure new commercial and trading routes to distant markets and societies. A number of seafaring powers and their commercial interests, led initially by the powerful kingdoms of Portugal and Castile, were determined to enhance their political and economic strength at home by success beyond the seas. But to sail to Eastern markets, Europeans faced the obstacle of rounding Africa.

As they sailed progressively south during that century, Europeans encountered an African coastline of almost unimaginable vastness and physical variety. And it was a coastline which offered great commercial promise, with the added advantage of being a stepping stone onwards to Asia. Step by step, Europeans established a number of trading bases and communities at important points along the African coast. By the end of the fifteenth century, the Portuguese were trading at Arguin and they had rounded the Cape, many thousands of kilometres to the south. At any number of locations in-between, Europeans were busy exploring the geography and the available commercial prospects, but their presence on the African coast was often tentative and fragile. Indeed, throughout much of the era of the Atlantic slave trade, Europeans barely clung to a few places on the westerly edges of the African continent. At first glance, it is tempting to imagine that Europeans exercised a secure and powerful presence, most strikingly in the form of their medieval-like fortresses, which now began to proliferate, especially along the Gold Coast. They also developed a trading and colonial presence in a number of coastal communities, along some of Africa's mighty rivers, and in the towns which slowly grew up around the European settlements. Yet even these towns and forts, symbols of apparent power and domination, are deceptive. What crucially shaped the Europeans' ability to settle, or even to set foot, on the coast was the nature of the topography they encountered and, above all, the assistance and co-operation, or hostility, of the Africans.

Europeans were faced by a diverse physical landscape which presented enormous dangers alongside the seductive commercial prospects. Even the most worldly and experienced of explorers were often daunted by the surprises in store on the coast. At times, the realities of Africa surpassed even the astonishing myths about the continent which had circulated in Europe for centuries. Europeans were surprised to discover that it was a world of 'towns, mosques, river boats, metal foundries, horse traders and armed cavalry', a world of 'expansionist kings' and successful empires not unlike Europe's own.[1] But that is not always what those first explorers thought or saw as they edged gingerly along the coastline. Moreover, much of what they saw was filtered, not so much through the haze of an Atlantic seascape, but through the (often distorting) lens of existing European mythology and expectations.

The coastline itself confirmed one central fact about the continent: here was a place of perplexing variety. For centuries to come, the European experience of Africa was defined primarily by what happened on, or very close to, the coast. With the exception of those who sailed up the rivers, few outsiders ventured into the interior. Even men who were lucky to survive many years on the coast admitted that they had never been more than a few kilometres inland.[2] The European first-hand familiarity was essentially defined by coastal Africa, even though many of the people they encountered and bought as slaves came from distant, inland locations.

In learning about the variety and complexities of the coast, Europeans quickly appreciated that the best – indeed the only – means of successful commerce was via the help and assistance of Africans themselves. In the business of acquiring slaves, or the more basic risks of simple survival in Africa, through to the process of loading and shipping the slaves, European traders and sailors needed local help and expertise. A casual glance at the evidence – of massive slave forts and of ships armed with powerful weaponry – might suggest that Europeans were the dominant force. In fact theirs was a presence which had little strength or command without local muscle and advice. Throughout, the slave traders were clients on the African coast.

Furthermore, the connections forged on the Atlantic coast between outsiders and Africans were more complex and far-reaching than they appeared. African dealings with the seaborne traders formed the last link in commercial and human connections that reached deep into the continent. For Europeans, this was the first point of contact with huge, unknown African networks. Portugal's first major position, the 'very beautiful and powerful fortress' on the island of Arguin,[3] was in effect the terminus of a trading system which stretched across a Sudanese empire reaching from the Atlantic to Ethiopia. Here was an example of what was to follow, later, at a multitude of locations on the coast and throughout the history of the Atlantic slave trade: Europeans only touched the continent's trade routes at their last extremity on the Atlantic coast. The reverse was also true. African coastal traders were making contact with seaborne traders whose own networks stretched to Europe, North America and even to Asia. Both sides, Europeans and Africans, were in effect plugged into human and commercial networks about which they knew virtually nothing, and whose geographic immensity they could hardly imagine.

From first to last, the encounters on the coast formed a two-way commercial business. Local traders wanted the European and Asian goods imported on European ships, and in return, they were happy to provide goods, including African slaves. It was, however, a coastal slave trade which did not fit a single or simple pattern, because commercial and social relations differed from place to place and were determined to a large extent by local physical circumstances, and by what local African communities wanted or allowed. The way slaves were transferred to the ships varied greatly and was largely determined by local geography. But everywhere, and whatever form it took, this movement of enslaved peoples was only possible via the help, approval or agreement of other Africans. Europeans needed local African know-how and experience (mastering the huge Atlantic rollers on the Gold Coast, for example) to fill their ships with goods and slaves. From the first days of exploration, through to the final days of the 'illicit' slave trade,

Europeans realized that, to trade successfully, they needed both to understand the topography of the coast and to co-operate with the people living there.

It was also clear that Europeans visiting the coast were hemmed in by two forces over which they had very little direct control. On the one side lay the physical dangers of Africa – above all, an environment of ferocious disease. Three-quarters of the men arriving to work in the forts were dead within twelve months.[4] From the first, Africa was as physically dangerous as it was commercially promising. Behind the Europeans stretched the enormity of the Atlantic Ocean, with its routes back to the European motherlands and, later, westwards to the lucrative slave markets of the Americas. But the ocean itself was dangerous and unpredictable. For almost four centuries, Europeans on the coast were effectively wedged between the dangers of Africa on the one side and the perils of the deep on the other. That they willingly confronted such persistent dangers, over so long a period, speaks to the commercial potential and promise of Africa.

As Europeans sailed south, beyond the edge of the Sahara, they encountered an ever-changing coastline – and very different peoples. With the huge Senegal and Gambia rivers they also found direct sailing routes into Africa itself. Once beyond the continent's most westerly point, Cape Verde, they began to experience that green lushness we associate with sub-Saharan Africa.

Each coastal region presented different navigational and commercial problems. South of Gambia, the inshore waters had dangerous rocks and shoals – all with risky approaches (and marked thus on modern Admiralty charts.) Further south and east, the coast consists of mile after mile of mangrove swamps, before breaking into accessible beaches close to the Volta River. Here was the start of the 'Gold Coast', the site of fabled wealth, and it was here that Europeans began to dot the coastline with forts. Further east, lagoons stretched as far as the Benin River, which itself provided access to a powerful local kingdom and culture and in time was to afford a lavish supply of slaves and other trading commodities. From Benin, the coast turns east towards the vast Niger delta – 'the biggest mangrove swamp in the world' –

overleaf: A chart and map of the Gold Coast of Guinea from Rio da Corsa to Ro da Volta 1744–46, The prospect of Cape Sta. Appollonia with an insert showing the coast at El Mina with the castle of that town and the fort at St Jago, 1744–6.

The Prospect of Cape St.ª Appollonia. The

a Village   a Village

A Particular Chart of the Coast
of Mina and Cabo Corso

Th Land

S abou R.

Rio Dana

Fort Conadtbrough
St. Iago

Rio Dolce

Fetu R.
Ps

Mouree
Fort Naſsaw

Fort Naſsaw

The Town of Great Comendo
Where the King Reſided

4 D. 45 M   Comendo R.

Mina

Mouree
Fort Royal

Cabo Corce
Caſtle

R.

Scale of 2 Leagues

The Town of
Mina

A C C A N E S

Pars   2

6 D

Cap. Alta
de Torra

Petit Comendo

A F R I C

Doulwaro R.

Comendo R.

Iguira R.

Warshas R.

Adom R.

Iffiny
R

Quaqua Pars

Coſta da Ora

The   G O L D   Adom R.

Axim R.

Iads R.

Comendo

E
C

5 D

Gamma

R. de Suera da Coſta

Beru

Iceing grande
& Villages

Abbiny

Jebbi

C. Appalonia
& Villages
Aſcananann

Aguinare

Fort Unrit

Dague

Fort
Axim

Fort
St. Antonio

Aceera

C. 3 Puntas
Frederickbourg
at Cama

Anta R.

Fort Bodeſteyn

Boutrol
Dickiny

Viliuria

Takoradi

Viliuria

Fort St. Sebaſtian

Santa
Ania
Burre
Anta

grand Comendo

Comendo

Villa de Torra

Burre
Grande

Anishan

THE   G U I N E A   S E A

4 D

...ree B. being at E.N.E. about 1¼ League

B

a Village

ACCANES R. PARS

R S

Cabesterra. R.

Acchimos. R.

Rio da Volta

Aquambous R.

Ningo R.

Sabo R.

E

P A R S

Anguina R.

M. Redonda

Aguata

D

Bya

Bribroru

Aragoa

Occoa

Sabou R.

Fanteen R.

Lampy R.

Accara R.

Guyney

Lou Monte

Ponpena

Chambre

Cocke

Amis. Villages Mission

Ant. de Ziebra

la Grande

Iames Fort

Fort Creveceur

Chrissansberg

Ozion

Dowa Fort

Dutch Fort

English Fort

Sucumivio

Fetu R.

English Fort

T

Cabo Coren Castle

Fort Royal English

Fort Nassau

English Castle

Fort Amsterdam

Moure

Mongee

Anniban or Adia

la Vedia

Cabo Cores Castle

Roodolee

Elmina

Commenun

Petit Commenun

Cape Rouge

Montigne ou Diablo

Cape Rougehead of 6

Doyen

Felitra Bay

Mango

Moufart

Iana

Langa

Barn de Iama

Ico de Iama

Batchera

Laqua

Wlumbi

Bran de Barracou

The Ethiopian Ocean

D

D

A Chart and Map of the Gold Coast
of Guinea, from Rio da Costa to
R°. da Volta.

o. Villages
◇ Forts
f. fathoms

A Scale of 22 Leagues

I. Kip fe.

4 D

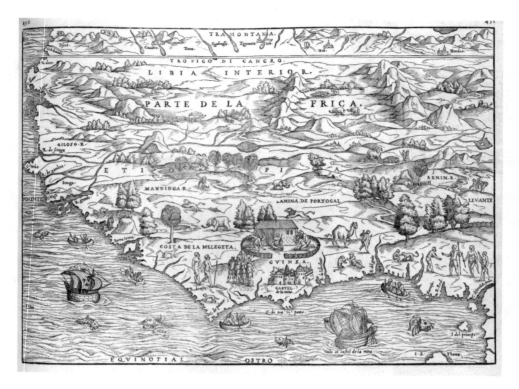

Map of Africa from 1565 clearly showing the fort at El Mina and boats off the coast, as well as details of the interior.

before curving into the Bight of Biafra, a treacherous, unhealthy trap for sailing ships, but enclosing big, inviting islands. This region – the infamous (for slavery) Bight of Benin (stretching along the coast of modern Ghana, Togo, Benin and western Nigeria) – was to yield millions of slaves for the plantations of the Americas.[5] Sailing on southwards, along the coast of what became known as Angola (an area covering today's Gabon, Congo, Zaire and Angola), another region presented itself which was to prove a rich source of slaves destined for the Americas, especially Brazil. But here early navigators had to battle against contrary winds and currents. Southerly winds, and the Benguela current running to the north, tested the mariners' sailing skills. These difficult conditions for ships heading south were, however, helpful to vessels sailing north from the Cape.

By 1500, Europeans had sailed along the length of the remarkably varied western coast, and information about it spread among mariners and merchants in all corners of European maritime trade. The problems of navigating the waters off Africa were widely discussed among European sailors. Printed accounts of voyages formed a new genre of publication which was to remain popular from that day to this: travel accounts which blended descriptions of the exotic and the unexpected with factual assessments of the commercial, and all larded with tantalizing prospects for future trade.

Risk was inescapable for European sailors and traders on the Atlantic coast – and not merely from African and oceanic dangers. Everyone sailing there was also exposed to other European competitors. Portugal, the pioneer, was naturally the first to find its position challenged by a succession of aggressive powers seeking their share of the spoils: Spain at first, then the Dutch, the French and the English. Each in their turn faced the same complexity of risks: the dangers of sailing to Africa, of trading and living on the coast, the uncertainties and menace posed by Africans themselves, and the physical threats from European competitors.

From the start, the Portuguese Crown had insisted on exercising trading monopolies in certain areas. But trade – especially the trade in gold – was too tempting to keep others at bay for long. Thus, in the course of the sixteenth century, all the major European maritime powers began to eat away at Portuguese positions in West Africa. As Portugal's global power declined, their military and commercial primacy succumbed to competitors from northern Europe, all keen for their own share of the commodities available from local traders but, above all, gold.

The initial Portuguese expansion had been a source of friction between Portugal and Spain, frictions partly resolved by Papal bulls and by a peace treaty in 1479. Now, other Europeans also found the news from West Africa irresistible, and it was impossible to keep them away from the coast. By the end of the fifteenth century, a number of nationalities were swarming around the trading positions on the African coast, all generating news (and sometimes secrets) about trade, and each angling for personal or national advantage. All needed some form of security on the shoreline, and the best method on the most valued stretches of the African coast was to follow the Portuguese lead: build some kind of defensive fortification. The first Portuguese fort was on the island of Arguin but the most famous fort was to be at Elmina.[6]

Today, the major slave forts have UNESCO World Heritage Site status and have become important tourist sites. Thousands of people

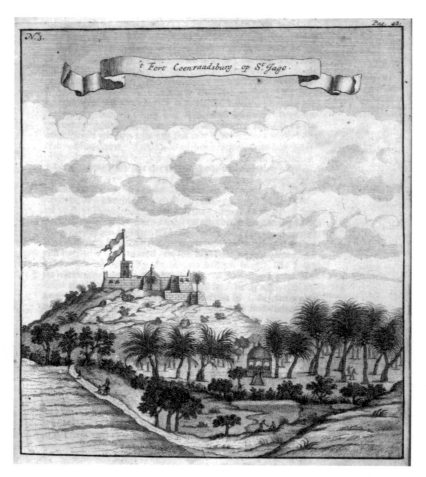

Engraving of Fort Coenraadsburg, St Jago, opposite the castle at El Mina,
Gold Coast, 1704.

– especially from the African diaspora – pay homage to lost and unknown ancestors, especially at Elmina and Cape Coast Castles in Ghana
and on Gorée Island in Senegal. Among those visitors, and indeed
among a much wider constituency around the world, the forts have
come to symbolize and to typify the Atlantic slave trade. They are at
once impressive and sobering places. Visiting the dungeons of those
forts, and gazing at the Atlantic Ocean through the 'door of no return',
is to be overwhelmed by thoughts of the horrors endured there by
generations of slaves. It is hard not be troubled by a sense that evil deeds
took place there. Even so, the history of those forts is not as straightforward as local guides and tourist officials would have the visitor

believe. Though the forts have come to represent the suffering and the inhumanity of the slave trade, they were not typical of the trade. Most captives did *not* pass onto the slave ships from slave forts, nor did anything like as many people pass through those prisons as the tourist literature suggests. The real key to an understanding of those forts was not slavery but European security, commerce – and especially gold.

In 1482, the Portuguese built a fort – El Mina (The Mine) – to protect their trade, on a protected bay (now silted) where ships could anchor. The existing neighbouring settlement quickly grew into a small town to service both the fort and the flotillas of ships which drifted in and out from the Atlantic. Initially, local people providing the Portuguese with gold wanted African slaves in return, and the Portuguese obliged by importing captives from more distant parts of the coast. Thus Africans from the Niger delta, from Kongo and Angola, were shipped to the Gold Coast. As that trade increased, and especially later when the Atlantic slave routes expanded, the original small fort was transformed by an army of European joiners, masons and builders – and African labourers, and Elmina became the formidable fortress we are familiar with today. Elmina's daunting structure was to prove invaluable to each of its successive colonial owners: Portuguese, Dutch

Illustration of the town and castle of El Mina, with ships and the harbour in the foreground and Fort Coenraadsburg behind, 1729.

and finally English – each seeking to impose their own dominance on the coast and on the local trade in gold and in slaves. But whichever European power dominated, the basic nature of trade on that stretch of coast was to remain the same for many years to come: 'a rough *modus vivendi* between black and white' in which European influence barely stretched beyond the fort.[7] Throughout all its incarnations, however, this fort (and many others like it) provided a relatively secure refuge for Europeans and their trade on the Gold Coast.

Over the centuries of European trading on that coast, the Portuguese, Dutch, English, French, Danish and Brandenburgers (from a part of modern Germany) built some sixty forts or castles, mostly concentrated along a relatively small stretch of the coastline from Beyin in the west to Keta in the east, with the forts passing from one dominant European power to another. Forts were also constructed at a number of other strategic positions. The English established one at Bunce Island, 32 km up the Gambia River, another at James Island, close to the mouth of the same river. But James Island was a mere 'slab of friable rock' no more than 110 m by 61 m, and often so badly defended that it was once captured by a pirate. Fortified bases reflected European rivalries on the coast. The French took Gorée Island, off the coast of Senegal, from the Dutch and developed it as a base, along with a new fort at St Louis, for the control and exploration of the Senegal River. St Louis itself was only 2 sq. km in area – but managed to offer accommodation to 2,500 people. Such desolate outposts loomed large in the imagination of planners in London and Paris.[8] The French and English fought a series of engagements for the fortifications which controlled the Gambia River, and similar struggles lapped around the fort on Bunce Island. In time, Bunce Island evolved into a major British fortification (against both French and African attacks) and was the departure point for more than 15,000 slaves transported to the Americas.[9] A number of other fortifications, Sherbro in Sierra Leone, for instance, were short-lived, and there were other, generally miserable, small trading posts, some little more than a shack. Such fortified trading positions dotted an enormous length of coastline, from Arguin in the north, to Ouidah in the south, and on to the island of São Tomé in the Gulf of Guinea.

Of course, similar forts proliferated wherever Europeans settled round the globe: in North America, in India and Southeast Asia, in the Caribbean and in South and East Africa, but the West African forts, though important, were *not* typical of how Europeans acquired slaves on the coast. The forts represent just one means – and a highly regional one at that – by which Europeans traded in and accumulated captives destined for the slave ships. Millions of people were bought, sold and traded in very different physical circumstances.

The slave forts present us, then, with a confusing story. At first sight they seem an impressive reflection of European strength and confidence. Yet the forts also expose a deep European fear *of each other*. Europeans feared threats to their trade (and gold) and threats to their territorial position posed by other European traders and colonizers. Of course, Europeans also deeply distrusted Africans, but that fear cannot explain the forts. Why, for instance, were the overwhelming majority of forts constructed on a relatively narrow stretch of coast that was famed for its gold supplies?

The slave forts embody the Europeans' need to safeguard their position, to secure their territorial claims, and to guard their valuables, but *not* necessarily to secure captured slaves. It is true that some of them became a useful and convenient means of holding, processing and dispatching batches of slaves onto the slave ships, while simultaneously providing relatively secure headquarters for slave-trading companies and their military support.[10] The irony, often overlooked, remains that the very fortifications which seem to announce European supremacy and strength also represent European limitations.

Even more curious, perhaps, is the fact that the slave forts had in some respects become redundant by the time the Atlantic slave trade boomed. They had been developed as bases and coastal headquarters for the various 'charter companies' – the monopoly trading companies which became the favourite means of global trade in the seventeenth century. They were designed to ensure monopoly supplies of captives destined for their nation's slave colonies in the Americas. But such trading monopoly was never able to satisfy the needs of the planters, and Europe's monopoly companies all found their role under attack both from European rivals and from independent traders. Once those trading companies' monopolies ended, and the trade in Africans was thrown open, slaves began to cross the Atlantic in ever greater numbers. But the forts, relics from the monopolistic past, remained in place, and the companies owning them struggled to maintain the heavy upkeep and staffing costs. The physical fabric of the forts easily weathered and corroded in the tropics (along with the resident military and·

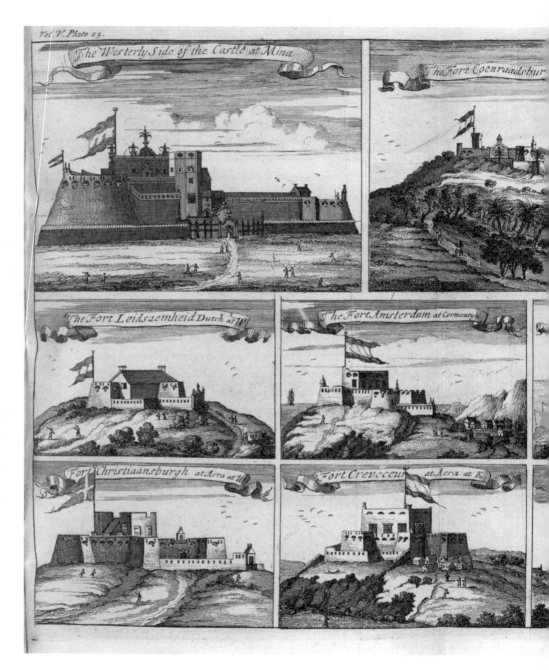

Illustrations of the various Portuguese, Dutch and English forts and fortified castles along the African coast, taken from Awnsham Churchill, *A Collection of Voyages and Travels* … (1746).

nd Gardens at W

Cabo Corso Castle and Fort Royall at E

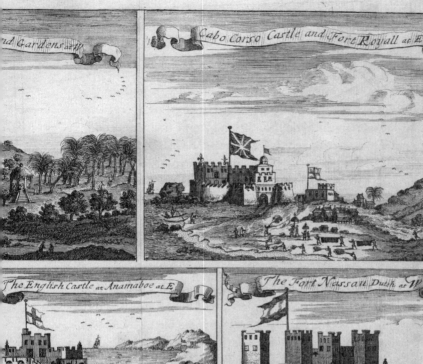

The English Castle at Anamaboe at E

The Fort Nassau Dutch at W

Fort Iames at Acra at E

The English Fort at Simpa at W

I. Kip Sculp.

administrative staff). In 1780, the small British fort at Anomabu – only a few kilometres away from the major base at Cape Coast – was described as: 'A disgrace to the nation . . . a nest for filth and vermin . . . laughing stocks for Europeans and the derision of the natives.' Yet this sorry-sounding fort was the departure point for 466,000 Africans heading to the plantations, mainly on British ships and destined primarily for the British Caribbean, especially Jamaica, though large numbers were also carried by vessels from Rhode Island.[11] Whatever their condition, and however numerous the cargoes of Africans they dispatched, the forts ultimately became a burden to the companies and nations controlling them. Even so, the forts remained the focus of national and military strength (and weakness) on the coast, flying their national flags in asser-tions of territorial and military power. But those flags often changed, as European imperial power and ambitions waxed and waned on the Atlantic coast, and elsewhere.

The forts became home to varied communities of people, from governors and clerics, soldiers and merchants, to resident African slaves. All the forts needed Africans (indeed, they could not function without them), not merely for the day-to-day running of the establish-ment, but for the vital commercial links to the interior, for gold and, increasingly, for slaves. All sorts of local people were understandably attracted to the European forts for work and for whatever scraps fell from the European tables. They undertook all the menial tasks required by the resident staff, bringing with them a range of African wares and foodstuffs and in general providing the services required by people living in the forts. The forts became an important social and commer-cial hub, generating business and livelihoods for the local community and for the offspring born of Africans and Europeans. Many of the slave forts also formed the kernel of new urban settlements: small towns which took on a life and a rationale of their own. Yet these cen-tres of apparent European dominance and control were exceptionally vulnerable and, in many respects, weak. European power sometimes extended no further than the main gate, but for all their weaknesses forts proliferated as the major European maritime powers scrambled to establish a secure presence on a critical stretch of the coast.[12]

The planning and construction of the forts followed the patterns established over the centuries in fort construction in Europe – though now transplanted to tropical Africa. Where Europeans felt the need for physical protection, they naturally turned to the traditional defences afforded by a fort. Despite the long history of the forts on the Gold Coast, such forts proved much less successful on other parts of the coast. In places, however, the environment was not suited to such constructions, though more crucially the Europeans' commercial and strategic ambitions did not require them.

It was the dramatic rise in the Atlantic slave trade in the seventeenth century which enhanced the initial importance of each European nation's position on the African coast. Despite the cost of maintenance, and despite the loss of life, forts seemed vital – if only to keep competing Europeans at arm's length. In the process, the forts became part of that global game of chess waged between all the major European maritime powers, each jostling and often fighting the others for position and supremacy. Forts were captured and lost, assaulted, rebuilt and repaired, and new ones founded, in the continuing search for ways of enhancing and expanding global power.

The irony was that the forts' role was bypassed by the rising importance of the slave trade. When the Atlantic slave trade really took off in the late seventeenth and early eighteenth centuries, the commercial weaknesses of African forts were quickly exposed. The massive expansion of plantation slavery in the Americas, notably in Brazil and the Caribbean, generated a voracious demand for ever more slaves, especially on sugar plantations. There was a similar substantial demand to fuel the expansion of tobacco (and later rice) production in North America, though on nothing like the scale of the slave trade to the sugar colonies. The monopoly companies, operating from their fortified trading posts, simply could not provide enough captives to satisfy planters in the Americas. Nor could they keep out a growing armada of interlopers, of all nationalities, anxious to break into the slave-trading markets and to ship slaves to the Americas. The forts retained their importance as centres of European military presence, as 'way-stations' for the movement of men, goods and information along the different oceanic legs of the slave trade (and on to Asia), and as a toehold in the wider European claims to empire. They were also important supply points for slave ships.[13] But they were not the main means of access to the supply of slaves. There were better, more efficient and profitable, ways of acquiring prisoners for the slave ships than via the forts. The Atlantic slave trade boomed when a relatively free trade in Africans was encouraged. A new generation of slave traders developed different systems of accumulating ever more slaves for their ships. European slave traders became adept at finding sources of slaves in very diverse coastal locations, developing specific trading networks which suited local conditions and local African communities. Slave trading thus differed greatly from one coastal region to another – and across time. It ranged from close co-operation and personal ties with rulers and monarchs, through to casual agreements with coastal peoples who simply announced the availability of slaves by sending up smoke signals to catch the attention of ships at sea. As one fruitful and profitable location for the trade dried up, slave traders had to look elsewhere.

Though the slave forts retain their power in the popular imagination, there were many other locations and ports which saw enormous numbers of Africans depart for the Americas. Many embarkation ports were not, strictly speaking, on the coast. They were to be found on islands, on lagoons, along Africa's massive river systems, or close to an inland town, all of which might be some distance from the coast and the awaiting slave ships. Even so, particular ports came to dominate the trade. Of the 12 million people embarked for the Americas, a staggering 4.7 million departed from a mere four slave ports, on an area of coast covered roughly by Angola: from Loango (400,000) and Cabinda (735,000) in the north, Luanda (2.8 million) on the central coast and Benguela (750,000) in the south.

The main embarkation point for an astounding number was the Angolan port of Luanda. Founded in 1575, the city seemed designed by nature for the task. Silt-bearing coastal currents had created spits of land and a bay, with the entrance to the bay protected by rocky sites – all helping to create a sheltered port. With easy links into the interior and thence onto the slave ships, Luanda became a major slave-trading entrepôt, especially in the eighteenth century. The town teemed with an incredibly transient population, of Portuguese and Brazilian traders and merchants and an ever-growing mixed population forged from the intermingling of African and European people. But there, as elsewhere, death rates were enormous. As hundreds of thousands of Africans passed through Luanda to the slave ships, large numbers of Europeans were also going quickly to their graves.[14] The enslaved, who had already passed through numerous hands en route to Luanda, now found themselves kept in slave pens (often shared with animals), which were scattered around the outskirts of the town and sometimes on the beaches. Further south, the most southerly of the major slave ports, Benguela, was the departure point for 750,000 Africans to the slave ships. There, too, the slaves were enclosed, along with pigs and goats, in the filth of communal holding pens. Death rates were inevitably high, and, in scenes of grotesque horror, slave traders found it cheaper to dump the dead in shallow graves or, worse still, in piles – on the edge of town or on the beach – for hyenas to eat during the night.[15] Huge numbers of Africans also passed through the town of Cabinda to the north, the town itself perched on a bay well suited to receiving and dispatching sailing ships. Again, the slaves were first kept in town before being moved from the beaches to the sailing ships. These embarkation points did not have to be large settlements to sustain a substantial flow of captives through to the slave ships. The small town of Ambriz, for instance, in the north of Angola, saw the embarkation of more than 200,000 people onto the slave ships.

The story of slave embarkation onto the ships differed greatly between African locations. By the end of the seventeenth century, for example, Ouidah (in modern Benin, on what became known as the 'Slave Coast') – had become the main slave port in West Africa, attracting traders from throughout Europe and Brazil.[16] But the town was actually inland, some distance from the coast, and while the Africans were awaiting removal to the ships, they were kept in secure buildings known as 'trunks' in town and sometimes in Ouidah's various forts. Later, in the nineteenth century, many slaves in Ouidah were kept in prisons built and maintained by European traders and known as barracoons. The slaves were then marched to the nearest beaches to be loaded onto canoes, manned by Africans, for the perilous ride through the Atlantic surf to the slave ships sitting offshore. Throughout, in the town, on the march to the coast, and on the beach itself, the slaves were under the control of African officials. More than 1 million Africans departed from Ouidah as slaves.[17]

Throughout the long history of the slave trade, the Atlantic slave traders exploited different coastal regions at different times. They switched from one location to another as supplies of slaves flourished or faded. Of course, the flow of people to the coast waxed and waned in response to internal African issues: wars and famine, the rise and fall of African slave-trading powers. But when supplies from one region declined there always seemed to be other sources available on other parts of the coast. Initially, Europeans drew their slaves from Upper Guinea (the area covering modern Guinea, Sierra Leone and Liberia), with large numbers also bought along the Gambia River (which was navigable for 200 km), and about 98,000 slaves were shipped from Galinas (in modern Sierra Leone), for example. But the Upper Guinea trade declined from the 1780s onwards. More fruitful still was the Bight of Biafra, which emerged as a major supplier of slaves when the British slave colonies in the Americas flourished, from the mid-seventeenth century onwards. Altogether, some 700,000 Africans were shipped from Bonny, 62,000 from Old Calabar and 142,000 from New Calabar.[18] The prime slave-trading location switched again after the British and American abolitions of 1807–08. Now the 'illicit' trade thrived by finding secluded places which were safe from the scrutiny of abolitionist naval patrols, and here again coastal geography was important. The creeks and swamps along the Gambia River offered ideal discrete locations. So too, between 1815 and 1850, did Lagos, which was shielded from the Atlantic and from prying warships by the shelter of a lagoon: 250,000 slaves left that city in those years.[19] Above all, however, it was the coast of Angola which yielded the largest and most long-lasting supply of Africans destined for the Americas.

Africans, then, were transferred onto the slave ships from a host of very different locations, along a coastal region which stretched from Senegambia (roughly modern Senegal and Gambia) to Mozambique. They embarked from forts and barracoons, from beaches and riverside jetties, from major towns and cities, and from isolated spits of land. It was as if the Atlantic slave traders and their African trading partners cast a net along a vast coastline, catching people where they could, and incarcerating them in a range of prisons, before dispatching them across the Atlantic.

Who is to say which was the most traumatic form of incarceration and departure from the coast: being shuffled into the dark, dank misery of a dungeon in Elmina or sharing the filth with the pigs and the corpses in the barracoons of Luanda? For millions of people, these were the last memories of Africa itself. But they were soon to find their lives transformed once again – and generally for the worse – by the months which followed on board a slave ship in the Atlantic.

THREE

Slave Ships, Cargoes and Sailors

The millions of people transported by the Atlantic slave ships brought about a fundamental population change to the Americas. But they did much more than that. Slave ships were used for different purposes on different legs of their voyages. They shipped huge volumes of imported goods to Africa, and they returned to their home ports in Europe and the Americas with slave-grown produce from the slave colonies. Slave ships were the agents for a complexity of human and social exchanges which transformed the face of the modern world. They were important in the transfer and development of goods from one corner of the world to another, and they helped make possible the expansion of crops, and forms of cultivation, in new and sometimes alien regions. Sugar, the most obvious example, was not native to the tropical Americas, but transferring and developing it there created the rapid growth of the Brazilian and Caribbean sugar industries – but only because of the related transportation of African slave labour. Here, then, was the 'Columbian exchange' of crops and plants, of foodstuffs, diseases, human beings and social habits – all these and more the very essence of the post-Columbus encounters between Europeans and the wider world.

The slave ship was the startlingly violent vehicle for a massive international movement of humanity, peopling swathes of the Americas with Africans. Those same ships were also conduits for diseases: microbes, germs and ailments making their way from Africa to the Americas and in the process cutting a devastating path through the shipboard Africans and crew long before landfall in the Americas.

The most obvious achievement of the slave ships was bringing together the economies and peoples of three continents. There were an estimated 40,000 such voyages and we have details of some 35,000 of them, spread over a period of four centuries.[1] We know that the prime destination for the slave ships was the Americas, but as we have seen, Atlantic slave ships also transported Africans to other destinations. Indeed, the earliest Atlantic slave trade involved Africans being transported from one African coastal region to another, to the Atlantic islands, and to Europe. That changed, however, with the European settlement of the Americas and the demand for labour to tap the tropical and semi-tropical lands of Brazil and the Caribbean. The first Africans to cross the Atlantic travelled as slaves or servants to Spanish explorers and settlers, though they sailed not from Africa but from Spain, to Hispaniola. The numbers involved were small on the initial Spanish and Portuguese voyages to the Americas, rising from about 2,000 during the first decade of the sixteenth century to 37,500 by the 1560s. No one had previously tried to move such large numbers of slaves across such huge expanses of ocean, and this early slave trade to Spanish America was clearly experimental. But it was a success, delivering growing numbers of Africans to places in need of labour and pointing out, to other nations and traders from other nations, how to carry large numbers of Africans across the Atlantic. Today, historians recognize that Spanish slave traders were the pioneers of this experimental transportation, but others quickly followed.[2]

The scale and the direction of the Atlantic slave trade was utterly transformed by the development of the Brazilian sugar industry. The Portuguese established early sugar plantations on the northeastern coast of Brazil, in Bahia and Pernambuco, on Crown land leased to planters. They, in turn, leased land to smaller planters, and they all planted sugar, but they all needed labour. With the example of the Atlantic islands and São Tomé before them, and aware of an *existing* slave trade on the African coast, they naturally turned to African slave labour. As Brazilian sugar expanded, so too did the flow of Africans across the South Atlantic. By the time the Dutch invaded Brazil in 1630, 262,000 Africans had been embarked on the ships heading for Brazil, the majority destined to work on sugar plantations. From the 1560s through to the final decline of the Atlantic trade in the 1860s, the Portuguese established themselves as the leading slave traders in the Atlantic. All told, Portuguese and Brazilian slave traders carried in the region of 6 million slaves from Africa. The British were the second major trader, carrying 3.25 million.[3]

Throughout the Americas, indigenous peoples seemed ideal labourers for the work the European settlers demanded, but from one new colony to another, labouring experiments with indigenous people, both free and enslaved, generally failed. They fled, refused to work at the pace and pattern demanded of them, or simply succumbed to the diseases unknowingly imported by the new arrivals, both European and African. Ironically, the Catholic Church's campaigning against the slavery of Native American peoples left the way open for the importation of African slaves. Even then, slavery did not dominate at first, and early sugar plantations used a mix of free, local and slave labour. But by the 1630s, African slaves dominated Brazilian sugar plantations, and planters demanded more slaves, so the number of Africans arriving in Brazil increased. In the mid-1580s, 166 African slaves had disembarked from one slave ship in Bahia; by the 1640s, six vessels delivered 2,134.[4]

A remarkable economy had emerged in the Atlantic by the mid-seventeenth century. As European sugar consumption expanded enormously, so too did the Atlantic slave trade. Despite the occasional blip in the data, sugar was a rapidly expanding industry which devoured Africans by the boatload. Its success inevitably attracted other European trading nations. The Dutch were the first, carrying 58 Africans to Portugal in 1596. Following the Dutch invasion of Brazil in 1630, the Dutch West India Company (WIC) established a regular trade to Pernambuco, and within twenty years they had embarked 30,900 Africans destined for the Americas: 25,000 arrived. Thereafter the Dutch slave trade boomed, greatly helped by the rapid expansion of other European sugar colonies in the Caribbean. Between 1625 and 1650, Dutch ships transported 26,000 Africans, the figure rising to 74,200 between 1675 and 1700. By the time the Dutch abolished their slave trade, they had shipped 554,300 slaves from Africa.[5]

By the end of the sixteenth century, the decline of Portuguese and Spanish global power opened the way for the emerging nations of northern Europe. In the course of the seventeenth century the Dutch, the British and the French all established their own tropical colonies in the Americas and elsewhere. All held island possessions throughout the Caribbean, and all laid claims to parts of North America, while the French and British established trading and colonial roots in India and the Dutch in Southeast Asia. All had learned from the earlier Portuguese experience in Brazil, and later European settlers

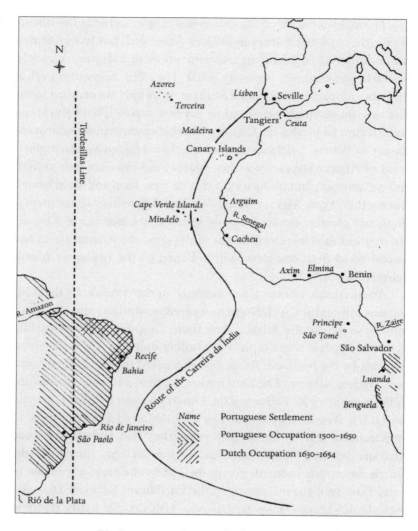

The Portugese Atlantic, 16th to 18th centuries.

and statesmen were conscious that tropical colonies seemed to offer commercial and material bounty to all who could successfully settle them and tap the luxuriant environment for crops which Europe devoured in ever growing volumes. Nowhere was this clearer than in Brazil, which, with a brief period under the Dutch, rapidly became the jewel in the Portuguese crown, its tropical wealth, above all its sugar, brought forth by Africans ferried across the Atlantic in increasing numbers. The Portuguese–Brazil trading axis across the South Atlantic was to become the largest oceanic slave route in the entire slave trade system.

W. Berryman, depiction of slaves cutting cane on a sugar plantation in Jamaica, between 1808 and 1816, watercolour.

By the mid-seventeenth century, the Dutch had become a major figure in the Atlantic slave trade, and the British had begun to stake their own claims in the enslaved Americas. Helped and influenced by the Dutch (though less so than has been traditionally thought),[6] the English acquired their own Caribbean islands, notably St Kitts, Barbados and, in 1655, Jamaica, the island that was to be their most prized possession in the region. Settlers in all the British islands followed the pattern established by the Portuguese and Dutch south of the equator by developing agricultural settlements and communities which experimented with a range of commodities, before realizing that their islands were best suited to sugar cultivation. A familiar pattern quickly followed. Sugar meant plantations, and sugar plantations meant African slaves and the gradual marginalization of other forms of labour, indigenous, free and indentured. By the end of the seventeenth century, the Caribbean islands had been utterly transformed.

Africans were imported in enormous numbers. By the time the British abolished their slave trade in 1807, they had shipped almost 1 million to Jamaica alone – another 458,000 to the tiny island of Barbados.[7] The French followed a similar path on their own Caribbean islands.

From small beginnings, the French slave trade exploded – especially to St-Domingue (the French western half of the island of Santo Domingo) in the eighteenth century. By the time they abolished their trade, the French had shipped almost 750,000 Africans to their colonies.

The British also developed plantation slavery in their North American colonies, landing more than a quarter of a million Africans there. Although slavery in North America was to become hugely influential in the subsequent course of American history, the number of slaves imported was relatively small, compared to the figures for Brazil and the Caribbean. Indeed, only about 4 per cent of the total Atlantic slave trade was accounted for by Africans transported to North America. They famously toiled for the tobacco planters in the Chesapeake, and later in rice cultivation in the Carolinas. Settlers had initially experimented with a mix of free, indentured and slave labour. The massive boom in North American slavery was to come after 1800, with the development of the cotton industry on the expanding western and southern frontier.

Wherever we glance, across huge expanses of the colonial Americas, from Brazil to the Chesapeake, slavery became an embedded feature of the human and social landscape. In the process, growing numbers of Africans were scattered across North and South America and throughout the arc of the Caribbean islands. Imported primarily to undertake the harsh work on plantations and, in some places, in mines, many of them, in time, moved out of those occupational beachheads and settled into other employment, sometimes in remote locations (as cowboys on the frontiers or enslaved sailors working the Atlantic shipping routes, for example). Indeed, Africans and people of African descent could be found in most jobs and locations throughout the enslaved Americas. Under the impact of these massive arrivals, from Europe and Africa, the native peoples wilted and declined. In places – notably on the islands – they simply vanished, succumbing to alien diseases. Elsewhere their numbers were greatly reduced, their empires and civilizations collapsed, and the survivors retreated at the advance of the African and European newcomers. Very soon, the native peoples of the Americas were reduced to pockets: small bands of strangers in their own lands.

Today, thanks to the remarkable *Trans-Atlantic Slave Trade Database*, we have precise details about the numbers of people caught up in this extraordinary trade. More than 12 million were loaded onto the

ships, and more than 11 million arrived in the Americas. They were
transported from Africa by ships from all the major European maritime
powers (and some minor ones) and by merchants from throughout
the Americas, but especially from Brazil and North America. We know
of 188 ports, on both sides of the Atlantic, which dispatched ships to
buy slaves, though the great majority – 8.5 million – were transported
by ships from a mere twenty major ports. Ships from Rio de Janeiro
top the list, carrying 1.5 million, with Liverpool a close second at 1.33
million. Other, smaller, ports were also involved. Ships from Cadiz, for
instance, transported 53,000 Africans. There were some ports which
readers might not associate with the slave trade: Lancaster and Lyme
Regis, St-Malo and Le Havre.[8]

Ships from all corners of the Atlantic headed to the west coast of
Africa to trade in slaves. Those ships were, at once, cargo ships which
also became floating prisons for the enslaved, often for prolonged periods both on the coast and during the Atlantic crossing. What happened
on those ships was – and remains – the most searing experience in
the history of slavery, endured and survived by more than 11 million
Africans. It was a seaborne ordeal characterized by brutality and suffering, death and disease, by violence and gnawing uncertainty. One
million did not survive the crossing, their corpses cast to the ocean to
the following sharks, which had learned of the rich pickings to be had
in the wake of a slave ship.

Just as the imagery of the African slave fort has become the popular perception of slave trading on the African coast, so too has imagery
showing the tightly packed slave ship *Brookes* helped to define the
experience of the slave ship. It is an image which deceives as much as
it reveals. The pictures of Africans crammed, sardine-like, into every
conceivable inch of space, filling the crowded decks like spoons in a
drawer, have been used time and again to convey the essence of a slave
ship. The main image of the *Brookes* was drafted originally for Quakers
in Plymouth as part of the initial attack on the British slave trade in
1788. Images of the *Brookes* quickly established themselves as a hugely
influential element in the abolitionists' propaganda drive – in Britain
and abroad. They presented a deeply shocking, disturbing impression
and proved to be a revelation for large numbers of people. More recently,
this image has been a regular theme in published accounts of slavery
and the slave trade and in historical discussions.[9] The *Brookes* has,
then, captured the grotesque sufferings of the African captives below

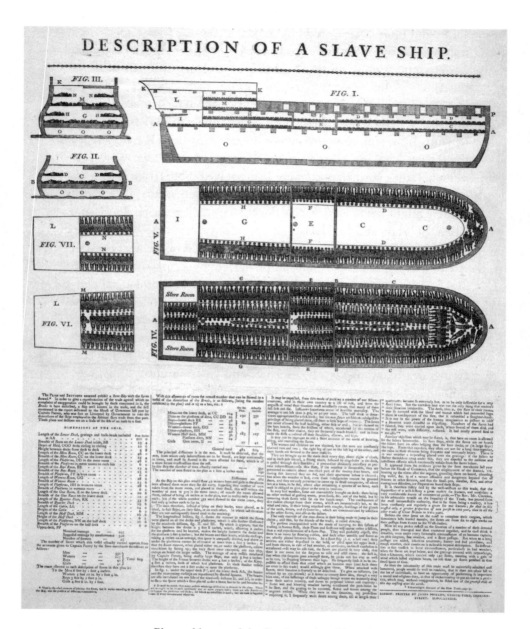

Plan and layout of the *Brookes*, printed in 1789.

decks. But these pictures are of the *Brookes* when carrying 482 Africans across the Atlantic (under the limitations imposed by Dolben's Act of 1788). In fact, the *Brookes* had recently transported 740 Africans across the Atlantic.[10]

At 297 tons, the *Brookes* was a large vessel for a slave ship, built in 1781 and named after its owner, the Liverpool slave trader Joseph Brookes. Over the next quarter of a century, she was to make ten Atlantic crossings filled with slaves – 5,163 Africans were brought on board, of whom 4,559 survived to landfall. On the 1785–6 voyage she carried a massive 740 Africans – 258 *more* than we see crowded into the decks in the 1788 depiction.[11]

We can gain some sense of how crowded this was by looking at details of the earlier Atlantic slave ships. At 297 tons, the *Brookes* carried one African per 0.40 tons. As early as 1586, slave ships to Spanish America were restricted to carrying one slave per ton. A century later, the Portuguese instituted a limit of 2.5 slaves per ton, though these restrictions were to fall into disuse with the passage of time. Of course, the *Brookes* was built at the apogee of Liverpool's late eighteenth-century slave-trading empire, and in a city which had mastered the art of constructing custom-built slave ships. At the height of Liverpool's slaving history, its most famous slave ship carried five times as many Africans per ton as slave ships of three centuries before. If the *Brookes* was typical, conditions of overcrowding for the African captives had got worse – not better – in the course of the slave trade.

In fact, an extraordinary variety of ships transported people across the Atlantic. We know of one Liverpool giant of 566 tons. But others were very small: one tiny vessel weighed a mere 11 tons. Yet it is important to recognize that they were slave ships for only one leg of a trading voyage. European ships generally did three legs: Europe to Africa, to the Americas and back to Europe. Ships from Brazil faced an apparently simpler voyage, to Africa and back, while ships from North America had voyages which often entailed stops en route in the Caribbean. Although they were fitted out and equipped in their home port, they only really *became* slave ships on the coast of Africa and when they sailed west across the Atlantic. On the outbound leg to Africa, they carried cargoes to be bartered and sold in return for slaves; ships returning to Europe generally had cargoes from the Americas. As a general rule, it was important to have ships which were flexible vessels, capable of carrying both human and other cargoes. And even when, in the case of

Liverpool at its slaving height, that city boasted an armada of custom-built slave ships, they too had to be adaptable for the outbound leg to Africa and the return from the Americas.

Organizing a slave voyage was a protracted commercial venture: raising the money to pay for the ship and its supplies, recruiting the officers and crew, arranging the necessary paperwork to underwrite the enterprise, drafting instructions for the captain and making all the preparations to safeguard the men and vessel in the months (sometimes years) they were away. Ships from northern Europe could expect to be away for the best part of a year. All this was time-consuming and costly – even before the ship cast off from its home berth. Early pioneers naturally made use of whatever vessels came to hand. When, for instance, the Dutch entered the trade, they used ships which had served them well in other forms of maritime commerce. Among the variety of ships used by the Dutch for carrying Africans, one particular model, the *fluit* (flute) – designed as a commercial bulk carrier[12] – was used in their early slave trade. By the eighteenth century, however, the Dutch were using barks, snows and yachts. When the trade was at its height, the most popular Dutch vessel was a small frigate, which, like other slave ships, was adapted for carrying humans by the ship's carpenter and crew during the course of the voyage. Though some Dutch ships made repeated voyages, half of the vessels we know of made only one voyage for slaves. Here was clear enough evidence that Dutch ships were general-purpose cargo ships, used for whatever task came to hand, and were not designed or earmarked solely for carrying Africans.

As the Atlantic trade evolved, slave ships changed, though the basic requirements were similar everywhere. They needed to be speedy, to effect as swift an Atlantic crossing as possible – with enough room to carry a substantial body of captives. Experience and the knowledge acquired from sailing the Atlantic slave routes naturally led to changes in ship design over the centuries. In the course of the seventeenth century, new arrangements of sails were introduced, allowing ships – the bark, snow and brig – to sail closer to the wind and enabling them to make the most of the Atlantic trade winds. Slave ships also got bigger in the course of the seventeenth and eighteenth centuries. In the case of Liverpool ships, the average size of 70 tons in the early eighteenth century had grown to 200 tons by the end of the century. The city's 'Guineamen' were larger than other ships trading from Liverpool.[13]

At the end of the eighteenth century, slave ships from all of Europe's major slave ports were much larger than their forebears in the early days of Atlantic trading. Slave ships from Nantes and Bordeaux ranged between 200 and 400 tons; so too did Dutch and Danish ships. By then, Liverpool dominated the North Atlantic trade, with one African in five crossing the Atlantic in a Liverpool ship. Liverpool's shipyards, turning out slave ships to the specific measurements and requirements of the city's merchants, formed a massive local industry and employed 3,000 shipwrights, alongside a host of ancillary industries, from rope- and gun makers to victuallers. Of the 8,087 British ships plying the slave trade in the eighteenth century, 2,120 of them (26 per cent) had been built in Liverpool. In the last twenty years of the century alone, Liverpool shipbuilders constructed 469 'Guineamen'.[14]

To modern eyes, all these ships seem tiny. Ships belonging to the Dutch West India Company in the early eighteenth century were a mere 27–37 m long. Dutch slave merchants used even smaller ships. Yet it was on such vessels, ranging from roughly 110 to 230 tons, that the Dutch transported 300 Africans.[15] Precise details of the ships are hard to find, though we have more data about them from the last years of the British slave trade (before 1807), a period when such trading came under critical and careful scrutiny from an inquisitive abolitionist lobby. The *Hall*, for example, constructed in Liverpool in 1785, was 375 tons (75 tons larger than its contemporary the *Brookes*. She measured 31 m in length and 9 m wide (a modern cricket pitch is 20 m long and 3 m wide). The *Hall* boasted a height between decks of 2 m. She also had a raised after-deck, providing a vital command position for the captain and crew, and a protective barrier, armed with swivel guns, for use against slave revolt. But, like other Guineamen of the period, the *Hall* could be readily switched from slaving to other, conventional, bulk trading. When a similar Liverpool vessel, the *Parr*, was launched in 1797, she was described by the press as 'a very beautiful vessel and the largest out of this port in the African trade for which she is designed'.[16] She was wrecked on her maiden voyage, but the 200 Africans on board (all unlikely to have thought of her as a 'beautiful vessel') were saved and subsequently landed in the Americas by other slave ships.[17]

In a trade that spanned three centuries, involving so many nations and spread across such an immense expanse of ocean, it was under-standable that the ships involved varied enormously. They ranged from the tiniest of ships, through to what were, by contemporary standards, oceanic giants. Whatever their physical differences in displacement, size or shape, all had a common thread. They were home to – and the cause of – human misery on a scale, and of a concentrated kind, that had never before been experienced at sea. Long-distance oceanic travel in the age of sail was normally a miserable experience for most people involved, but nothing remotely compared to the slave ships. Convicts shipped to the Americas in the seventeenth century, or after 1787 to Australia, troops shipped to distant postings, or the huge numbers of people heading westward to America from Europe in the nineteenth century, did not have endure anything like the seaborne miseries of millions of African slaves.[18]

For a start, the space provided for African captives was minute. Even in the last years of the British slave trade, the area allowed on Liverpool slavers was miniscule, and this on a ship which might be a mere 21 m long and 7.3 m wide. After 1788, when the British Parliament became seriously interested in the nature of the slave ships, their enquiries revealed that the average space allotted to each African was around 0.6 sq. m. (Reformers seeking improvements in 1799 demanded 0.7 sq. m.) These rough figures were very similar to data from French slave ships of the same era. There was an irony here, because in the eighteenth century slave ships got bigger, but this did *not* mean that they allotted more space for their captives. Indeed, quite the reverse. It was on the smaller, not the larger, slave ships that Africans had more space. Yet it was the larger ships which became a feature of the Atlantic slave trade in the late eighteenth century – the very period when the British (and especially Liverpool) dominated the trade. Put simply, as the British came to dominate the trade, the Africans on British ships endured more crowded conditions. Curiously, however, this crowding – 'packing' – of Africans on board a slave ship was *not* the key determinant of the levels of slave mortality on board the ships; the main factor was the length of time spent on board.[19]

Mere recitations of data about space and numbers can never capture the stinking claustrophobia of the slaves' conditions, which were more confined and crowded than the basic evidence suggests. Even contemporary sketches of slave ships fail to capture the essence of the on-board crowding. The available space between decks, and inside a hold, was altered by ships' carpenters and crew on the voyage out to Africa, or as the ship traded on the African coast.[20] To provide more space for the enslaved, rack-like shelves were put in place between the decks along the side of the ship, in order to squeeze in more Africans. While this provided added accommodation, it markedly reduced the room allowed for each person. It also meant that Africans lay on rough wooden shelves only inches above other captives lying on the deck, with no room for movement or manoeuvre when they were seasick, or when afflicted by the stomach ailments that were the common feature of all Atlantic slave ships. Here were physical arrangements which seemed designed to maximize human misery, even before a vessel nosed out into the uncertainties of a protracted Atlantic crossing.

The mortality rates among the Africans on board slave ships declined gradually over the history of the Atlantic trade. This improvement, between the days of the pioneering Portuguese and the last phase of the Brazilian slave trade, was partly a reflection of a better-organized, more competent industry. As crude as this claim may seem, the Atlantic slave trade became an ever more efficient business. The slave traders of the nineteenth century were better than the slave traders of the sixteenth century at the enforced movement of people: they had learned the best way of sailing a ship filled with Africans to the Americas, quickly and efficiently. Of course, it was in the slave traders' interests to keep their captives alive and well until they could sell them in the Americas. For all the deadly horrors, for all the brutality and the levels of endemic sickness on the ships, the ships' masters' aim was to get the Africans to market in the best possible condition for a good sale.

The early slave traders of the sixteenth and seventeenth centuries were pioneers, experimenting with a mass transportation of people in ways that had never been attempted before. It was a system which evolved by trial and error. Those who suffered throughout were the African victims of these experiments. The early slave voyages tended, for obvious reasons, to be longer than later voyages and thus had higher death rates both among Africans and crew. The rule of thumb which characterized the slave trade was that, the longer a ship was at sea, the higher the death rate would be.[21] Ships heading for North America – a substantially longer haul than sailing to the Caribbean, or to Brazil – had higher levels of shipboard mortality, but even this does not tell the whole story. Deaths on the ships also reflected the physical health of people when they were brought on board a ship on the coast. Africans who had endured a long, taxing journey to the coast, from their point of initial enslavement, and who were, as a result, sick or physically diminished, were likely to join the sick and the dying when thrust on board a slave ship.[22] Physical examinations of captives offered for sale on the coast thus became a basic feature of the slave-trading regime: ships' doctors and experienced crewmen conducted humiliating, public, physical examinations of Africans before the captains agreeing to buy them. They knew that sick Africans were unlikely to survive and might, at worst, infect other Africans in the filth and intimacy of the slave decks. In the early years of the trade, there were also marked differences in death rates of Africans leaving from different parts of the African coast. For reasons that are not entirely clear, slaves from some regions of Africa seemed to be healthier than others, a fact reflected in different levels of mortality on board the slave ships themselves.[23] Africans going to the Caribbean from the Gold Coast and the Bight of Biafra in the seventeenth century had twice and three times the death rates of those leaving from Upper Guinea respectively.[24] Through all these variations, the journey length at sea was critical. When the time taken to cross the Atlantic was shortened in the late eighteenth century, largely because of improvements in sailing and navigation (the years when the British were the ascendant power), there was a consequent fall in shipboard mortality. Thus, by the last phase of the British trade, death rates on ships heading to the British Caribbean had fallen to 8 per cent (though they remained much higher on vessels sailing to Dutch and Spanish possessions).[25]

The most striking trend was that, as Atlantic crossings got swifter, mortality rates declined. But then, paradoxically, something unusual happened in the very *last* phase of slave trading in the nineteenth century. After British and American abolition in 1807–08, both the Royal and the U.S. Navies adopted an aggressive abolitionist policy chasing and impounding 'illicit' slave ships, mainly Portuguese and Brazilian, heading overwhelmingly to Brazil. The slave ships which escaped this naval attention (and most did) were faster than ever, for two reasons. First, they were sailing the shortest, most direct, routes between Africa and Brazil, plus many were new, custom-built, fast-sailing ships, notably the Baltimore Clippers – designed and purchased for fast Atlantic crossings and able to outrun the naval ships. Because of their speed and the faster crossings, they ought to have experienced *lower* slave mortality among the Africans on board. But they did not.

After 1831, when Brazil itself abolished the trade, the trade to Brazil was not only illegal but it developed a callous brutality perhaps unmatched in any other period. The levels of slave mortality on slave ships to Brazil in the last years of Atlantic trading actually *increased*.[26] This last generation of Atlantic slave traders appeared less solicitous of the Africans' well-being. They were careless about provisioning and crowding, sometimes even unconcerned about murdering captives (by jettisoning them overboard when being pursued[27]). At a time when the slave trade, and even slavery itself, came to be viewed as an ethical and religious abomination, the very years when the slave trade was under severe attack throughout the Western world, 850,000 slaves endured some of the worst levels of sickness and death seen in the entire history of the Atlantic trade.[28] As the Atlantic slave trade entered its final phase, as we shall see, the stories that emerged from the coast of Africa and at sea in the South Atlantic were among the most chilling in the history of the trade.

Efforts to make such comparisons may seem pointless. To suggest that one phase of the slave trade was worse than another, or that the slave-holding pens of Angola were perhaps worse than the slave forts of Ghana, may seem both futile and meaningless. After all, every single African on board a slave ship endured his or her own unique form of hellish suffering: how could one be worse than another? Yet the data that historians have managed to tease from the documentation of the slave trade over the past generation reveal marked differences in what unfolded on board the thousands of slave ships in the Atlantic. Africans heading to Brazil in the nineteenth century endured some of the harshest conditions we know of in the entire history of the Atlantic slave trade.

In the process of studying the victims of the slave trade, we have also learned a great deal about the people who were their tormentors: the men who sailed the slave ships and who manhandled the Africans from the moment they stepped on board to the moment they stumbled ashore in the Americas, or were cast to a watery grave en route. The suffering of the Africans on board the slave ships is now the stuff of common legends. Less well known is the fate of the men who herded them like cattle in their transit to the Americas. They too suffered startling levels of mortality and ill health. Indeed the death rate among sailors was generally higher than among the Africans, in large part because of the ferocious diseases of West Africa which afflicted the sailors both on the coast and thereafter on the Atlantic crossing. In 1788, Thomas Clarkson proved that of the 5,000 men who left Britain on slave ships in 1785, only 2,329 returned.[29] In the generation before 1807, some 20,000 sailors died on British slave ships. Clarkson thus destroyed the traditional arguments that the slave trade was a nursery for the Royal Navy, and this evidence helped to win over the Prime Minister, William Pitt, to abolition. By comparison, the late eighteenth-century peace-time strength of the Royal Navy was about 30,000, but quadrupled in size in the war years of the 1790s.[30]

Sailors on slave ships of all nationalities suffered higher death rates than sailors on any other ships – including men who sailed to and from Africa on other business. The deaths of Africans and of sailors was an inevitable accompaniment to any slave voyages, from the moment the ship arrived in West Africa (but especially when Africans first came on board) to the day the last one was discharged into American slavery. For huge numbers of people, black and white, the slave ship was a tomb, a floating charnel house, with corpses regularly cast overboard, especially on the coast, to the awaiting predators. Everyone involved in the slave trade knew of the dangers. Merchants in the major slave ports of Europe and the Americas had to plan for it, sailors worked surrounded by such dangers on a personal, daily basis, and the Africans endured it in the fetid squalor of the slave decks. Slaves had no choice in the matter, of course: they had been forced on board. But the sailors had *chosen* to join the ships. Moreover, since slave ships originated in all the major ports of the Atlantic world, from Amsterdam to Rio, the stark realities of life and death on a slave ship was also common gossip and knowledge clean around the Atlantic. There was no secrecy about death and the slave ship; how could there be, when so many men simply disappeared over the horizon, never to return to their home port? Why, then, would anyone in their right mind choose to work on a slave ship? Yet hundreds of thousands did.

The slave trade has been described as 'the most international of all commercial activities before the nineteenth century'. Its ships were drawn from all corners of the Atlantic world, and the goods loaded on board were themselves gathered from the most distant parts of the globe, all with the intention of acquiring slaves. Portugal was the main organizer of slave ships (two out of five Africans crossed in Portuguese ships), though the great majority of Portuguese ships were actually organized in Brazil. Slave ships also sailed direct to Africa from the Caribbean and from North America.[31] Indeed, some 46 per cent of all Atlantic slave voyages were organized from the

Americas.[32] In such an international trade, with slave ships drawn from a mixture of nations and people, the seamen on board slave ships were equally cosmopolitan. Captains and officers tended, understandably, to be of the same nationality as the ship – Dutch if commanding Dutch vessels, Britons commanding British. They were the men chosen specifically by the ship's owners and backers in the ship's home port, and entrusted with the substantial money invested in the vessel and its cargoes. Masters were often partners in the voyage, sometimes via an investment, by a bonus, or in the form of slaves they were allowed to buy and sell on their own behalf. These men had a personal stake in a voyage, and, like the merchants back in their home port, it was in their interest to ensure that Africans were carefully examined and chosen on the coast, were suitably housed and treated, and later, when approaching land in the Americas, to ensure that they were prepared for a profitable sale.

There were, then, powerful reasons, notably the economic self-interest of the main people involved, to look after the slaves from the minute they boarded a ship. The ship's owners expected it, and the officer class on board benefited from it. Yet the history of the slave ships is not only a story of casual brutality, but, more crucially, of endemic suffering and death and even occasionally catastrophic casualty levels. Who was responsible for the sufferings endured by the Africans?

Slave ships were infamous as the most gruesome of all sailing ventures, and sailors joined from grim necessity. Nothing 'but necessity compels them . . . especially to Guinea'. Drunk, in debt, at the risk of being jailed, too young to know better – desperation in one form or another propelled poor men towards the slave ships. Many sailors were cheated, deceived or forced onto the ships, but most found themselves heading to Africa from dire necessity. Not surprisingly, they came from the poorest ranks of society, on both sides of the Atlantic, described by John Newton as 'the refuse and dregs of the Nation'. Hugh Crow thought them 'the very dregs of the community'.[33] To such men, the offer of cash – wages in advance – for joining a ship was virtually irresistible, to clear debts, to sustain impoverished families or merely to keep dockside debtors (tavern keepers and crimps, recruiters for the ships) at arm's length. The real cost of agreeing to join was hidden and was to be paid later, off the coast or in mid-Atlantic, as, one after another, numbers of them succumbed to African diseases and to the infections which swept through their ranks.

On British slave ships sailors were drawn from across the British Isles, but they also came from Britain's far-flung colonies and settlements. There were Africans, Lascars, Americans and Europeans from as far afield as Sweden and Sicily, alongside freed slaves from the Caribbean. To modern eyes the presence of African sailors might seem the most unusual presence on a slave ship. But Africans were vital to the whole slave-trading business: slave ships needed more hands on the Atlantic crossing to the Americas than they had on the first outbound voyage to Africa itself, normally the easiest part of a slave voyage. Africans were sometimes used to step into the gaps left by crewmen who died on the coast.[34]

The black presence on ships in the Atlantic was also important for another particular reason. Throughout the centuries of Atlantic slavery, a life at sea was sometimes the only means of escaping from slavery – or from the oppressive difficulties of being a free black in societies dominated by slavery. The sea meant freedom. Whaling ships proved particularly attractive to freed slaves, and we know of some whose crews were 50 per cent black.[35] The best-known former slave who turned to a career at sea – both as a slave and as a free man – was Olaudah Equiano. His varied career at sea, on no fewer than eighteen ships, took him from the eastern Mediterranean to the Arctic, and throughout the Caribbean islands, to Central and North America. Even a sailor's basic garb conveyed the impression of freedom. When Frederick Douglass escaped from North American slavery in 1838, he dressed up as a sailor.[36] A career at sea, then, had unique qualities which attracted Africans and men of African descent. It was the most international and most democratic of occupations, where men from all corners of the world rubbed shoulders with other men of different colour and backgrounds. They lived in conditions of close and generally squalid intimacy, sometimes beset by life-threatening terrors, all bound together by the strenuous and dangerous life on board a sailing ship. Men at sea needed each other – often for mere survival – in ways that did not happen on land (except perhaps in military combat).

The slave trade also ensured that Africans were scattered around the world, and not merely in the Americas. By 1700, when millons had been shipped to the Americas, small African communities had taken root in distant ports and cities, with dozens of black people dotted among fashionable homes in Europe and the Americas as domestic servants. On the back of the slave trade an African diaspora had emerged, and not simply in the slave quarters of the Americas. Equiano, for example, had sailed in Arctic waters; there were men of African descent to be found in the first convict settlements in Australia after 1787. Black soldiers served in European armies wherever they fought around the world. Africans who once seemed exotic had, over the centuries, become familiar. Why, then, should Africans *not* appear in the crew rosters of the slave ships? Indeed, by the early nineteenth century, in the last phase of the slave trade, there were significant numbers of slaves working as sailors on the slave voyages across the South Atlantic to and from Brazil.[37]

Though we know with some precision the numbers of African slaves carried across the Atlantic, we can only guess at the numbers of sailors involved. In shipping some 3.5 million Africans to the Americas, 350,000 men may have been employed on British ships. Of those, it has been estimated that about 210,000 would have been rank-and-file sailors.[38] Each ship needed a small inner core of skilled and experienced men: master, junior officers and mate, a carpenter (a critical figure in fitting out the facilities to house the slaves) and a cooper to handle the ship's vital water barrels.[39] (More space was allocated to barrels of water on a slave ship than to any other item – including the people on board.) Though the crew of slave ships varied in size, slave ships needed more sailors, per ton, than any ships engaged in other forms of maritime commerce, for fairly obvious reasons. Trading on the coast and, more especially, sailing from Africa to the Americas, in a ship filled with distressed and turbulent Africans, was quite unlike another other voyage at sea. Sailors did not normally have to worry about cargo. On a slave ship the 'cargo' was human. The slaves lay in fettered ranks, in communal squalor, released according to a daily regime for food and exercise – weather permitting. Many were sick, some of them mortally. And all were brimming with a truculent resentment when not utterly traumatized and depressed.

Once a slave ship arrived at its trading locations on the coast, and began to receive Africans, the sailors' role changed crucially. They were no longer ordinary seamen, but had become jailors in a floating prison gradually filling with understandably resentful and vengeful captives. The dangerous, violent and often disastrous events that unfolded on those ships continued until the last Africans were discharged in the Americas. The ship itself had changed. The first leg of most slave voyages was much like other trading voyages, except for the large numbers

Frontispiece from *The Interesting Narrative of the Life of Olaudah Equiano or Gustavus Vassa, the African, written by himself* (1789).

of sailors on board. The voyage began with the outfitting of the ship not merely with the essentials for the journey, for crew and Africans, but with the goods required to trade and barter on the coast. Slave ships left their home ports brimming with commodities demanded by African coastal traders. Moreover, those traders had very clear ideas about what sort of goods African merchants wanted from the Atlantic ships. Trading for slaves involved an exchange of *specific* imported commodities, not cheap baubles. Like the ships and the sailors, those goods came from all points of the compass.

The slave ships carried a variety of cargoes: goods from Europe, Asia and the Americas, all destined to be traded for slaves. The nature and variety of those goods provide important clues about the nature of the slave trade itself and are revealing about the complexity and sophistication of commercial transactions on the coast. From an early date, Africans were very specific about what they wanted from the Europeans; they could not be bought off with cheap, throwaway goods. Once Europeans began the search for slaves for the Americas, African merchants and traders quickly developed a keen commercial sense of what they could demand from the ships. In their turn, Europeans scoured the markets of Europe – and of Asia – to provide what Africans demanded. In the early seventeenth century, Dutch slave traders imported a great variety of textiles and other goods from Asia to Upper Guinea: Indian textiles (which had been dyed in Holland); textiles from Flanders, England and Spain; woollen cloth from Rouen; raw cotton from Cape Verde; calico from Gujarat; cloth from Bengal and Seurat; satin from Persia; striped cotton cloth from Sindh; taffeta and bedspreads from China; woven cloth from North Africa; shawls from southern India. In the same period large volumes of beads were traded in Upper Guinea; there were beads and semi-precious stones from India, coral, cowrie shells and pearls. Such luxuries arrived alongside more prosaic goods: hats and cloaks, stockings, belts and shoes, codfish from Newfoundland, fruits, wines and foodstuffs, paper and French brandy.[40]

Shipping goods from the wider world to West Africa was pioneered by the Portuguese and Dutch. Though the British had traded to Africa since Elizabeth's reign, their role was strictly minor until the mid- and late seventeenth century, when they quickly overtook their European rivals on the back of their own expansive commercial and imperial growth. London was the engine which propelled that maritime trade, its finance, commercial houses, political elites and myriad trades fuelling a massive expansion of shipping and commerce in all corners of the Atlantic – especially to the Americas. British traders wanted more and more Africans to feed their Caribbean slave colonies but were unable to push aside the Dutch on the African coast until the formation of the Royal African Company – with its combined strength of the City and royalty – after 1672. Thereafter, the British established themselves as the major European presence on the slave coast.[41]

Ships now left British ports, but especially London in the early phase, filled with goods from a wide range of industries, two-thirds of them English by the early eighteenth century. The most valuable export to Africa was English woollens and textiles, followed by a range of iron-ware, weapons and gunpowder, and then textiles from Asia, re-shipped through London. Metalware of all kinds – iron bars, raw metals, manu-factured ironware (from nails to guns and shot) – all found their way onto ships departing for Africa. For all this variety, textiles dominated: it has been calculated that in the seventeenth and eighteenth centuries, 50 per cent of the value of *all* goods imported into Africa consisted of textiles, followed in importance by alcohol, manufactured goods, then armaments. When, after 1740, Liverpool emerged as Britain's major slaving port, its rise was in large part because of the city's proximity to the textile regions of Lancashire and Yorkshire.[42]

The African demand for specific goods meant that European traders could not easily find a suitable cargo from within their own local or national economies. No nation produced the full range of goods wanted by Africans. Hence traders needed, from an early date, to trans-ship a range of commodities acquired in other parts of the world. They bought cool Indian fabrics, Swedish iron bars (to be fashioned into metal instru-ments by African blacksmiths), French brandies and liquors, Brazilian tobacco and cowrie shells from the Maldives. Most of these items had themselves been purchased from other European merchants who had shipped the goods to Europe from distant trading posts.

Slave ships thus headed for the African coast with their holds filled with goods from all corners of the known world. Ships from Rio loaded Brazilian produce alongside goods imported from Asia and Europe for the voyage across the South Atlantic to their favourite trad-ing area in West Central Africa. Traders from Pernambuco dispatched rolls of Brazilian tobacco to exchange for slaves. Merchants from Bahia traded for Africans in the Bight of Benin, where locals had acquired a taste for Brazilian tobacco coated in molasses. Ships from Barbados bought slaves in exchange for Barbadian rum.[43]

The early British monopoly of the Royal African Company, from 1672, was never able to provide enough Africans to satisfy the planters, and so free-trading interlopers, confident that they would not be caught or prosecuted, were quick to step in. By 1698, the British trade was thrown open, in return for a levy imposed on exports to Africa. Thereafter, London's trade to Africa was eclipsed by merchants and shippers from Bristol and Liverpool, though the capital continued to play a major role in the African trade. At the same time, ships from North America and the Caribbean conducted their own trade to Africa, exchanging rum and other local produce for slaves. (The irony was obvious: slave-grown produce – rum and tobacco – was traded to Africans in return for yet more African slaves.)

The growth of Liverpool's trade to Africa in the course of the eighteenth century was massive. In 1709 one ship of 30 tons traded to Africa from Liverpool; a century later that had grown to 134 ships and 34,966 tons. Again, outbound cargoes provide a snapshot of the remarkable range of commodities demanded by Africans in return for slaves. Though cargoes bound for Africa formed only a small proportion of the city's overall export tonnage, the *value* of those cargoes was high, largely because much of it consisted of manufactured goods. Time and again, the inventories of both small- and large-scale Liverpool shippers tell a similar tale: of ships loaded with textiles, metal goods, guns, knives, silk and cotton goods, brass goods (mainly cooking pots) and copperware, bottles of beer and liquor and clay pipes. Many of these items were manufactured by craftsmen and small industries in and around the city of Liverpool, with local trade directories tracing the proliferation of those industries over the course of the century. Other goods were transported to Liverpool via the coastal trade from smaller ports up and down the west coast of Britain, the Isle of Man and Ireland. In addition, England's newly constructed canal system made possible the transfer of bulkier goods to Liverpool from the far reaches of Lancashire, Yorkshire and even as far away as the Midlands. When we add to the economic data details of the sizeable ship-building industry in Liverpool, we can see that something like 10,000 people in Liverpool – one in eight of the population – depended on the trade to and from West Africa. About 40 per cent of the city's income was derived from the same trade. (Not surprisingly, there was widespread opposition in Liverpool to the campaign against the slave trade after 1787.[44])

Whether operating under the seventeenth-century monopoly, charter companies, or the more open trade of the eighteenth century, ships sent to trade for slaves were more costly investments than 'normal' trading ventures. As the trade evolved, and as African traders became highly selective about what they expected from the ships, the outbound cargoes became more costly. At times, cargoes amounted to upwards of 65 per cent of the total cost of a voyage – a much higher cost than other forms of maritime trade. In fact, the slave trade was the most costly of overseas trades. That it grew so rapidly, and was so fiercely defended and promoted by European states, provides a clear indication of its potential value and of the importance everyone attached to the acquisition of Africans on the coast.

However we study it, here was an extraordinary international trade. At first glance the Atlantic slave trade appears to be a product of communities fringing that Atlantic ocean. But those societies were themselves part of complex networks which extended far beyond the Atlantic world. After all, Europeans had first set foot on the West African coast en route to the more distant markets of Asia. The trades which evolved around the coastal peripheries of the Atlantic take us deep into the interiors of *all* the communities involved in that trade. Liverpool's links to the towns and villages of Lancashire and North Wales, of Yorkshire and Cheshire, offers just one, British, illustration. It is an example which could be multiplied wherever we look at the complexity that was the Atlantic trading system. Trade on the African coast itself was only one aspect of an emergent global trading and imperial system which, though orchestrated from the main centres of European trade and governance, embraced far-flung settlements and trading outposts. On the African coast, in India, in North or South America, Europeans developed commercial dealings with local peoples whose own trading systems stretched deep into regions beyond the Europeans' reach. Pelts and furs, foodstuffs and tobacco from the native peoples of North America, luxuries of all sorts from the inaccessible interiors of Central Asia and China – all found their way to European trading posts, thence to be transshipped via Europe to West Africa.

Rulers and merchants on the African coast were quick to spot goods they liked, items they could enjoy or use to advance their own strength or wealth. In return, they were happy to provide whatever supplies of slaves reached them on the coast via interior wars, raids or trading systems. Thus, European slave traders carefully packed their outbound ships with the appropriate goods needed to lubricate the machinery of slave trading on the coast. The goods arriving in Africa on the slave ships may have come from all corners of the globe, but the demand they sought to satisfy was *African*. In return, Europeans acquired slaves who were destined to transform the face of the Americas and to toil at activities which enriched their colonial masters and their metropolitan backers. But before that could happen, millions of Africans had to endure the unspeakable terrors of the Atlantic crossing.

FOUR

The Sea

The 120 people who crossed the Atlantic on the *Mayflower* from Plymouth in 1620, in about 65 days, had endured what all (save the baby born on the way) agreed was a hellish voyage. At landfall they gave relieved thanks to the Lord for their salvation (not knowing, however, that almost half of them would be dead before the first winter was out). They celebrated by singing Psalm 100:

> For the LORD *is* good;
> His mercy *is* everlasting,
> And His truth *endures* to all generations.

By that date, more than 160,000 Africans had been forced onto (mostly Spanish and Portuguese) slave ships, the great majority also destined for the Americas. But they had little to give thanks for on arrival – except perhaps that landfall brought an end to their seaborne experience.

Every single one of the over 11 million enslaved Africans who stepped ashore in the Americas had endured prolonged distress which, to this day, remains difficult to envisage or recapture. Even the most experienced of writers and historians have struggled adequately to describe what happened. What is often called the 'Middle Passage' (the voyage across the Atlantic) continues to defy efforts to convey the human experience. Allowing the worst evidence to speak for itself can verge on the pornographic, while simply reciting the raw demographic data seems callous and uncaring. It sometimes feels as if the victims ought to be left in peace, and that their suffering ought perhaps to be left unspoken. Yet it was the experiences at sea which *defined* Atlantic slavery. Whatever the upheavals and pain of African enslavement and travel to the coast, nothing could have prepared slavery's victims for the terrors of being at sea in a slave ship. Not surprisingly, in the years since slavery the slave ships have anchored themselves in popular memory, as a defining image of slavery itself. Ask for a popular concept of what slavery meant, and you are likely to be told about a slave ship. What is rarely understood, however, is that many slave ships spent longer trawling for slaves on the coast of Africa than crossing the Atlantic. For many slaves, the longest period on a slave ship was spent riding at anchor, in sight of Africa.

People of all sorts and in all conditions, men and women and children, often from diverse and unknown backgrounds and communities, found themselves sharing the bleak squalor of the slave decks. All found themselves imprisoned in a vessel the likes of which most had never seen before, and all at the mercy not merely of brutal and terrified white men, but beleaguered by oceanic terrors they could hardly understand. The sea could bring even the most hardy of experienced sailors to a state of howling fear; many of the captives on board the slave ships had never seen the sea before, still less experienced its dangers. They now found themselves loaded onto a ship that was to be, by turns, a prison, a torture chamber and, in many cases, their last known place on earth.

Most captives spent a considerable time on the ship even before they departed on the Atlantic crossing. At many trading points on the coast there were no facilities for holding captives before they were sold to the slave ships. As we have seen, slave forts – 'factories' in the contemporary parlance – or ready-made barracoons capable of holding large numbers of people until a ship arrived and a deal could be done, were unusual. For many, perhaps most, the main method of detention was on the ship itself. Africans were bought by slave traders and then brought on board to be held until final departure. Some ships were anchored offshore as a permanent sales platform and factory, with Africans later moved to departing ships. Marshalling, containing and controlling large numbers of prisoners – even if they arrived in dribs and drabs – demanded new forms of incarceration. Indeed the numbers of Africans were so vast that what emerged on the slave ships was an experiment in penal policy. Britain (and the rest of the Western world) had not devised a penal policy for its own criminals at home, though loading them onto rotting ships – the hulks in the Thames – or shipping them to distant settlements provided solutions. Slave ships occupied much the same position: they became prisons where large numbers of sullen people were forcibly detained in dire physical conditions until they could be disposed of elsewhere – in the Americas. It was no accident that a number of contemporary critics viewed the ships as floating dungeons, and that sailors who exchanged an English prison for life on a slave ship thought they had swapped one prison for another.

African prisoners might spend many months on the coast. Slave captains rarely found a full complement of slaves waiting for them on arrival. Instead, they had to barter and trade, here and there, for individuals or for groups of slaves, in a series of protracted negotiations with African 'headmen' and traders. They dispatched sailors onto dry land to follow leads – rumours from departing ships and from traders already on the coast – about where captives might be had. Their arrival offshore could also attract local interest, with fires lit onshore to inform the ships that slaves were available. African canoemen swung alongside the ship, offering not only foodstuffs but slaves. Crewmen travelled some distances onshore and upriver to locate fresh captives and organize their movement to the ocean and onto the awaiting ship. Anchored just off land, the captain now adopted a new role, switching from mariner to commercial dealer and negotiator, always trying to stick to the ship owners' instructions while having to adapt to local conditions. A captain often left his ship in another officer's charge while he went onshore to buy slaves. Just as the captain became a negotiator, the men on his ship became jailors.

When John Newton's ship, the *Argyle*, finally made landfall at Sierra Leone on 23 October 1750 (after a two-month voyage from Liverpool), he clambered aboard another slave ship, the *Cornwall*. The latter's Captain Duncan told Newton that he had already been on the coast for six months, and had ranged as far south as Anomabu on the Gold Coast, but still had only fifty slaves for his efforts. Two days later Newton went ashore and bought his first slaves, two men and a woman. He finally embarked on the Atlantic crossing in late May 1751, a voyage that took six weeks. If they survived, the first three Africans he purchased had been on board for six months *before* they even left the African coast. Newton had intended to buy 250 Africans: he managed to secure 156, of whom 146 survived.[1]

This example was not unusual, and similar patterns could be found throughout the seventeenth and eighteenth centuries. In the seventeenth century, ships of the Dutch West India Company spent an

Fishing canoes at El Mina, with slaves being carried aboard the waiting ships. The slave forts can be seen in the background. Etchings taken from Awnsham Churchill, *A Collection of Voyages and Travels* ... (1746).

average of 120 days on the coast, while British ships averaged 94 days trading there in the same period. A century later, ships stayed even longer: the Dutch averaged 200 days, while 230 French ships averaged 143. A much larger sample of British ships (in the years when Newton was trading) spent an average of 173 days on the African coast. Ships were detained longer on some stretches of coastline – Loango, for example – than others. However, ships trading to and from the major slave forts tended to have a quicker turnaround, because the forts could generally deliver larger numbers of Africans more quickly. Sometimes, captains sold Africans purchased earlier to other slave ships, allowing them to make up their cargoes and depart from the coast.

Through all this discussion about 'coasting' – about the prolonged time slave ships spent on the coast – one central fact stands out: untold numbers of Africans spent many months 'at sea' long before they lost sight of land. The first Africans to be brought on board could spend many months on a slave ship before the voyage began. Moreover, those were hazardous, terrifying months when the encounters between sailors, Africa and Africans produced a perilous brew of ailments and contagions. It was here, on the coast, that crewmen were struck down by tropical illnesses, and where slaves also succumbed in large numbers. The sailors had entered a new disease environment and contracted illnesses to which they had no resistance. Africans not only faced those same medical problems, but many of them were in a feeble state despite having been 'examined' for purchase: all had already endured the physical and mental distress of enslavement and the often months-long trek to the Atlantic coast. The problem was at its worst when an anchored ship was struck by a contagious disease, brought on board either by a sailor or African captive. On the very last day of 1729 smallpox was discovered among the slaves on board the Dutch ship *Brandenburg*. Seven Africans died before the ship cast off for Surinam a month later. By the time the ship reached its destination, 38 more (from a total of 409) had died of the disease.[2]

As a slave ship swung at anchor in sight of Africa, sailors and slaves began to die, often in large numbers. We know that on Dutch ships, some 5 per cent of the slaves died during this prolonged stay on the coast.[3] The Dutch ship *Vergenoegen*, trading off Loango in 1794, took on board a handful of Africans every day for four months. But only days after the first one came on board, smallpox broke out. Of the 390 Africans purchased, 50 contracted the disease and 26 died before the vessel sailed. (Eight crewmen had died on the African coast.) The sick offered a revolting spectacle. In the captain's words, 'Some looked like monsters, raw from top to toe as if they were skinned alive, and a stench that was hardly bearable. We have to turn them over with . . . old rags.'[4]

Sometimes, Africans found themselves passed from ship to ship, in a confusion of trading between friendly traders or via conflict and warfare among European rivals and enemies. In February 1781, the British impounded a Dutch ship, the *Zorgue*, close to Cape Coast. She was already carrying 244 Africans, who had been on board for months past. Yet the ship, now renamed the *Zong*, did not quit the African coast until 18 August. By then she was packed with 442 slaves and began a disastrous voyage that was to last 113 days and see the ranks of captives thinned out – largely by murdered by the crew with an insurance claim in mind – from 442 to 208. If some of the original Africans managed to survive to landfall in Jamaica by late December 1781, they would have been at sea for well over a year.[5] Although the level of African mortality on the coast was high, it was generally lower than the level suffered when crossing the Atlantic, but it still formed a substantial slice of the overall African death rate on the slave ships. Somewhere between 18 and 30 per cent of all African deaths 'at sea' occurred *before* they embarked on the Atlantic crossing. There was, then, a grisly apprenticeship taking place on the ships off the African coast. Africans were incarcerated on board, on an ocean which offered its own dangers and fears, and all the while, as the numbers of Africans increased, sickness and death haunted the ships.

Organizing life on board a slave ship changed as the ranks of the enslaved increased. The early handful could be marshalled relatively easily. Large numbers, however, created unique logistical and human problems – for the crew. For the Africans, the ship meant something entirely different. They were naked, or near naked (clothing might hide a dangerous weapon), and they lost their names. Henceforth Africans entered that strange twilight world where someone else decided what they should be called. On the ship, they were given a number. They were listed, and entered into the ship's documentation, in numerical sequence as they came on board: numerical rank, gender and physical condition. This doleful litany echoes through all the documents of the slave ships. John Newton again illustrates the process. In late December 1750, his ship's small boat brought alongside six Africans: '1 woman, 2 boys, and 3 girls, all small, No. 38 to 43.' In early New Year 1751 he bought a 'woman slave', 'tho she has a very bad mouth. Could have bought her cheaper.' She was number 46. Newton's African captives entered his accountancy as numbers and stayed that way during any subsequent illness, as in: 'No. 27, being very bad with a flux . . .'. The dead departed his accountancy in the same fashion: 'in the morning buried a boy slave (No. 66) who was ill with a violent flux the 3rd day after he came on board'. Later they buried 'a man slave (No. 33), having been a fortnight ill of a flux, which has baffled all our medicines'.[6]

Once brought on board a slave ship, the Africans passed through the next phase of a prolonged uprooting which had begun with their initial capture and enslavement. Numbered, not named, in life, sickness and death, they were removed ever further from their defining identity. They now found themselves rolling and swaying on a ship at anchor for months on end, their ranks swelling as regular handfuls of Africans clambered aboard. As their numbers grew, though regularly diminished by death, they became subject to a tightening shipboard discipline which, at its worst, was brutal and terrifying. Their miseries stemmed largely from the crew, but their tormentors were themselves under increasing strain. Sailors on a slave ship were, by definition, the roughest of all men to be found at sea – no mean feat. On the African coast they too had to change, of necessity. For a start, sickness began to erode their physical strength and their numbers. Time and again, captain's logs recorded the sudden onslaught of terrifying tropical sickness, of bouts of screaming delirium – and sudden, painful death, followed by a swift burial. It was vital, for security, that crew numbers be maintained, and that any shortfall did not become obvious to the Africans. Yet this same band of men, their numbers decreased, their individual strength sapped by sickness and the tropical conditions, faced growing numbers of angry Africans, keen to escape from their prison. Bit by bit, shipboard discipline tightened; bit by bit, a fatigued and wary crew viewed the Africans with increased concern – and fear.

After a few weeks on the coast the crew on most slave ships found themselves outnumbered by their African prisoners. In the process, relations between the crew and the Africans changed. The initial, casual forms of incarceration gave way to more rigid routines. Women and children were always a sizeable proportion of a slave 'cargo' (the women easy sexual targets for sailors long deprived of female company) and were generally allowed more latitude. But the men were treated with greater caution – and increased severity. Daily routines of feeding and exercise were established; so too was that regime of imprisonment below decks, using the well-known hardware of the slave ships: the chains, shackles and manacles so familiar in the popular imagination. This ironware – the chains of slavery – appears at first sight to speak to African defeat and submission. But it also illustrates something more profound. Without those restraints, the slave ships could not survive. Restraining the growing ranks of Africans by manacles and chains was the only way in which small bands of sailors could hope to maintain any semblance of control.

As the ship slowly filled with Africans, she changed. What had once been an unexceptional cargo ship – largely indistinguishable from any other – was now a characteristic slave ship. She was a prison which teemed with people and echoed with the (often distressing) noises of

a prison and an infirmary. The slave ship also gave off its own distinctive smell – the stench of crowded, unwashed and sick humanity.
And all this – fetid ranks of distressed people, packed into a small,
noisy, stinking ship as it swung at anchor – in the tropical waters off
the coast. As bad as this may seem, it was to get worse, much worse,
when Africa disappeared from view and the ship finally slipped into its
Atlantic crossing.

When a master decided he had enough Africans on board to begin
what he hoped would be a profitable venture, when he was satisfied
that his ship was adequately provisioned (and especially had enough
water to sustain the people on board), he turned his ship towards the
Americas. Thereafter, he and everyone on board was at the mercy of the
elements. Even the most experienced of masters, and the best-drilled
crew, could not guarantee what might happen when they embarked on
an Atlantic crossing. Indeed, in large measure, the course of the slave
trade was dictated as much by the natural weather patterns of the
region as it was by the wishes of planters or navigators. The Atlantic
was divided by two major weather systems which imposed themselves
on the movement of shipping in both the North and South Atlantic.
In the North Atlantic, the prevailing currents worked in a clockwise
motion which directed sailing ships south from Europe, thence across
the ocean towards the Caribbean and then northwards to North America.
Ships sailing to West Africa were helped by the warm current which
they entered off the northwest coast of Africa. Leaving West Africa
for the Americas involved picking up a South Equatorial Current
heading northwest towards the Caribbean. The major currents in the
South Atlantic flowed anticlockwise, the Benguela current feeding
into the Brazilian current and propelling ships onwards towards Brazil.
These two movements of water – the North Atlantic clockwise, the
South Atlantic anticlockwise – were associated with major prevailing
wind systems, which compounded the work of the Atlantic currents.
It was as if sailing ships were propelled by massive weather systems
which acted like paths and signposts across the immensity of the
Atlantic Ocean.

Ships that kept within one of the major weather systems, north or
south, enjoyed the quickest of Atlantic crossings. Thus a ship sailing
from Upper Guinea to the Caribbean and North America (by remaining within the northern system) could, typically, cross in about six weeks.
And so too would a vessel leaving West-central Africa for Brazil (that

is, remaining within the southern system). Ships which moved from one weather system to another, however, significantly increased the time of the Atlantic crossing. Ships from the Gold Coast and the Bight of Benin to Brazil took two months to cross. The most protracted and therefore the most lethal of all slave voyages were those which hauled Africans huge distances from southeast Africa (Mozambique) or those which had complicated voyages across both weather systems. Ships that dropped down from the Gold Coast and the Bights of Benin and Biafra, south into the Atlantic, thence west into the Atlantic, before moving into the northern weather system, sometimes took three months. They inevitably lost a high proportion of their captives.[7]

Within these Atlantic weather systems, sailors and navigators struggled to plot and sail to specific destinations – hoping to avoid a host of threatening obstacles en route: storms, and especially the annual hurricane season; hidden rocks and sand bars on the coasts of Africa and the Americas; and sudden and unexpected changes in the wind and current which could, in a flash, drive a ship to disaster. Experience and assistance became available to the wider seafaring community in the form of printed manuals and guides, though fixing a ship's longitude remained a rough-and-ready science throughout much of the history of the Atlantic slave trade.

> The great End and Business of NAVIGATION is to instruct the Mariner how to conduct a Ship through the wide and pathless Ocean, to the remotest Parts of the World, the safest and shortest Ways, in Passages navigable.[8]

Even the best navigators at sea were, ultimately, in the hands of the Atlantic weather systems.

The master of every slave ship was keen to cross the Atlantic as quickly as safety allowed. Everyone involved in the trade quickly learned that the longer a slave ship was at sea, the worse the death rates among the Africans. In general, the Atlantic crossings became quicker over the history of the slave trade – and the death rate on board declined accordingly. The Middle Passage was nonetheless a time of dire suffering for most of the Africans involved. They suffered grievously when the weather turned foul, when a ship was delayed, becalmed or in danger. If a ship was gravely threatened by a storm, it had to be lightened as a measure of last resort and Africans were even jettisoned overboard –

much like any other item of cargo (a loss for which, by the late eighteenth century, ship owners could claim compensation under the conventions of British maritime insurance). In storms, the Africans remained below decks, the hatches and air vents closed, shackled together for days on end. The crew were too busy keeping the ship afloat to attend to the needs of the Africans, or even to remove the dead. Unfed, unwashed – effectively ignored until the storm abated – hundreds of Africans were thrown this way and that, crashing against each other in fettered filth along the bare boards of the deck, or pressed into their rough wooden racks. At such times the slave decks became an abomination: more like a neglected stable than a human habitation, a place which even slave surgeons (men possessed of a strong stomach) found hard to enter. In such pestilential conditions, old illnesses flared again, and new ones took hold.

The ships were a breeding ground for disease. Communal feeding, the filth of the slave decks, the practical difficulty of using the 'necessary tubs' while in chains and on a heaving ship, all helped to generate epidemics of the 'bloody flux' (amoebic dysentery) which both fouled and haunted the slave ships. Africans laid low by, and succumbing to, the disease were a commonplace on the slave ships. Many had stepped on board the slave ships with dormant ailments which readily flourished in the ships' squalor. Each African had been 'examined' before purchase, but such scrutiny was generally rudimentary. Slave surgeons or an experienced sailor were looking for imperfections and physical problems that might diminish the African's value, or might bring sickness onto the ship. It was no surprise if they did bring sickness on board. Many had trekked huge distances before they arrived at the Atlantic coast. Others, enslaved closer to the ocean, though avoiding a long overland journey, often had to wait a considerable time in poor, confined conditions before entering a slave ship, where they faced another protracted delay. Being detained in a slave barracoon, a slave fort or a holding pen was itself a demoralizing and debilitating process. Enduring the claustrophobic gloom of a cell in a slave fort, or sharing the company of pigs in Angola, was a recipe for sickness. There were, then, many reasons for sickness and distress among the Africans on a slave ship – even before they lost sight of land. Once on board, any weakness or imperfection a slave might be harbouring would be cruelly exposed and made worse by shipboard conditions, whatever the master, the crew or the ship's distant owners might do to maintain health and survival among the

Africans. It was one of the great ironies of the slave trade that all those involved – and especially those with money to make from the trade – had every reason to maintain the health and well-being of their seaborne captives. But the system devised and perfected for transporting Africans to the American markets contained its own inescapable ingredients for sickness and death. In time, those factors were diminished (mortality rates declined by more than 40 per cent over the history of the trade), but they never vanished completely and remained an inherent threat to every African being shipped across the Atlantic.

Africans taken to North America faced a long haul from their various departure points (which ranged from Upper Guinea to West-central Africa), with the ships normally stopping en route in the Caribbean. Those long voyages consequently registered some of the highest levels of African mortality.[9] There were, however, some strange blips in the data: Dutch ships to the Caribbean took longer than voyages to other islands – yet the mortality rate was lower.[10] Similarly, though mortality levels on slave ships declined in the eighteenth century, the length of voyages did *not* decline. There were also marked differences in the experiences between national carriers. The British lost about 8 per cent of their Africans on ships to the Caribbean, while those heading to the Dutch and Spanish Caribbean lost upwards of 20 per cent. This seems to be explained partly by the rising British abolitionist pressure, after 1783, to improve conditions on British ships, and the fact that traders to the Spanish Caribbean bought their Africans from regions with traditionally high levels of mortality.[11] The duration of crossings to the Caribbean began to fall significantly towards the end of the slave trade, by which time slave traders were using newer, faster vessels.

The largest movement of Africans was to Brazil and there, at the peak of the trade, the mortality levels were lower than they were for Africans shipped to the Caribbean and North America. This was largely because it was far quicker to cross the South Atlantic: Brazil was much closer to its supplies of slaves than Central and North America and Atlantic crossings were about 40 per cent shorter – ships were helped across greatly by the powerful South Atlantic currents. On the Brazilian crossings, mortality rates dropped markedly in the late eighteenth and early nineteenth centuries.[12] All that was to change in the second quarter of the nineteenth century, with a revival of startling levels of mortality, levels which can stand comparison with any period of the Atlantic slave trade. There was a revival of harsh brutality towards Africans on Brazilian and Portuguese ships as the 'illicit' vessels sought hurriedly to pack up and outrun the abolitionist navies.[13]

At times, all this data – providing as it does the building blocks for the historical reconstruction so vital to any understanding of the slave trade – seems oddly sterile. It is as if the victims, the living and the dead, have somehow vanished under a pile of statistics. The difficult task for the historian is to strike a balance: to shape from this flinty data a meaningful historical narrative which does justice to the African victims and, equally, makes sense of the actions of the perpetrators of the trade. What did all this mean for the Africans?

The great majority of Africans survived the Atlantic crossing, though their condition on arrival raises other fundamental questions. But something like 1 million Africans died at sea, either on the coast or mid-Atlantic. These are grim figures by any comparison we care to make. Yet even to offer a total figure – to add up all the deaths and offer them as a rounded figure – fails to capture what the seaborne crossing meant to each *individual* survivor, not to mention those who died. What sort of memories – mental scars and inescapable nightmares – did the survivors carry into the unknown world they entered at landfall, weeks and months after their ship had slipped away from the African coast?

We can only speculate about what went through the captives' minds as their ships made their way across the Atlantic. How many had even seen the sea before they were marched to the coast? And though most had perhaps become accustomed to the rhythms of being at sea when incarcerated in an anchored ship on the coast, that was fundamentally different from sailing the Atlantic. How could they know where they were? Even had crewmen told them that they would soon step ashore, what sense would that make? For all they knew, they were merely biding their time as their shipmates fell sick, died and were thrown into the sea. How could they be sure that they too would not join the sick and the dead in some kind of diabolical ritual? All this is speculation – guesswork about what went through the minds of millions plunged into an unimaginable horror story. But it is surely not idle speculation to feel that thoughts about the Atlantic crossing embedded themselves deep in the personal and communal folk memories of the African survivors, to emerge as the stuff of nightmarish accounts across the slave communities of the Americas.

No one in charge of a slave ship wanted or planned for the foul conditions on a storm-tossed ship. Yet the slaves' conditions *were* made worse by the crew. But the crew also found themselves struggling against circumstances they could barely control. For a start there were rarely enough sailors to pay adequate attention to the needs and well-being of each African – especially on a rough crossing. The depletion of crew numbers, on the coast and in the Atlantic, frequently left the crew short-staffed, with the surviving ranks often weakened by illness. The crew found themselves greatly outnumbered by ranks of slaves who were with good reason defiant and hostile from the moment they came on board. Every sailor knew that they could not trust the Africans. Even young children could be used to assist an escape, a revolt or an outburst of violence. Tools and implements – even a stray piece of wood – could become a dangerous weapon in the hands of an African slave. The crew had to be permanently wary and distrustful: a moment's carelessness would lead to a slave outburst and a danger to life, even to the very existence of the ship itself. Though most officers sought to maintain some semblance of control over their men, and the way in which they treated the Africans, it often proved impossible to keep nervous sailors in check. Random violence, sexual assaults, capricious cruelties – all and more were doled out to the Africans by sailors who were, at once, terrified and nervous of them. They feared the worst and were always ready to get their retaliation in first.

Slave ships crossed the Atlantic not only beset by the changing moods of the ocean, but oppressed by their own on-board climate of fear and loathing. Officers managed the crew with an iron discipline (though this was true on all contemporary ships). John Newton recorded on 1 November 1750, 'Gave two of my gentlemen a good caning and put one (William Lees) in irons.' Masters had to balance such punishments with the need not to allow the Africans to detect divisions among the crew: 'a mark of division amongst us was a great encouragement to the slaves to be troublesome'.[14] The crew handled them with a mix of terror and hatred, and the Africans regarded the crew, of all ranks, as their diabolical tormentors. Given the chance, Africans would lash out, remove their tormentors and escape. Of course, the slaves were not of one mind through this tumultuous experience. Many did not understand each other; some got by via a patois used by shipboard crew and Africans employed on the ships. (There were Africans who were used as interpreters and go-betweens both in Africa and at landfall.) But, in the main, all captives struggled for their own survival in the bleakest of physical conditions, arguing among themselves, and fighting each other, about space, about provisions, about movement on the slave decks. All had to cope with the unimaginable problems of being hemmed in by sick people who relieved themselves where they lay. Theirs was a world designed to create personal frictions.

Africans spent their time on slave ships in the company of that universal seafarer – the rat. The European rat had travelled on board ships heading to the wider world and settled a host of distant locations, plaguing societies and environments unprepared for them. In places, rats overwhelmed their new homes (Peru in the sixteenth century, for example) and almost destroyed fledgling colonial settlements (Jamestown in 1609, and Port Royal, Nova Scotia, at much the same time). Rats from a slave ship were thought to have escaped and rapidly proliferated across Jamaica by the mid-eighteenth century.[15] Later still, rats swept through the settlers in Sydney in 1790.[16] But rats seemed to feel especially at home at sea – and a slave ship provided an ideal breeding place for them. In the process, they brought incalculable torments to the ranks of manacled Africans. On eighteenth-century British warships it was calculated that the rats outnumbered the crew – and never left the ship unless she sank. Along with termites and other pests, rats ate their way through a ship's food supplies, damaging anything they could sink their teeth into, from water barrels to ammunition. They had especially rich pickings on the slave ships. John Newton took cats with him on the *Argyle* bound for Africa in 1750, but they too, like his crewmen, died on the African coast, and the ship's rats multiplied: 'We are quite over-run with them and can not get a cat upon any terms.' They even ate their way through the spare sails. As the months passed, and as the number of Africans on board steadily increased, the ship's rats continued their onslaught on everything remotely edible. In May 1751 Newton recorded, 'At work all spare times mending the sails, yet cannot repair them half so fast as the rats destroy.' Even more troubling, the rats had begun to attack people on board: 'We have so many on board that they are ready to devour every thing, and actually bite the people when they catch them asleep, and have even begun to nibble at the cables.'[17]

We can only imagine what all this meant for the wretched Africans. While still in sight of land, they were trapped, guarded by brutal and frightened sailors and shackled for long periods alongside other tormented Africans, many of them gravely ill. As if all that were not bad enough, they now found themselves plagued by rats scurrying around the decks, flourishing on the ship's abundant filth and boldly nibbling at the flesh of sleeping Africans. Rats were, then, yet another hideous torment (curiously, however, they are hardly ever mentioned by historians of the slave trade).

As the Africans crossed the ocean, for week after week their dead companions were unceremoniously dumped over the side (sailors had a more decorous ceremony and went to their grave with religious incantations uttered over the corpse). When possible, the crew released batches of slaves for exercise on the deck – but always remained alert. It was then, as they scanned the horizon, that the Africans could see . . . what? The Atlantic Ocean, North or South, in all its heaving immensity. Day after day, weeks, months even, of unchanging expanses of ocean, broken only by the swell and the waves of the ocean's movement; no land in sight, not even an accompanying bird, until they began to approach the Americas. For all they knew, they had entered another world where land had vanished and had given way to water. At night, shackled again below in the pitch-dark slave deck, they were assailed by the sounds of the ocean, by that unfamiliar cacophony of wood and sail cutting through the water, the night-time silences periodically broken by the groans of fellow prisoners and the shrieks of the dying. It was a hellish world from which only the strongest or luckiest were to emerge unscathed. If anyone doubted the physical loathsomeness of a slave ship, they only had to smell it. The men on board became accustomed to it. One captain warned a shipmate that 'the smell would be unpleasant for a few days', but 'when we got into the trade winds it would no longer be perceived'.[18] This stink was evident for some considerable distance, the foul stench drifting downwind for some kilometres from a crowded slave ship.

Oceanic voyages were always perilous, despite the best efforts of the crew. The sickness and death which haunted all slave ships sometimes endangered the ship itself. As sailors died on the voyage, especially after they had left Africa, ships often found themselves dangerously short-handed. Captains worried that their control over the Africans might become precarious if the captives sensed that the crew was diminished. But what happened when the captain died? The death of a ship's master, or that of senior officers, could imperil the entire venture and everyone on board. Although there was a clear line of descent for shipboard authority in such cases, with designated ranks and named men stepping into the dead man's role, such events could, and did, threaten a voyage. The disaster which overwhelmed the Africans on board the slave ship *Zong* in 1781 (when 132 of them were murdered by the crew) was in large part due to the death of the captain and the subsequent navigational confusion among inexperienced men at loggerheads with each other.[19] Mistakes at sea cost lives. Prolonged voyages depleted the provisions – especially the water (vital in such fetid, crowded and tropical conditions). Navigational errors led to conflicts and even loss of the ship. Sailing too close to an enemy colony in wartime (and Atlantic history was peppered with wars throughout the era of the slave trade) could lead to attack, capture and confiscation of the ship and its Africans.

Above all, natural dangers presented the greatest threat, especially to a depleted crew deprived of experienced navigators by sickness or death. Ships simply disappeared into Atlantic storms, leaving no trace of the vessel or her people. Less spectacular, but deeply troubling for all on board, were the doldrums, the area of equatorial calms in the mid-Atlantic which ships needed to cross as they moved from the southern into the northern weather systems. Ships found themselves trapped by the weather, waiting for the winds to pick up. The ship's ventilators, which normally directed fresh air into the slave decks when the vessel was under sail, were now useless as everyone on board lay becalmed on the equator. There was no relief from the stifling heat. Provisions, notably water, began to run low, and meagre allocations were rationed further. As time lagged, and the voyage prolonged, death rates rose. There was simply no escape until the winds picked up and came to their rescue. Sometimes the wind became their enemy.

Storms and shipwrecks were terrifying enough. For Africans chained below decks they were unbearable. There were times when, even though a slave ship survived a serious storm, the slaves, battened below, were so neglected as the crew fought to save the ship that large numbers died. In 1838 reports reached London that 300 Africans had died of hunger and suffocation on board a storm-bound slave ship from Mozambique recently docked at Havana.[20] There were even more terrible accounts of the crew abandoning a sinking ship, leaving Africans entombed below. The crew – fighting to the last to save the ship and, finally, desperate to save themselves – felt they could not afford to release hundreds of terrified Africans. The crew feared being overwhelmed by huge numbers of freed captives who were no less anxious to escape the tempest. The grim reality was that Africans remained manacled below decks as slave ships were destroyed on rocks, sandbars or shoals, or were torn apart by an Atlantic storm. In January 1738 the Dutch ship *Leusden*, bound for Surinam, was driven onto rocks in a storm. The crew and fourteen Africans who had been helping the crew on deck escaped; 702 Africans perished, chained below as the vessel foundered.[21] Such stories surfaced regularly, especially during the years of the illicit trade in the nineteenth century, when large numbers of Africans were left to a terrible fate. Crews managed their own escape by ensuring that the Africans remained shackled or imprisoned below decks. As late as 1838, the Royal Navy went to the rescue of a Spanish slave ship, wrecked on the Pedro shoals south of Jamaica. The vessel had broken up and vanished along with all 300 African captives. Others had been luckier: 'The crew had taken to their boats and landed at Black River.'[22] We know of 148 slave ships that were totally lost – and when everyone on board perished. Another 443 ships were shipwrecked (though sometimes the slaves were rescued by other slave ships and merely continued their onward journey into a lifetime's bondage). Piracy also posed a major threat to the slave ships, and many were seized by pirates or other privateers – again with the captives merely passing from one slave trader to another.[23]

Through all this misery, the slave ships evolved their own organized rituals and routines. As the trade in humanity evolved into a major commercial practice, ships from all countries developed roughly similar patterns of shipboard life. There were well-established routines of physical inspection, incarceration, daily exercise and twice-daily feedings. Equally important, the officers and crew were keen that their captives should be made aware of the crew's mastery and dominance. Guns were located at critical strategic points, capable of firing on any turbulent slaves, and African miscreants (as we shall see) were the objects of cruel and public physical punishments and execution. Everyone involved recognized that here was a brutal system which, despite its profit motive, contained its own built-in losses.

There were occasions when the crew felt they had to sacrifice Africans in full view of the others: as punishment, as deterrent – and from simple self-interest. Life on board a slave ship was brutal and dangerous, for all concerned. In their turn, slaves quickly learned that dissent and truculence provoked punishment and death. But the crew also appreciated their own exposed and dangerous position, and thus, each side, the enslaved and the crew, cagily scrutinized each other for months on end – on the coast, clean across the Atlantic, and right up to the moment the Africans left the ships.

The crew tried to reassure the slaves, notably via other Africans used as intermediaries and translators, but the unremitting seaborne wretchedness of the captives only ended when the ship made landfall in the Americas. Even then, their troubles did not so much end, as change. The crew, relieved that they too were in sight of land, set about their next macabre chore, of preparing the Africans for landing and sale. Though the sailors disliked the job, the victims must have hated it, because, once again, they faced a further round of personal physical humiliation. The crew inspected, scrubbed and oiled them, preparing them for sale. The condition of the Africans was all-important and would determine the price they would fetch at sale. As on the African coast, the Africans were physically scrutinized for imperfections and illnesses. The past months at sea had been a cruelly arduous process, likely to test the resolve and stamina of even the strongest person. We have no idea how many escaped unscathed from these ordeals and were unblemished by the ailments of those around them, or unharmed by the dangerous conditions in which they had lived. Even more imponderable is the psychological damage the crossing may have inflicted. Again, we will never know, and can only guess that many bore mental scars just as they carried physical wounds.

Every single African trapped in the system endured a long, drawn-out process, months on end; for some, more than a year. On the coast, the captives became miserably accustomed to the bleak realities of life on an increasingly crowded ship, but they also learned how best to survive the physical privations and how to cope with the personal dangers posed by their nervous captors.

When the African coast disappeared from view they were assailed by a very different torment, apparently lost in the middle of a dangerous ocean. And even when landfall might have seemed to offer the prospect of relief, the survivors found themselves exposed, yet again, to another round of humiliation, manhandling and onward travel, through alien waters and lands. Landed at myriad locations, from the British North American colonies to the southern edge of the hemisphere, and countless locations in between, survivors had travelled immense distances under the control, and at the behest of, people they could barely comprehend. They were, throughout, reluctant voyagers in this massive transfer of humanity to the Americas. From the first, however, they learned how to show their dissent and how to resist the miseries that had engulfed them. Slave resistance peppered the history of the Atlantic slave ships.

FIVE

Mutinies and Revolts

A slave ship was an immensely dangerous place for everyone on board. Above all, of course, it was hazardous for the Africans. But it was also dangerous for the crew. They faced not merely the threats of disease and tropical death, but the ubiquitous perils posed by the slaves. In the words of John Newton,

> One unguarded hour, or minute, is sufficient to give the slaves the opportunity they are always waiting for. An attempt to rise upon the ship's company, brings on an instantaneous and horrid war.[1]

The dangers were visible in the very structure of the ship itself, in the daily routines of the people on board, and were constantly repeated in the commercial and descriptive literature spawned by the slave ships. Even before the ships left their home ports, their owners paid great attention to the risks posed by the Africans. Their captains were specifically cautioned against those dangers, and the ships departed with equipment to keep the captives in check. Indeed it is that equipment – notably the chains and manacles – which to this day symbolizes the slave ships themselves. The repressive machinery of the slave ship – canons, swivel guns, hand guns, cutlasses, chains, manacles, thumbscrews – speaks not only of the fear of the ship's owners and crew but points us directly to the essential reality of the slave ships. The millions of people who found themselves incarcerated in a slave ship were likely to do anything to escape. Indeed, they took whatever opportunity arose to free themselves, to revenge themselves, to strike back – and even to kill themselves.

From the first moment of contact, the crew of a slave ship were wary of the Africans' every move, suspected what they said (when they understood it) and feared them throughout the voyage. This atmosphere of suspicion derived not simply from a vague, inherited anxiety about people who were utterly alien, but was based in harsh experience of shipping them in large numbers. Africans resisted their bondage in a complexity of ways, and the crew needed to stay one step ahead of them. Sailors knew that vigilance and preparedness, plus a willingness to be brutal, was their main guarantee of staying alive in the teeth of dangers from the slaves. Describing the process of shackling them, one slave captain remarked, 'these are not cruelties: they are matters of course; there's no carrying on the trade without them'.[2]

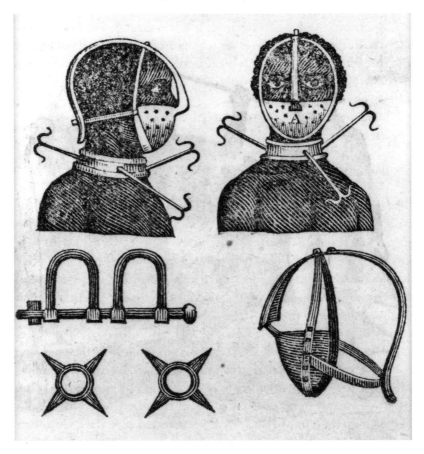

Iron mask, collar, leg shackles and spurs used to restrict slaves; woodcut taken from Thomas Branagan, *The Penitential Tyrant, or, Slave Trader Reformed* (1807).

Alongside the varied cargoes destined for the African coast, slave ships took on board huge volumes of equipment designed to quell and control the slaves. In 1784 the *Comte du Nord* left Liverpool loaded with '110 leg irons, 110 pairs of handcuffs', along with iron collars and chains.[3] They also loaded smaller items of ironware for 'management' purposes: thumbscrews for persuading slaves to reveal details of any plotters on board and a *speculum oris*, normally used by surgeons to deal with lock-jaw but used on slave ships to force-feed a resistant African. When Thomas Clarkson purchased one in Liverpool, the shopkeeper told him that

> the slaves were frequently so sulky, as to shut their mouths against sustenance, and this with a determination to die, and that it was necessary their mouths should be forced open to throw in nutrition.[4]

Clearly, there was no secrecy about the violence that took place on slave ships. The men who manufactured the repressive equipment vital to the slave ships – the iron industries of Britain which turned out this equipment by the ton – and the merchants and shopkeepers who passed it on to the ships, plus many others besides, were privy to their intended purpose. Armies of people who lived thousands of kilometres away from the slave routes knew that slaves fought back against their enslavement, and that they could only be restrained and kept under control by an assortment of vicious equipment manufactured in Europe and loaded onto the slave ships.

The ships' owners urged their captains to care for their captives, not from benevolence but from economic self-interest. Ships' captains, however, had to rely on crewmen who lived in daily fear of their lives and were not inclined to treat their charges compassionately. Quite the reverse. The crew now became armed guards, posted by the master at strategic points to supervise the Africans. They regularly searched the Africans and their living quarters.

Sailors on the slave ships were responsible for the most unpleasant of tasks (those same tasks were doubly unpleasant for the slaves). They manhandled Africans from first to last. They shackled and unshackled them, and they organized the intimate rituals of physical examination and of cleaning the slaves and alleviating the filth on the slave decks, though at times it was too dangerous to undertake such necessary cleaning work. In the course of every voyage sailors worked in close, sweaty contact with the Africans, the two sides locked into a repellent intimacy which bred disgust and anger. Sailors hated the work, while Africans hated the violations involved. It was a recipe for mutual detestation. Not surprisingly, revolts on slave ships were common.

Until recently, however, there has been a reluctance to recognize that slave revolts were any more than incidental episodes in a much bigger narrative. Today, it is accepted that slave revolts were frequent, and that the *fear* of such revolts haunted the entire history of the trade. The evidence suggests that there were more revolts than we can actually document. We know of around 500 slave revolts, though what we know of some of them is sparse. How, for example, can we interpret a single line from an agent in West Africa writing of Captain Branfill's ship: 'His Negroes rose'? English newspapers, which recorded the departure and arrival of ships from all corners of the world, sometimes provided fuller details: 'The Scipio, Stewart of Leverpool, from Africa for America, was blown up on the coast, occasion'd by an Insurrection of the Negroes.' And again, from 1765: 'the sloop Sisters, Jackson, had an Insurrection on board, and several were kill'd on both sides'.[5] These three different cases expose the central problem of evidence and interpretation. What do we *mean* by a slave revolt? They ranged from brief, personal spasms of violence, quickly repressed and punished, through to massive conflicts – a fight to the death – between African captives and a desperate crew.

Control of the Africans on slave ships posed enormous difficulties from the outset. The crew often had to leave the ship to work on shore: exploring local villages, meeting African traders and taking the ship's smaller sailing yawl, or a local canoe, to a distant location for trade. Crew numbers were stretched even before the inroads caused by tropical sickness.

Slave traders knew that slaves would try to escape and realized that many had already tried to escape from their African captors even before they reached the coast. Resistance to slavery was manifest. Villages and communities threatened by slave traders took elaborate precautions to prevent residents being enslaved. Barricaded villages, canoes prepared for a swift escape, hiding in the bush, sending away the vulnerable to a place of safety – all this and more spoke of the determination not to be enslaved. Equally, many of those who were captured tried to escape when they were marched or shipped down to the Atlantic, prefiguring the pattern that would become more striking on the coast itself. There, in forts, barracoons and slave pens, Africans had to be guarded against escape. Even as they were being ferried to the ship, they tried to flee:

> The negroes are so wilful and loth to leave their country that they have often leap'd out of the canoes, boat and ship, into the sea, and kept under water till they are drowned, to avoid being taken up and saved by our own boats which pursued them; they having a more dreadful apprehension of Barbados than we can of hell. We have likewise seen divers of them eaten by the sharks, of which a prodigious number kept about the ships in this place.[6]

On the ship, the crew faced immediate difficulties of control, of maintaining their hold over their captives, and of preventing their escape or suicide. As the ship lingered on the coast, the sight of Africa proved tempting. Thomas Phillips described how, in 1693, 'we shackle the men two and two, while we lie in port and in sight of their own country, for 'tis then they attempt to make their escape and mutiny.' Guards were placed close by with a store of small arms 'ready loaden and prim'd constantly lying at hand upon the quarter deck together with some granada shells; and two of our quarter deck guns pointing at the deck'. Mealtimes, at mid-morning and early evening, were often dangerous, and the crew stood by, armed and ready for trouble. Sometimes, the master placed informers among the slaves, hoping to pick up gossip and hints of potential trouble.[7] But all this preparation offered no guarantee.

If they could not escape, some tried to kill themselves – easily accomplished offshore by leaping from the ship: 'a stout man slave leaped overboard and drowned himself'. Others simply abandoned hope and starved themselves to death. In the pitiless gloom and violence of the slave ships, many were plunged into deep despair, feeling that life promised nothing but more torment and misery. Surgeons and masters took note of those who seemed afflicted by 'despondency' or 'melancholy' (they used a variety of words to describe the slaves' depressions) and who seemed likely to put an end their bleak existence. One African swore 'he would never go with white men'.[8] Some seriously harmed themselves – slashing their throats, hanging themselves, refusing to eat (despite efforts at force-feeding by the crew). But the easiest, and quickest, way out of the mental turmoil of shipboard enslavement was to jump overboard.

The men most familiar with the Africans on board were the ships' surgeons, whose task it was to keep them alive until landfall. Their testimony confirms that suicide was a regular feature of their medical work on the slave ships. Suicides, and failed suicides, were just one more loathsome result of the suffering on the slave ships.[9] But everyone involved in the slave trade recognized the risks of African suicides, and captains received specific instructions about the risks. The most common precaution was to sling nets at critical points round the ship to catch any would-be suicide. With a ship offshore there was always the remote possibility that a captive could reach land – and freedom – before the crew could man a boat and retrieve them. More likely, however, they would drown or be devoured by sharks. Even if they managed to reach the coast, they could fall prey to local slave traders – and be handed back to the ship, where they faced severe punishment.

The crew did not guard against slave suicide for compassionate or humane reasons. Everyone on board realized that the master had paid good money for the captives – they were a valuable investment which needed to be safeguarded and preserved. That investment was most seriously threatened, not by individual suicides, but by slave revolts which threatened to destroy the entire venture. In some conflicts, the crew showed no hesitation in killing and severely harming large numbers of Africans. Here was a grotesque paradox of life on a crowded slave ship. In order to safeguard the ship, and to ensure its successful commercial mission, there were times when rebels had to be killed, often in the most hideous of fashions – as punishment, as an example, and as a deterrent to others. Africans who harmed or assaulted the crew, or, worst of all, those who rose in revolt, could expect nothing but barbaric reprisal.

Even so, slave revolts rocked the slavers' ships throughout the history of the Atlantic trade. Some revolts engulfed and destroyed everyone on board. Others were mere violent flickers of frantic people at the end of their mortal tether, but quickly repressed by punitive savagery. In all the revolts, however, we can see the reactions of people determined to assert themselves: to affirm their right not to be treated like cattle and to reclaim the freedom taken from them.

Most revolts took place when ships were still on the African coast, or when they had recently departed on the Atlantic crossing. (We need to remember that slave ships spent more time on the African coast than they did on the 'Middle Passage'.[10]) The sight and smells of Africa lent a glimmer of hope to despairing people. For all they knew, it might be their last chance of freedom. The explanation seems obvious. Slaves on a vessel anchored for months offshore saw people coming aboard most days, with small boats and canoes ferrying people and goods back and forth between the ship and the coast. The land they had recently been wrenched from was still within sight – and within reach. Their natural home might, of course, remain far distant, deep beyond the coast itself. Nevertheless its apparent proximity could be seductive and might persuade captives that escape was still within their grasp – however perilous and improbable. Oddly, slave traders felt more secure with their ship at sea, out of sight of Africa. They believed that 'the negroes Ignorance of Navigation will always be a Safeguard'. But since many Africans felt that death would take them home, 'there has not been wanting Examples of rising and killing a Ship's Company, distant from Land, tho not so often as on the Coast'.[11] Some ships were commandeered by the rebels and driven ashore, where the captives were then able to escape. There were ships that simply vanished – sailing on, with no one on board able to navigate, until storm or death overwhelmed those on board. Other revolts totally destroyed the ship, killing all the crew and the Africans. In 1786, a group of English sailors fought to regain control of a rebellious Dutch slave ship off Cape Coast, but a massive explosion killed all on board, 'upwards of three or four hundred souls'. Such disasters were unusual. More common by far was a failed revolt followed by punitive violence against the survivors.

There were regular reports of slave ships being 'cut off' on the African coast. The phrase embraced a variety of events, from an attack on the ship by Africans from the shore, through to the more common seizure of the vessel by slaves already brought on board. So: 'The *Sally* [Captain] Draper and the *Fly* [Captain] Jones of Liverpool are both Cut Off on the Coast of Africa.' In 1750, it was reported that the *Ann* 'was cut off by the Negroes on the Coast of Guiney. The Captain kill'd on the spot, and all the Crew murdered'.[12]

The threat of African upheaval was a permanent fear for everyone involved in the slave trade, from the ship owners in distant ports down to the roughest of hands on board. Slave violence could imperil the entire enterprise: it could produce a financial disaster and offered an example that slaves on other ships might find infectious. The crew also knew that each and every African would, given the chance, try to escape. As the numbers swelled, as conditions on board the ship became more and more crowded and stressful, and as the crew found itself increasingly outnumbered, the dangers multiplied. This is not to claim that every African was rebellious – even though all wanted to be off the ship. Untold numbers were already too sick, too depressed or dispirited. We will never know how many were lost souls, doomed and beyond salvation. Yet for all that, the slaves harboured a persistent rebelliousness which the crew might be able to contain but which they could never eradicate. The crew's essential task, for months on the coast and then at sea, was to maintain some semblance of control and domination. At the same time, they wanted to ensure that the Africans would survive in a reasonable condition for sale in the Americas. It looks, in retrospect, a hopelessly ambitious task. Yet the fact that the great majority of Africans *did* survive the crossing, and that most *were* sold into American slavery, speaks to a system which had evolved from its initial experimental form into a well-oiled commercial routine. The irony remains that Africans, the source of the system's commercial success, were also the very people who threatened it, via their truculence, their violence and their revolts.

The crew tried to reassure newly boarded Africans that they were safe from harm (many feared they were about to be eaten), and that they were merely being transported to work in a distant place. But what sense did this make to terrified people? Comforting words rang hollow in the face of the visible realities of a slave ship. From the outset Africans could see clearly that they had entered a bizarre and violent system: they were hemmed in by an intimidating display of equipment designed to control and threaten them. It was obvious that the slave ship was an alien and dangerous world from which the captives wanted to escape. The odds, however, were stacked heavily against them.

Ships of all nationalities experienced revolts. We know of Portuguese and Brazilian ships off Angola being overwhelmed by captives, who then managed to run the vessel aground and escape. Some ransacked the ship before they fled, taking whatever food and clothing they discovered on board. But setting foot back on African soil brought new dangers. Some immediately fell into the hands of slave traders, who controlled huge stretches of the Angolan coastline, and were promptly resold to other slave ships. Certain Portuguese sailors became so wary of revolts on the coast that they tended to keep Africans locked below

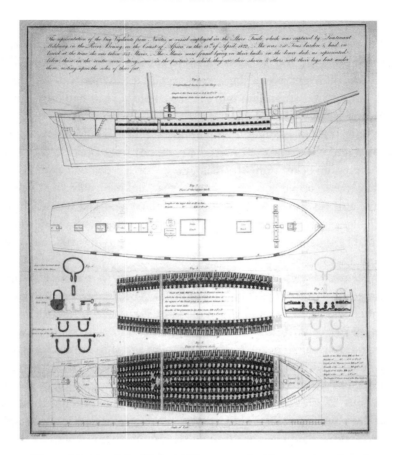

Plan and layout of the *Vigilante*. The text reads, 'the representation of
the brig Vigilante from Nantes, a vessel employed in the slave trade,
which was captured by Lieutenant Mildmay in the river Bonny on the
coast of Africa, on the 15th of April 1822 : she was 240 tons burden &
had on board at the time she was taken 345 slaves: the slaves were found
lying on their backs on the lower decks, as represented below, those in
the centre were sitting, some in the posture in which they are there
shewn & others with their legs bent under them, resting upon the soles
of their feet.'

until the ship was well out to sea.[13] We have good evidence about revolts
on Dutch ships, and, again, most of the revolts took place within sight
of the coast, though the pattern of revolt varied. Initial African success
sometimes led to disastrous disappointment. In 1769, 21 Africans escaped
from the *Zang Godin*, but they were recaptured on the coast by other
Africans and offered for resale. On another Dutch ship, the *Vigilante*,
in 1780, the 200 slaves put the crew to flight. The crew, not the Africans,

escaped to the shore – and the ship was wrecked. Revolts sometimes led to catastrophe. Shortly after leaving the African coast in 1741, a revolt among the 260 Africans on board the *Middelburgs Welvaren* led to the death of 213. Not a single crewman died: when threatened, they had simply fired at random into the slave holds. They had only thirty Africans for sale when they arrived in Surinam.[14]

Slave traders assumed that shipboard rebels would be male, but women and children often played a part, not least because they had more freedom of movement – trust, even – on a crowded vessel. They could carry an implement or tool to the shackled men, allowing them to escape and revolt. Some captains particularly disliked women from particular tribes, because they were 'fully as ferocious and vindictive as the men'. As far as possible, they tried to avoid buying Africans from groups that had rebellious reputations. There was some substance to such feelings. We now know that shipboard revolts were more common among captives from particular regions of Africa. Slaves from Senegambia, Sierra Leone and the Windward Coast accounted for more than 40 per cent of all known shipboard revolts. The reputation of certain groups of Africans went before them and ship owners, captains and surgeons were alert to the dangers posed by them. Some thought Gambians 'will attempt any Thing, tho' never so desperate, to obtain Freedom'.[15] Alexander Falconbridge, a slave ship surgeon, thought that Africans from the Gold Coast were 'Very bold and resolute, and insurrections happen more frequently among them, when on shipboard, than amongst the negroes of any other part of the coast'.[16]

Precautions were taken to separate and guard slaves deemed particularly dangerous.[17] There was no guarantee, however, that even the most intrusive and careful management could prevent revolt. When the *New Britannia* was anchored off Gambia, African boys passed 'some of the carpenter's tools' to the manacled men and revolt ensued. In 1753, 87 slaves slipped their shackles on board the *Thomas* anchored in the Gambia River, attacked the crew (who numbered only eight) and drove them ashore in their long boat. Two other slave ships tried to recapture the vessel but had to struggle against Africans who were now in control of the *Thomas*'s guns.[18]

Many Africans brought on board had been enslaved initially in military combat and it seems clear enough that numbers of them had had some form of military experience in African conflicts. Healthy young men with a military background made for dangerous prisoners on a crowded slave ship. Equally, men who had once held positions of authority in an African conflict or army were potential leaders of shipboard revolt.[19] It was apparent that some even knew how to handle the ships' guns – not surprising given the amazing volumes of weaponry which the slave traders themselves shipped into West Africa. At the height of the slave trade, it has been estimated that Europeans brought between 283,000 and 394,000 guns *each year* to West Africa[20] – some African communities were awash with weaponry. More generally, the longer slaves spent on the ship as it lingered on the coast, the more familiar they became with the workings of the ship itself, with its physical layout, with its crew and their routines, and with the equipment on board. Many of them acquired a quiet confidence that they could act effectively against their oppressors.

There were of course other, spontaneous slave outbursts – a sudden flash of anger prompted by an injustice, perhaps an act of violence against a slave – when an African simply lost control or could not resist the opportunity to strike back. But such moments tended to be personal: an individual reaction, a moment of anger or frustration. It might be the spark for a bigger conflict, but a *revolt* among a large group needed more than a moment's anger. It is hard to tell how much plotting went on, but there were clearly more plots than revolts. It is also true that the crew, like planters in the Americas, were nervously *looking* for plots. In the febrile anxiety of a slave ship, the crew were permanently on guard against trouble from the slaves and were far too ready to see plots and dangers where none existed. Did such suspected mutinies have any substance? Or were they largely a figment of a captain's worried imagination? When John Newton thought a revolt was brewing on his ship on the coast in 1752, he took the suspects aside and 'put the boys in irons and slightly in the thumbscrew to urge them to a full confession'.[21]

Shipboard revolts germinated in a complex mix of human and physical forces: the nature and backgrounds of the Africans themselves, the specific conditions under which they were detained and treated, and the nature of the crew (plus the ratio of crewmen to slaves). In addition there was the element of unpredictable and haphazard circumstance, such as a female or child slave stumbling upon, and secreting, a misplaced metal tool, then passing it to the male slaves held below. Equally, there could be present a particularly powerful man (occasionally woman) who wielded a rebellious influence over other Africans.

Of course there were countervailing factors which served to *divide* the enslaved and inhibit revolt: gulfs and confusions between people of different backgrounds and cultures, to say nothing of personal frictions and disputes, all of which left the slave house divided. Nonetheless, there were critical moments when Africans found themselves united – confronted by a moment of stark choice, now or never, and apparently able and willing to tackle their oppressors. What followed was a violent outburst which might engulf everyone on board, might even lead to freedom, but more usually could lead to defeat and a savage crushing of the thwarted rebels.

A slave ship was a floating tinderbox, likely to burst into flame from the least expected and surprising spark. The crew was always aware of the risk of revolt, but they never knew when or how it might erupt. They lived in a state of permanent anxiety, acutely conscious of the risks but never really knowing which direction they might come from or what form they might take. This friction – sparring – continued month after month, each side beadily watching the other, the one looking for an opening, the other for an indication of impending danger. Long before a slave ship had its full complement of Africans, the crew were greatly outnumbered by imprisoned slaves. At times, the imbalance was extreme (for example, seven sailors controlling 250 Africans), but even with a 'better' balance, everyone on board knew that the crew were in a tiny minority. It was obvious to the most untrained of eyes that the crew were clearly vulnerable and, at critical moments, very exposed indeed. Newton wrote of his relief that his captives had not rebelled 'upon the coast when we had often 7 or 8 of our best men out of the ship at a time and the rest busy'.[22] Others were less fortunate. Africans on the *Eagle* in 1704 rose up when twelve crewmen were away from the ship. In 1759, with half the crew of the English ship *Perfect* on shore, the slaves rebelled, killing a number of sailors and running the ship aground before escaping. In August 1786, there were only five sailors in charge of 270 Africans on the French ship *Ville de Basle* when an unsuccessful rebellion resulted in the killing of 36 rebels.[23]

A depleted crew could also aggravate the slaves' miseries, affect slaves' health and enfeeble them and, more obviously, weaken the ship's defences.[24] When large numbers of sailors on the English ship *Benjamin* fell sick, 'so the Africans were Neglected'. They rebelled and killed an officer. When the *Sandown* was trading off Sierra Leone in 1793, the crew were affected by a yellow fever epidemic. All the men were sick, and medicines ran out. The fifty Africans on board rebelled and eight sailors were killed.[25] Stormy weather, or a navigational crisis, meant all hands were fully occupied sailing the vessel. A damaged ship, in need of extra hands, sometimes turned to the Africans for extra manpower. But that was a risky decision. When slaves, heading for Maryland on the *Phoenix*, had been employed in this way in 1762, they rebelled: fifty of them were killed before the revolt was put down.[26]

Africans were alert to the changing moods on the ship, scrutinizing the sailors for signs of any weakness or a decline in their numbers. They also made the most of dissent and disunion among the crew (a crew mutiny, for example, or an aggrieved sailor revenging himself against a violent or tyrannical master by helping the slaves). Freedom sometimes beckoned when the ship was attacked by privateers or by a warship. Much more likely, however, was an unpredictable moment: a sailor's negligence or lapse of attention, allowing the slaves to pounce. Unshackled Africans up on the deck, helping with a strenuous chore, slaves freed for bathing or eating, a simple piece of wood found on deck – here was a mix that could spark a revolt. Such opportunities could present themselves in an instant, and had to be seized before they vanished forever.

Revolts sometimes escalated into wholesale battles, with no quarter given, and with Africans and sailors slaughtered and thrown overboard. As fighting ebbed and flowed, the Africans sometimes seemed to have won, only for the fighting to turn against them. A small handful of sailors, trapped in a strategic position and with good firearms, could beat back waves of rebels. Sometimes, especially on the coast, other ships were drawn into the battle, attracted by the tumult and the explosions. Order was usually restored, normally at the cost of dozens of African lives and a number of the crew.

Although the crew maintained tight control of the ship's formal weaponry, there was an abundance of informal weapons available to the captives. Practically anything could be used as an offensive weapon. In 1721 Captain Messervy was attacked by the Africans, who 'beat out his Brains with the little Tubs, out of which they eat the boiled rice'. In the following revolt, eighty were killed before order was restored.[27] Cooking implements, tools used by the carpenter and cooper, even an abandoned anchor – all were used in a revolt. In the teeming environment of a crowded slave ship, with space at a premium, it was easy for a crewman to store an apparently innocent item in a spot accessible to the Africans. One simple act of forgetfulness could lead to disaster. A barrel of knives, accidentally stored in the slave quarters, enabled the Africans to rise on the *Ruby* in 1787. But much less obvious items were recruited to the fight, from razors to buckets, from shovels to bowls and boiling water, even the chains that bound the slaves. Anything that could be used to harm a sailor was deployed.[28]

To have any chance of success, captives had to release themselves from their manacles. They frequently managed to pick themselves free with an implement passed to them by other slaves. Even if this noisy business had not alerted the crew – and guards were posted at critical points to maintain a watch over them – the Africans then had to break out from the holds (the gratings were locked overnight) before they could confront the crew on deck and in other parts of the ship. When that happened, what followed was the crew's worst nightmare: a crowd of vengeful Africans, pouring onto the deck, prepared to brawl their way to freedom. The tumult and noise, the shrieks and screams, sweeping across the deck terrified the sailors. As the slaves tried to overwhelm the sailors, they in turn sought to batter them back towards the hatches and then below deck – and to prevent other Africans joining the ferocious melee. Slaves had the numbers, but the crew had the weapons. Cutlasses for close combat, pistols, guns and swivel guns for more deadly fire from behind the protective barrier which all slave ships erected for defence at such moments. With luck and brute force, the slaves might be able to overpower the crew. But if the crew had been killed, wounded or thrown overboard – what then? It was obvious that they needed some of the crew to help sail the alien and complex sailing ship.

Surprise and timing were crucial in a revolt. Night-time, with the crew asleep, was best, though mealtime revolts were also common, but even the best planned and most violent initial attack was rarely enough. The crew, no less than the Africans, were battling for their lives and fought back savagely. There were no holds barred as the crew struggled to regain control of the ship. If they beat back the rebels and could pin the insurgents into a confined space – in a corner of the deck, in a cabin or (best of all for the crew) back in the hold – they could then rain fire and destruction on them. The crew fired guns point-blank through the gratings and lowered themselves in boats along the side of the ship to rake the decks through the ventilators. Scalding water, fat, boiling oil, gunpowder – all and more were poured onto the insurgents whenever the crew had them trapped in a confined space.

One captain effectively suffocated the slaves by sealing the hatches and filling the holds with powder and pepper.[29]

The very great majority of slave uprisings were crushed, generally with dire consequences for all the prisoners on board. Revolts were sometimes betrayed to the crew and nipped in the bud. Even when the Africans seemed to be gaining the upper hand, help for the crew was often close at hand. Other ships – slavers, warships and even the vessels of enemy nations – were sometimes close enough to come to the crew's rescue. Embattled crews sent out a series of inventive distress signals to neighbouring or passing ships. While the crew knew that any other ship or local military would hurry to support them against insurgent slaves, Africans could not hope to rally allies to their rebellious side. The fight had still to be won, but with the arrival of other vessels the odds, and the tide of battle, firmly shifted against the slaves.

The stamping-out of an African revolt on a slave ship was followed by rituals of brutality of a kind that was horrifying even by the standards of the Atlantic slave trade. The masters and crew of a slave ship saved from servile insurrection were determined that punishments would be gory and exemplary and would be carried out in front of as many Africans as possible. The lessons of defeat had to be learned by all. Their violent actions were not a secret kept within the maritime community. From the late seventeenth century onwards there was a stream of publications, by sailors, captains and others, describing in graphic detail the violence on rebellious slave ships and the exemplary punishments that followed. The bloodshed that was an essential feature of the slave trade was widely known and discussed, on both sides of the Atlantic.

Slave-ship masters believed that mere execution and floggings were inadequate means of dealing with rebels. The entire process had to be extreme. When a sailor was killed on William Snelgrave's ship at Anomabu in 1721, Snelgrave asked eight neighbouring ships to marshal all their captives on deck. The main rebel was then hauled to the yardarm, where ten sailors shot him. Then,

> The body being let down upon the Deck, the Head was Cut off, and thrown overboard. This last part was Done, to get our negroes see, that all who offended thus should be served in this manner.[30]

Attrib. Isaac Cruikshank, *The Abolition of the Slave Trade; Or the Inhumanity of Dealers in Human Flesh Exemplified in Captn. Kimber's Treatment of a young Negro Girl of 15 for her Virjen Modesty*, 1792, etching. A sailor on a slave ship suspends an African girl by her ankle from a rope over a pulley. Captain John Kimber stands on the left with a whip in his hand.

By that date, rituals of execution and dismemberment were a well-established tradition on the slave ships. Limbs hacked off, torsos raised to the rigging and left there for days, and minor rebels lashed to within an inch of their lives in sight of the reeking human remains. Wounded Africans had open scars and lacerations rubbed with pepper, salt and ashes. On a French slaver, the *Affriquain*, the rebels' gashes were rubbed with 'cannon powder, lemon juice, and brine of peppers, mixed together with a drug prepared by the surgeon'.[31] Experienced captains even recommended such severity in printed accounts, offering examples of extreme punishments as the only way of intimidating Africans on board: 'The way of making it clear to them, I mean the form of punishment that scares the Africans most, is by cutting up a live man with an axe and handing out the pieces to the others.'[32]

Such barbarities jostle for space in the catalogue of slave-ship reprisals. Slaves were starved to death, dangling from the rigging, and severed heads passed hand to hand among surviving rebels; they were set alight, garrotted, drowned.[33] There seemed no end to the ingenuity of slave captains determined to punish and to kill in the most terrible of manners – and to ensure that other Africans looked on. Even in a

Western society hardened to corporal and capital punishment, where public executions were commonplace, and where heads and body parts were routinely displayed around English city walls, what happened on the slave ships was extreme.

There is an obvious paradox, however, about the bloodletting on the slave ships. The sole purpose of the voyage was, as we have seen, to deliver Africans safely to the planters of the Americas. Indeed, it was in the interests of everyone on board to keep Africans alive: bonuses, profits, extra pay, and more, depended on the safe delivery of the human cargo. The death of an African involved a financial loss. And yet it was equally clear that there were times when Africans had to be killed: the crew felt obliged, for their own salvation, to kill them as a gory warning to others. Without force and violence the slave trade could not survive. Killing Africans was an inescapable fact of slave trading. In an all-out assault, a battle between sailors and slaves holding nothing back, Africans were killed at random: shot, stabbed, incinerated – killed in any manner available in order to regain control. But, such extremes aside, the revenge killings were not capricious or random. They were calculated and targeted: victims were chosen and killed with an eye to both punishment and deterrence.

We know of revolts which resulted in hundreds of deaths, but most revolts were suppressed with dozens rather than hundreds of casualties. Equally, there were revolts where masters took pains *not* to kill Africans, but to bring the insurgents under control by threats and non-lethal means. Once trouble was suppressed, of course, the captain was free to select the ringleaders for exemplary punishment. It is impossible to know what effect these public displays of death and punishment had on the people forced to watch. They must surely have had no illusions about what would happen to a defeated rebel, nor any doubt about the crew's willingness to inflict the most grotesque of sufferings. There was, however, much more to the mutilation of African bodies than simply offering a daunting deterrent to other Africans.

Here was an illustration of the extreme power of the white masters, displayed not merely in killing rebels but in desecrating African bodies. The intention of these on-board executions was not simply to kill an offender, but to have the survivors understand what happened to a defeated African's body. Europeans knew little or nothing about Africans' beliefs, but there was a common understanding that they believed that, in death, they would return to their homelands (if, for example, the body was thrown overboard). To dismember and desecrate the body was an attempt to dishonour the dead publically and to destroy any chance of an afterlife.

This litany of suffering and violence did not end with the suppression of a slave revolt. With order restored to a rebellious slave ship, rebels who had escaped with their lives, and who had survived the initial murderous cull of ringleaders and supporters, faced another unexpected round of horror. What was to be done with wounded slaves? Africans were selected for their commercial value when landed in the Americas. An African with obvious wounds – not facial markings or old wounds from a previous life, but recent marks acquired in shipboard violence – presented the captain with problems on landfall. Planters and others did not want wounded or disfigured Africans. Any physical reminder that a slave had been involved in fighting on the ship, even if they were in reasonable general health, would instantly detract from their value. One merchant openly complained that many of the recently arrived Africans had survived a rebellion, and those 'who lived to be brought to market had wounds in this bodies which gave an unfavourable impression'.

Some ships' masters resolved the problem by simply killing the wounded before arrival. The captain of a Bristol ship, fearing that the wounded would 'have sold for nothing', threw them into the sea. Similarly, a revolt on the slave ship *Nassau* had left many survivors with gunshot wounds. After examination by the ship's doctor, the most severely wounded were deemed worthless – and thrown overboard.[34] Such killings did not mean, however, that the dead constituted a total loss to the ship's owners, because most were covered by the ship's insurance. Here lies another vital source of information that confirms the importance of slave revolts in the story of the Atlantic slave trade.

Ship owners insured their ships and their cargoes – including their human cargoes – against loss. The expansion of maritime trade in the seventeenth and eighteenth centuries had seen the emergence of maritime cover as a distinct branch of insurance. Naturally enough, legal arguments and disputes about insurance increased as maritime trading itself flourished. A standard insurance policy was first printed in 1680–81 and did not change for a century, though a 'Memorandum' was tagged to the end of each policy listing the specific details of the ship and its cargo. The phraseology of both the policy and the Memoranda were, however, archaic and confusing. Even judges versed in the complexities of English law found maritime insurance puzzling. Yet it was this policy which was the standard document used by ship owners to insure their ships – and the Africans on board.

The policy allowed ship owners some flexibility in making a claim for losses. It was an accepted practice that there were times when cargo had to be jettisoned. When a vessel was in danger of capsizing or running aground and needed to lighten its load, it was necessary to jettison the cargo to save the ship. Though the standard policy issued by Lloyd's did not cover 'common mortality', or the loss of a perishable cargo, the jettisoning of a cargo was allowable under certain conditions.[35] In practice, this meant that slave traders who took out this policy were insured for the death of Africans killed in a revolt, or who died of their wounds. Merchants could recover the cost of the dead Africans on the ship's insurance. The major legal text outlining the law of insurance in the late eighteenth century described the matter thus:

> The insurer takes upon himself the risk of the loss, capture, and death of slaves, or any other unavoidable accident to them: but natural death is always understood to be excepted – by natural death is meant, not only when it happens by disease or sickness, but also when the captive destroys himself through despair, which often happens: but when slaves are killed, or thrown into the sea in order to quell an insurrection on their part, then the insurers must answer.[36]

Underwriters sometimes specifically *excluded* insurrections from their policies, but in general the system was clear. Slaves who simply died or who committed suicide on the ship were *not* covered by the insurance policy. Those killed during a revolt or its aftermath were covered, and the owners could claim their value back from the insurer.

French slave traders, and French insurance, followed a roughly similar pattern. The *Ordonnance de la Marine* of August 1681 had laid down the basis for maritime insurance for French slave ships. The irony was that, although the lives of crew members could *not* be insured, the Africans could, because they were cargo. Thus slaves were insured for their purchase value and were covered in case of death by killing, drowning or other 'unnatural means'. In practice, insurers would not pay for slaves who died of disease – if the death was 'natural'. Nor would they pay if an African died from depression, but if slaves died in a storm, in a sea battle or during a slave revolt, the ship owners could claim for their loss.[37]

Through the fog of legal jargon and dispute, one central fact stands out. The insurance of slave ships by insurance companies and underwriters, both in England and France, accepted *as a matter of fact* that revolts were a basic feature of the slave trade. Indeed, slave revolts and their consequences came to be enshrined in the way English commercial law dealt with the complex matters of the slave ships. It was assumed that there would be losses: the practice was that there could be no claim on the first 5 per cent of slave losses, but above that figure, the insurers were liable. More critically, African deaths during and after a slave revolt would lead to a claim against the insurers.

The story of shipboard mutinies can be told simply as a list of failed revolts – of defeated Africans, pushed back into the holds and, when not killed or wounded, forced to continue their voyage, under even more vigilant guard, to their various American destinations. But what of *successful* slave revolts? Indeed, what do we *mean* by such a success? Even if slaves succeeded in overwhelming a crew, they faced the daunting (sometimes impossible) task of sailing the ship to safety, back to Africa or on to the Americas. Whichever side of the Atlantic rebellious slaves might land, east or west, slavery beckoned. Returning to Africa might merely involve a return to bondage, while the American slave colonies (their destination in the first place) were perhaps even more dangerous. But who, except experienced sailors, could safely sail and navigate such vessels across the Atlantic, or back to the African coast?

The enslaved wanted their freedom, but how could they secure that on a slave ship? Even when they had succeeded in seizing control – and we know of at least thirty such cases – and even when they used surviving crewmen to help their escape, their chances of real freedom were remote. We know of massive battles followed by tense negotiations to be transported back to the shore, either by longboat or by driving the ship aground. There were disputes among the Africans, uncertainty about *where* they were and chaotic efforts to leave the ship and reach land. Seizing a ship was often followed by episodes of panic and tumult, with nervous decisions made to seek a safer landing spot or to put back to sea to escape approaching slave ships, which were seeking both revenge and the plunder of a ready-made cargo of Africans. Time and again, Africans found their triumph short-lived: merely the first step in what sometimes became a prolonged struggle to beat off other slave traders. At times, full-scale and sometimes prolonged naval battles followed, with slaves manning the ships' guns to beat off attacks. In 1764 one ship was in African hands for ten days before the rebels were finally defeated. Thirty years later, the *Thomas* was controlled by Africans for 42 days before the revolt was quelled by two other ships.[38]

Away from land, with no visible marker, rebels were, quite literally, all at sea; at the mercy of the Atlantic's winds and currents – and storms. It was then that they needed experienced help. Without such help – with all the crew killed or pitched overboard – the rebels were doomed to a miserable end. Some ships just vanished; others were found, months later, floating aimlessly with a few wretched survivors, barely alive, finally taken into port (and presumably enslaved again).[39]

Even though we know that the majority of such revolts did not lead to freedom, a remarkable number did. There were at least 120 slave up-heavals which resulted in freedom for some of the Africans on board. Yet it would be wrong to assess these revolts simply in terms of success in gaining freedom. Here, after all, were desperate efforts by thousands of people, spread over the entire history of the Atlantic slave trade, to kick against a violent system which had snatched them from their homelands, thrust them into the belly of floating prisons and threat-ened to ship them – they knew not where. The success of revolts lay not merely in the numbers fully freed, but in the persistent assertion by all involved of their rights: they denied the authority of their oppressors to treat them as slaves. Africans thrust into seaborne slavery demanded the right to be treated differently – to be free. For most, those demands were crushed by systemic violence which sought to break the body and the will of rebels. That revolts continued throughout the history of the slave trade speaks to the Africans' unquenchable desire for freedom.

SIX

Landfall

C rewmen were greatly relieved to see land after an Atlantic crossing. It meant that the most dangerous part of their journey was almost over. What it meant for the Africans, however, was utterly different. For a start, they remained below decks, only able to see the approaching land when brought on deck for washing and preparation, or they learned of it with the arrival of birds and the general excitable hubbub of the crew preparing the ship for docking.

Even when Africans saw land on the horizon, what did it mean to them? They had no idea of where they were, although sometimes, thanks to the imperfections of navigation, the crew were almost as ignorant. Ships often made landfall many kilometres distant from their intended destination, a serious problem in an Atlantic world wracked by warfare and territorial disputes and when the land ahead might actually be enemy territory. Even so, for the crew, land meant eventual safety. For the Africans, land brought a new and utterly unknown twist to their continuing miseries. It is tempting to imagine that the end of the Atlantic crossing meant that the Africans' travels had ended. In fact, it heralded a continuation of their journey. Landfall did *not* bring an end to the Africans' physical sufferings, and for many months to come the Africans continued to be haunted by the problems of the slave ships.

The past months on the ship had taken a terrible toll, and survivors showed signs of the physical damage of the Atlantic crossing. Huge numbers of them were sick on arrival, though the precise numbers varied from ship to ship. It had been the surgeons' task to keep sickness at bay while the Africans were on board, but it was an uphill struggle in the face of shipboard conditions. Try as they might, it was simply impossible to eradicate shipboard sickness. Yet prospective buyers in the Americas (some of whom had already ordered Africans in advance) wanted *healthy* Africans. Thus, at the sight of land, the crew set about trying to give the Africans an appearance of health and vigour: to make them more presentable, more saleable. For the Africans, this entailed yet another humiliating routine of washing and scrubbing, plus physical examinations which rode roughshod over any sense of personal delicacy or privacy.

To claim that crewmen busied themselves preparing the Africans for sale masks a much cruder human violation: of calloused sailors manhandling Africans – shoving, bending and twisting, lifting and lowering naked limbs – as they inspected and cleaned, scrubbed and sluiced, trying to bring some semblance of cleanliness and health to people who for months past had been penned and treated like cattle. As John Newton's ship, the *African*, approached the Caribbean in May 1753, the process began. 'Washed the slaves which the weather has not allowed us to do this fortnight nearly.' A day later the crew 'Shave the slaves foreheads'.[1]

Washed and cleaned, with a liberal application of oil to restore a healthier gloss to the skin, Africans were thus made ready for their next ordeal, though, again, they had no idea what lay in store for them. For some, it was too late:

> the sick, or refuse slaves, of which there are frequently many, are usually conveyed on shore, and sold at a tavern by vendue, or public auction . . . at so low a price as five or six dollars a head.

Refuse slaves – the ultimate throwaway category of the slaving system: Africans so physically reduced that they were virtually worthless, discarded for small change to anyone willing to take a gamble on their slim chance of survival. Sometimes they could not be sold. A planter came on board to look over the refuse slaves 'but did not like them'. Not surprisingly, many who were put ashore in this condition did not survive long. For them, landfall brought relief of a different kind.[2]

More attention was paid to those Africans likely to bring a good price. In the days before landing, they were brought on deck in batches and even allowed small pleasures, such as tobacco and food. And when this grisly business had concluded, when the ship had docked, and the master had cleared the quarantine formalities with the local authorities

Anonymous engraving of slaves exposed for sale at an 18th-century market; men, women and children are all present.

and agents, the planters and their representatives set about picking and choosing the best Africans. Whether sales took place on board the ship, or on land, either via 'scrambles' (a disordered rush to grab slaves) or more formal auctions, the Africans were once again scrutinized and examined. As if to compound their miseries, landfall heralded yet another cruel round of examination, another demoralizing and often terrifying regime of sale.

> The Planters buy them out of the Ship, where they find them
> stark naked, and therefore cannot be deceived in any outward
> infirmity. They choose them as they do Horses in a Market; the
> strongest, youthfullest, and most beautiful, yield the greatest
> prices.[3]

For many months past, the imprisoned Africans had known little of their ultimate fate, save for what they could see within the physical limits of the ship itself plus the occasional glimpse of the Atlantic, all larded with whatever gossip and rumour they were able to glean via intermediaries who had some grasp of the sailors' language. Now they were on terra firma, but it too was an alien landscape. Moreover, being ashore did not bring freedom. Africans quickly discovered that they had merely exchanged owners, had simply taken the next step in an onward journey which might last for many more months. Like the slave ship, this next stage was also dogged by death and sickness.

The very great majority of all Africans carried across the Atlantic were landed at a relatively small number of coastal locations in the Caribbean and Brazil. In effect, the slave ships were channelled towards a string of ports which served as staging posts for the onward movement of Africans to other locations across the Americas. Most Africans did not live and work where they first landed, and their disembarkation point was, for most, simply the next step on a journey which must have seemed endless.

Africans were disembarked at 179 known ports in the Americas, though the overwhelming majority (8,325,000) in the entire history landed in only twenty of those ports. The largest numbers by far disembarked in Rio de Janeiro (1,839,000) and in Salvador (1,550,000). Kingston, Jamaica – the largest British port of entry – saw 886,000 Africans arrive on slave ships. The largest French port was Cap-Français – today's Cap-Haitian – which absorbed 406,000 Africans. Havana saw 464,000 disembark, while Charleston, with 186,000 arrivals, was the major entry point in North America.[4] Now, for many, came the onward travel. Once colonial society had settled, and as local economies thrived and diversified, the demand for slaves grew in new and distant locations, far away from the main ports: in the rural hinterlands, in mines or on distant settlements and plantations. As smallholdings gave way to larger plantations, as other forms of cultivation developed (food and animal husbandry), as new regions of the interiors were explored and settled (higher altitudes were ideal for coffee cultivation, for example), or remote valleys explored for plantation development, and as logging industries opened up in densely forested regions, Africans were moved on. And all this was in addition to the search for precious metals, which continued throughout the slavery period in Brazil and in the Andes. In one form or another, all turned to slavery, though often in league with other forms of labour.

In Rio, large groups of slaves were initially herded into local warehouses. But their proximity to local homes led to complaints, and new slave pens, located away from local dwellings, were erected to process new arrivals. In such pens, as on board ships, they were scrubbed and inspected, valued and bid for, thence sent to wherever their new owners might decide. Africans landing in Dutch Curaçao and other Caribbean ports found themselves shipped on, once again, this time to Spanish possessions and thence along the Pacific coast to Peru. The Dutch were also active, until late in the history of the trade, on the northeast coast of South America, along the rivers of the modern-day Guianas region, feeding Africans into raw and troubled settlements in Essequibo, Berbice and Surinam.

The massive growth of the British slave trade in the eighteenth century fed the voracious demand for Africans throughout the British Caribbean. By 1700, as many as a quarter of a million Africans had been imported into the British islands. Their arrival there also involved the routine of inspection, holding pens, 'scrambles' by potential buyers – in pens and on ships – and the inevitable terror among people who had no idea what was happening. In a scramble, planters and their agents rushing to grab their targeted Africans laid claim to them by roping or tagging the terrified victims. It is, again, hard to decide which system of sale was most distressing for the Africans: the scramble or, for example, the auction system of South Carolina, with planters pouring into Charleston to bid for slaves fresh from their quarantine on neighbouring Sullivan's Island. Many arriving in North America had been trans-shipped in the Caribbean, where their ships had stopped for provisions and new instructions. The sale of Africans who finally landed along the Chesapeake Bay in Virginia, a region which lacked a major port, tended to be prolonged. Africans were kept for upwards of two months before they were bought – often by merchants who then moved them to new locations for yet another sale, thence onwards to their new owners.

What clearly made conditions worse for all the new arrivals was the sheer concentration of people poured into the holding facilities. At times, the numbers involved could not be processed quickly, with potential purchasers or their agents having to travel great distances to assess their potential slaves. Local merchants often had trouble holding and maintaining large numbers of Africans when they arrived in a relatively short space of time. This was especially bad on St-Domingue (Haiti after 1804). In the second half of the eighteenth century, the local sugar and coffee industries boomed on the back of massive importations of slaves, with Africans pouring into Le Cap (Cap-Français) on the north coast in unprecedented numbers. There, they were held in crowded holding areas until they were moved by sea and by trekking into the colony's difficult mountains, to distant sugar and coffee plantations. By 1789 the slave population of St-Domingue stood at almost half a million (by then, one half of *all* the slaves in the Caribbean lived in St-Domingue). The colony quickly developed a reputation not only for its wealth and importance to France, but for the harshness of life for its slaves, no mean achievement in the world of American slavery. The price was to be paid for that treatment in the volcanic slave eruption after 1791.

Africans had been shipped to South America, initially via Spain, from the earliest days of European settlement. In the course of the sixteenth century, in the region of 150,000 were shipped into the Spanish Indies. Then, between 1595 and 1640 (when the Crowns of Spain and Portugal were united), Portuguese merchants shipped upwards of 300,000 into Spanish colonies in the Americas. Africans had been imported into the Río de la Plata (the river dividing modern-day Argentina and Uruguay) as early as 1585 – a pattern that continued for the best part of three centuries. Many had made the crossing from Angola. For some arriving in Buenos Aires, landfall heralded an even more spectacular onward journey – overland, clean across South America, to the region that is now Bolivia and Peru. They were marched from Buenos Aires, inland to Córdoba, then on to the Andes, where they were used in the mines in Upper Peru (modern-day Bolivia). Quite apart from the vast distances involved, it was a severe trek, with slaves force-marched in caravans on journeys which involved huge climatic and altitude changes. However, more Africans entered slavery in the Spanish empire via the Caribbean, through Santo Domingo, Havana, Vera Cruz, Porto Bello (now Portobelo, Panama) and, above all, Cartagena, where half of all Africans entering Spanish America before 1640 arrived. From those ports, they were moved on either overland or down the Pacific coast of South America.

In so vast and diffuse an empire as Spanish America, slaves were employed everywhere, and in a host of occupations, notably in the major cities of Mexico City and Lima, as skilled workers and domestics. Indeed, urban slaves eventually constituted upwards of a quarter of the population of Spain's main cities in the Americas: Lima, Mexico City, Quito, Cartagena and Santa Fé de Bogotá. Large numbers worked in the mines of New Spain ('bad to have them, but much worse not to have them'5). And, as elsewhere, the coming of sugar-cane cultivation, in the Spanish Caribbean and in New Spain, went hand in hand with slavery. But, whatever the work, major areas of Spanish economic development in the Americas were forged with African labour, both free and enslaved. That Africans had been indispensable to that empire is now well known, though much less noticed is the enormous distances those people had to travel. By the mid-seventeenth century there were some 150,000 Africans in New Spain, and 30,000 in Peru. They, or their African forebears, had undergone epic journeys which had taken them, in various stages, on journeys at sea, and by foot, from Africa to the Pacific.

The Spanish experiment of introducing Africans – first as servants, then in mines, later and most dramatically in sugar cultivation – established a pattern which was copied from one European settlement to another. There followed a veritable contagion of slavery throughout the tropical and semi-tropical Americas. As ever more Africans arrived at the major ports of arrival, they found themselves driven on to those locations which were in greatest need of their labour.

Spain's American empire had started in the Caribbean, in that arc of islands stretching 3,200 km from Florida to South America, and Spain remained the dominant power in that region until the seventeenth century. In that period more than 200,000 Africans arrived, but most slaves went to Spanish territories via *Asiento* trading agreements which allowed other nations to import Africans to Spain's American colonies. It was, however, the rise of rival colonial powers, notably the English and the French, and the rapid development of their slave islands centred on sugar production, which saw truly massive numbers of Africans arriving in the Caribbean. By the time slavery ended, more than 2.3 million Africans had stepped ashore in the British Caribbean, 1 million in French islands and three-quarters of a million in Cuba.[6] However we arrange or shuffle these figures, however much they are divided into different categories, phases and chronologies, they form an astounding aggregation of humanity. There had never before been such epic enforced migrations of people by sea.

These staggering overall figures nonetheless mask a host of curious features. Barbados, for example, although a tiny island no bigger than the Isle of Wight, and the critical pioneer of British colonial slave production, received almost half a million Africans.[7] Jamaica, the major British slave-trading hub in the eighteenth century, absorbed more than 1 million Africans. In peak years, Africans flooded into Jamaica in enormous numbers – 16,000 a year in the last years of the century (though many were shipped onwards to other colonies).[8] Such an *intensity* of African arrivals, as much as the overall numbers, offers a clue to the crowded tumult which characterized the slaves' experience at first landfall in Jamaica. Slave ships jostled for space, and slave merchants were pressed for room to accommodate the regiments of Africans, especially those arriving in Kingston. Not surprisingly, contemporaries often used military imagery to describe the African workers. They were disgorged from the ships like an invading army, their ranks marshalled into military-like units, and then thrown into the brutal task of imposing profitable agricultural discipline onto the island's luxuriant habitat.

It was, however, St-Domingue which had the most intense and crowded arrival of Africans. In all, three-quarters of a million Africans were landed there, a quarter of a million in the 25 years after 1751. During the next 25 years, the numbers rose even higher, to a third of a million.[9] The bigger Caribbean islands and colonies catch the eye because of the sheer scale of these arrivals, but it was a pattern which was repeated right across the region. Massive numbers emerged from the Atlantic slave ships in all the European colonies. Even the tiniest of islands – Nevis, Tortola, St Vincent, Dominica – found reason to turn to African slaves, either for local work or for onwards movement to other colonies. Indeed, it was the economic potential of slavery in those colonies that persuaded European powers to vie for possession and control of the colonies themselves. Throughout much of the history of Atlantic slavery, those colonies were disputed, fought over, exchanged in peace treaties and seized by military action. Many had distinct strategic importance, but most were rendered valuable primarily by the labour of imported slaves. Remove the Africans – and the colony's value and importance vanished. Hence the regular arrival of the slave ships, loaded with sick and bewildered Africans.

Brazil received the largest number of Africans. By the last years of the seventeenth century, in excess of 700,000 had arrived, and the graph of arrivals went ever upwards. Over the course of the next century, a further 1,805,000 Africans stepped ashore in Brazil. Yet even those immense numbers were to be surpassed, in the years 1791–1856, with the arrival of 2.3 million more. Altogether, the slave ships delivered a little short of 5 million Africans to Brazil.[10]

The story of African arrivals in North America offers a stark contrast. Modern students are often surprised to learn that North America received a relatively small number (around 390,000) of Africans from the slave ships. Fewer than one in thirty of all the Africans who survived the Atlantic crossing disembarked in the region that was to become the USA in 1776,[11] and yet by 1860 there were 4 million enslaved people living in the USA. The great majority of Africans destined for North America had landed in the century prior to the American Revolution in 1776, though small numbers had been landed in the early seventeenth century. Until about 1720, they tended to arrive via the Caribbean, but thereafter there was an expanding direct trade from Africa to North America. The first Africans were settled initially around the massive shoreline of the Chesapeake Bay – in Virginia and Maryland – and employed primarily in tobacco cultivation. Most had travelled in English ships, especially from London and Bristol. That changed, however, after 1730, when most went to South Carolina, to labour in the expanding coastal rice industry. But in both the Chesapeake and South Carolina (and then in Georgia – which came later to slave cultivation), Africans undertook substantial journeys *after* they had landed. Indeed what happened there provides a clue to what happened to millions of slaves throughout the hemisphere.

As American settlers, planters and land holders fanned out from initial coastal and hinterland settlements, they established new properties which were ever more distant from the Africans' point of entry. The American frontier was pushed further and further away from the coast, and from the shoreline of the major rivers. In many places it was pushed back by slave labour, which had been marched from the point of disembarkation into the American interior, for example to the Piedmont region of Virginia and into the backcountry of South Carolina. Landless settlers removed themselves from established communities in the coastal regions of Virginia and South Carolina, moving inland to settle new properties – where they needed labour. Slave merchants, searching for potential buyers for their available Africans, found them, increasingly, on the distant frontier. By the 1770s it was claimed that two-thirds of newly imported Africans were being sold to the interior regions of South Carolina.[12]

Merchants in Charleston sold batches of Africans wherever they could: to smaller ports and quaysides up and down the Atlantic coast. They also contacted settlers in the backcountry, advertising slaves for

THE SLAVE DECK OF THE BARK "WILDFIRE," BROUGHT INTO KEY WEST ON APRIL 30, 1860.—[From a Daguerreotype.]

The *Wildfire* was captured and bought to port in Key West in 1860. This illustration of 1860, taken from *Harper's Weekly*, shows African slaves on the upper deck. There were thought to be 510 slaves on board when it was captured; they were soon to be freed.

sale in newspapers (which were liberally distributed in the backcountry). Sometimes they used other agents to move the Africans by boat along the river systems, then by foot into the hills and beyond. Merchants also travelled the backcountry, visiting remote locations along with their new slaves, selling them as and when they could to local settlers. Settlers used friends and contacts to fetch Africans from Charleston to their new properties. They even trusted friends to buy them, displaying a degree of trust in friends and neighbours that today seems remarkable but which, in an age of poor communications, was a vital ingredient in commercial and business dealings. In 1777, William Ancrum wrote to an overseer on his plantation that he was sending him 'a Negro Woman named Ruth & her female Child by Mr Rose's wagon'. Africans were thus shifted by riverboat, then by wagon and on foot to their new workplace, far away from the spot where they first landed. We know of cases where they travelled upwards of 480 km into the backcountry – and this soon after they had landed from Africa – via the Caribbean.[13]

These treks into the interior were rugged, haphazard affairs, in regions where roads – little more than tracks – were poor. The slaves likely had to camp and to eat and drink as best they could: there were few formal places for rest or refreshment and on such treks they effectively camped out overnight and were fed by the campfire. Sometimes, however, they rested at homesteads and plantations along the way en route to their new homes. Either way, it was a rugged and simple system which, though lacking the terrors of the slave ships, offered nothing in the way of basic comfort. Such treks also provided opportunities for escape: runaway advertisements for newly arrived Africans were common.[14]

Smaller numbers arriving in North America were shipped to New York and Philadelphia, from where they moved out into the 'Middle Colonies' (of New York, Pennsylvania, New Jersey and Delaware). An even smaller number – perhaps 10,000, many of them coming via the Caribbean – landed in Boston and were destined for New England.[15]

These patterns of onward migrations of Africans landing in North America were repeated, in different forms, throughout the Americas. For example, the horrors of the Atlantic crossing were often quickly followed by transfer to smaller, local ships for onward export to other colonies. The French island of Martinique was a regular first stopping point for slaves before they were shipped to Guadeloupe. Similarly, the small Danish islands re-exported Africans to other Caribbean colonies.

A slave sale in Charleston, South Carolina, from a sketch by Eyre Crow in the
Illustrated London News, 1856.

Spanish colonies, in particular, depended on the slave ships of other
European powers – initially Dutch and Portuguese – for their supplies of slaves. The Dutch island of Curaçao, for example, became a
major entrepôt where Atlantic ships transferred Africans to smaller
vessels for transport to Spanish colonies. Similarly, Jamaica was not
only a massive and expansive slave colony, with remoter parts of the
island being developed by newly imported labour throughout the
slave period, but it was also a major re-exporter of Africans to Spanish
settlements. Africans entered the Spanish Americas from Jamaica
through Porto Bello, Cartagena, Cuba and Puerto Rico. Most of
those shipped on from the British Caribbean were transferred 'more
or less directly from a transatlantic slaver to a colonial sloop'. The
numbers involved were enormous. In the years 1716–90 an estimated
1,679,000 Africans were shipped on to new destinations after arriving in the Caribbean.

Here was a system designed to bewilder its victims. Africans carried
in British ships found themselves quickly transferred to Spanish owners, Dutch traders exported Africans to the French islands, and the

British dispatched Africans to islands throughout the Caribbean, to the Spanish mainland and, of course, onwards to their own colonies in North America. Of the 268,937 slaves brought to the North American colonies in the eighteenth century, some 21,515 had been imported via the Caribbean. Slaves brought to Jamaica by British traders were sometimes sold on to the French colony of St-Domingue, from where some were then re-exported to Spanish colonies.[16]

It is hard to reconstruct the lives of the Africans flung into this protracted turmoil of travel and upheaval, each stage marked by the inevitable casualties and torments. Yet each stage was also shaped by the various slave-owners' desire to keep them alive, for onward sale and labour. Slave merchants in auction houses in Charleston or Rio, like slave masters on the slave ships (and even the drivers en route to distant American properties, inland Brazilian settlements, Peruvian mines or Caribbean plantations), had a powerful commercial incentive to keep the enslaved Africans alive. Even so, everyone in charge of these transient people faced enormously complex problems of health and well-being. For all their physical mastery over the slaves, owners were confronted by risks and dangers they could rarely control, especially the diseases and ailments which swirled around people whose travels began in one continent and now found themselves in another, thrust into disease environments to which they had no natural immunity. On top of all this, there was the sheer wear and tear, the physical decline brought on by protracted travel under the most stressful and dangerous of conditions.

There was often a twilight period for Africans between the Atlantic voyage and settling into their lifetime's labour, one which has been largely overlooked by historians but which formed yet another punishing ordeal for them. Slave merchants in Brazil, for example, became accustomed to losing upwards of 10 per cent of their newly arrived Africans. The worst time – when slave dealers *expected* Africans to die – was in the immediate aftermath of the Atlantic voyage, when they were herded ashore into warehouses or barracoons – or simply kept on board the anchored slave ship, awaiting onward sale. Even when they survived that dangerous phase, sickness and death, related to the recent voyage and travels, continued to haunt the slave quarters. It has been calculated that between 10 and 15 per cent of the gangs of Africans trekking into the Brazilian interior from their disembarkation points died before reaching their final place of labour.

Thus it soon became apparent, from the earliest days of slavery in the Americas, that Africans needed to rest and recover on their epic journeys from Africa. They needed to recover their strength, at a number of stages, for the next leg of the journey. Once at their final destination, they needed to rest again before they were thrust into the taxing work for which they had traversed such vast distances. Planters everywhere were forced to take drastic measures to prevent further losses of Africans who had reached their workplaces – to 'season' them gradually before confronting them with the full rigours of plantation labour. Such 'seasoning' periods became an established phase in the transition from the ship to life in the Americas.[17]

So, planters knew that freshly arrived Africans were not fit for the more gruelling and arduous work on plantations, especially with sugar during the crop season, the very work they had been purchased for. Many planters nonetheless simply threw their new labour battalions at whatever work was required. The cost was soon revealed in the alarming death rates. Edward Long, writing in 1774, claimed that upwards of a third of freshly arrived Africans died within their first three years in Jamaica. Proof was on hand on one of that island's more prosperous and durable sugar plantations, Worthy Park. Having invested huge amounts of money in 225 new Africans in the early 1790s, the owner, Rose Price, watched as 56 of them died within two years – largely from the 'bloody flux': the dysentery that was the scourge of the slave ships. Desperate to stop the losses, he ordered the survivors to be relocated at the property's provisioning grounds at Spring Garden 'for a change of air'. Worthy Park's slave doctor, Dr John Quier, trained in Leiden and Edinburgh and a pioneer of smallpox inoculation among the slaves, was in no doubt that the problems derived from the slave ships, from 'the bad habit of body these people have contracted from long confinement, bad food and improper treatment on the voyage'.[18]

To make matters worse, the quarantine restrictions imposed on slave ships in Kingston and other British ports were notoriously lax (compared, for example, to the stricter restrictions at Cartagena or Charleston), allowing contagious Africans to be released into Jamaica's slave communities – or onwards to other destinations.[19] Smallpox was a permanent threat on the island until the late eighteenth century, when inoculation was widely imposed on the slaves. Unlike the free population of contemporary Britain, Jamaican slaves were in no position to object to what was, in effect, a medical experiment being conducted on them. Nonetheless, it worked and effectively eradicated smallpox among the slaves. Earlier attempts to tighten quarantine foundered on the resistance of slave merchants whose economic interests demanded a more flexible entry system for Africans. The result was predictable: regular disastrous outbreaks of smallpox caused by infected Africans stepping off a slave ship. When Simon Taylor bought seven Africans for the *Golden Grove* sugar plantation in Jamaica, he soon discovered that 'they brought the smallpox out of the ship with them'. One-third of the Africans on that ship perished from the disease.[20] Advertisement for African sales understandably stressed their freedom from smallpox: 'The utmost care has already been taken, and shall be continued, to keep them free from the least danger of being infected with the SMALL-POX.'[21]

Those lucky enough to survive smallpox were effectively safe against further attack and generally carried visible proof in the form of facial scars and damage. Outsiders could tell a smallpox survivor by the marks on the victim's face. In a bizarre twist to the problem of smallpox and slavery, such scars – in effect, a guarantee of future health – enabled slave holders selling Africans to advertise those markings as an extra advantage. On both sides of the Atlantic, smallpox scars added to the value of slaves. Even slaves in England were promoted by their smallpox scars. In 1761, the *Daily Ledger* offered for sale 'A healthy negro Girl aged about fifteen years; speaks English, works at her needle, washes well, does household work, and has had the smallpox.' A year later, a twelve-year-old boy, sold at a Covent Garden barber's shop, was described as 'sensible and handy, speaks English well, and has had the small Pox'.[22] Smallpox scars also helped to identify slaves. A Jamaican runaway in 1790 was described as 'a NEGRO SAILOR MAN, of the Coromantee nation; he is about 5 feet 5 inches high, his face furrowed with the small pox marks'.[23]

Smallpox, however, was only the most spectacular problem which spilled forth from the slave ships. More routine – unexceptional, perhaps – was the simple struggle to survive. Slaves and their owners grappled with the physical consequences of the voyages: the Africans struggled to stay alive, while their owners cast around for ways of getting Africans fit enough to sell and to work. The most common solution was a reliance on the 'seasoning' mentioned above: the period of less intensive workloads and less hostile management – and all in a less adverse environment. Even then, and even without the dramatic intervention of contagious diseases, death among newly arrived Africans remained stubbornly high – as commentators recognized – from one slave colony to another.

The death of recently arrived Africans formed a persistent problem which drew puzzled comments from slave owners everywhere. It naturally caught the attention of doctors, who offered advice about how best to avert such losses. Cleanliness, better food, clean clothing and housing, less arduous labour and fewer severe punishments – and more – were periodically recommended and tried. Nonetheless, even the more enlightened doctors and planters continued to struggle against high levels of African mortality. John Richardson, a Jamaican planter who lost 141 of the 190 Africans he purchased over a period of fourteen years, thought that 'prudence & Industry are highly necessary'. But he, like most people involved, realized that keeping Africans alive derived 'from a lucky combination of circumstances'.[24]

Those most intimately involved in buying and selling Africans in the Americas knew that the essential cause of these casualty rates were the slave ships. But few knew how to solve the problem. Newly arrived Africans continued to die in large numbers, as long as the Atlantic slave trade survived. Clement Caines, a planter in St Kitts who was unusual in his criticisms of the slave trade, noted that, even when 'few died in their passage from Africa, multitudes die in consequence of it'. It was on the Atlantic slave ships that the seeds were sown 'of debility and despondence, of sickness, and of death'. Nor was this purely a physical matter: 'The melancholy and despondence cannot be ruled out . . . They pine and droop, linger rather than live, and shortly sink into the grave.' Caines thought that a generation of Africans died in less than 'a fourth part of the age of man'.[25]

Though they died in the Americas, the Africans died under the shadow of the slave ships. As hard as they tried, slave owners were unable to prevent legions of slaves dying from what were, in effect, ailments transplanted into the Americas via the slave ships. Millions of people had to undergo the complex process of adaptation to the new world they had entered. Nothing in their previous lives, not even slavery in Africa, could have prepared them for life as an enslaved person in the Americas, but the most severe test they *all* faced was simple survival. Those who had survived the Atlantic crossing in reasonably robust health, who had stepped ashore without the lingering ailments of Africa or from the slave ships, stood a decent chance of survival. But huge numbers were sick and vulnerable. For them – again unnumbered and effectively unrecorded – landfall heralded further physical misery and death. A route which Joseph Miller has aptly called a 'way of death' continued long after landfall in the Americas.[26]

Survivors had endured unparallelled upheavals, and immense journeys, but even they could never be sure that their travels were finally over. Nor could their descendants – slaves born in the Americas. Indeed, major upheavals and long-distance travel continued to haunt slave communities throughout the Americas. This was to be exposed most brutally by the internal slave trade which developed in both the USA and Brazil in the nineteenth century. In both countries overland slave routes developed which saw huge numbers of people moved great distances. When the USA abolished its own slave trade in 1808, the new Republic had no further need to import Africans because locally born slaves were available in abundance. The explosive growth of cotton production in the nineteenth century stimulated a new, *internal* slave trade, not from Africa, but from the old eastern slave states (Maryland, Virginia and the Carolinas) to the new cotton states of the South. Like their African forebears, many American slaves were now confronted by the trauma of further upheaval and forced, long-distance migration. Armies of slaves were uprooted, yet again, much as those before them had been. Although this was not an oceanic migration, they were again dispatched, against their wishes, to work on new cotton plantations far from their homes. Some U.S. slave owners relocated to the cotton frontier in the company of their slaves, but the major slave migrations were of slaves being sold to distant cotton plantations, with all the incalculable dislocation and hurt caused by family break-up and personal upheaval. The numbers were, again, enormous. In the years 1790–1860 three-quarters of a million North American slaves were driven along these internal slave routes. One slave marriage in five, from the slave-exporting states, was wrecked, and one child in three was separated from a parent. The main purpose of uprooting the slaves and selling them to distant plantations was simply to make a profit. Once a family member had been sold and moved away, they might just as well have crossed the Atlantic. They were lost forever to their loved ones and friends. It was a ghastly reprise of what had happened to their African ancestors.

The men who orchestrated this, the slave merchants of the U.S. South, were unmoved by the human tragedies which unfolded under the noses. Indeed, they were not unlike the merchants and slave captains of earlier centuries. They were men who chose not to consider the human distress they created but who instead looked simply at the accountancy of their businesses. For Africans, and for those born in the Americas, these upheavals and enforced onward journeys caused incalculable grief. Personal and family suffering were part of the fabric of slave life. The USA offers perhaps the best-known example of such upheavals, but the story was repeated whichever region of the enslaved Americas we look at. What happened in Brazil, for example, was no less dramatic. Notwithstanding the large numbers of Africans arriving, an enormous internal slave trade emerged in Brazil in the years between Brazilian abolition of the Atlantic trade in 1830 and the end of Brazilian slavery in 1888. Following the rapid growth of the Brazilian coffee industry in the early nineteenth century, large numbers of slaves were shifted from the older, established slave regions of Bahia, Pernambuco and Amazonia to the southeast of the country. Upwards of 300,000 were removed by sea, by river and even by train, along internal slave routes from old slaving regions to the new coffee-growing areas of the country. And all against their wishes. They too were forced to abandon homes and families, partners and children. In the two largest slave-holding countries in the Americas – the USA and Brazil –the threat of upheaval and enforced migration hovered over the slaves as long as slavery survived as a viable economic system.

Millions of Africans had survived the Atlantic ships, and the onwards journeys which took them from their African homelands to the very edge of the American frontier, and even to the western rim of the American continent. But wherever they settled, they, and their offspring, could never feel secure. There was no stability, no sense of rest or certainty. Slaves had no protection against the threat of removal and upheaval. All of them knew that they could be shifted onwards, carried along by the changing economic and social fortunes of the people who owned them. It was difficult to put down roots and feel at home. Africans, and their American-born children, were scattered around the world of American slavery, not knowing where their next stop might be. While the most horrific experiences of all had been in the slave ships, landfall in the Americas brought not so much a resting place as a new variant of further insecurity and enforced travel.

Stepping from the slave ship was clearly the end of a terrible journey, but there was no permanent 'final leg' of the journey for the enslaved peoples of the Americas. Though the epic oceanic journey from Africa eventually ended, slaves could never be sure that their wanderings were over. Not one single slave in the Americas had a guarantee of permanent settlement and rest. They were, from first to last, the possessions of others, and they might – and often were – simply uprooted and driven onwards. Millions must have asked themselves: where and when would it all end?

SEVEN

Resistance

One of the most puzzling questions about the history of Atlantic slavery remains the issue of control. How did such relatively small numbers of slave owners maintain their control and dominance over huge numbers of servile people, both at sea and in the Americas? In most slave societies in the Americas whites were outnumbered by Africans. The exception, with a few local variations, was colonial North America. But in Brazil and the Caribbean, Africans and their local-born offspring were in a majority. At times, the imbalance was enormous, with hundreds of slaves facing a mere handful of whites, often in remote, isolated rural communities, far from the major centres of colonial military power. Slave owners, especially planters, could call up the local military and militia and harness the savagery of slave laws for support. But that took time. On a daily basis they had to confront and contain their enslaved labourers alone and with neighbours, using methods of their own making.

Slave holders everywhere exercised control via a combination of methods which ranged from inducements for good behaviour (time off work, food, clothing – even cash – and better treatment) through to punishments for transgressions. Brutality in all its forms was always available and often mirrored the pattern of the slave ship. Yet rewards and punishments, and everything in between, are not sufficient to explain why and how such large communities were kept in enslaved subjection for so long. The durability of slavery for centuries in the Americas is, however, deceptive because, wherever we look, slavery was contested and resisted by the slaves. Indeed resistance was a ubiquitous characteristic of slavery, and the fear of slave rebelliousness remained a nagging concern of all slave owners. Slaves were not people to be trusted, and

William Blake, 'Flagellation of a Female Samboe Slave', depicting the flaying of a
female slave in Surinam, 1796.

although many owners were often lulled into a false sense of security, the dread of slave defiance cast a long and persistent shadow across the lives of slave owners throughout the Americas.

Africans landing in the Americas nursed deep resentments which had festered since their initial enslavement in Africa. Their lives henceforth were shaped not only by the harsh difficulties of adapting to utterly strange conditions, but by the need to cope with the dangers and threats which confronted slaves everywhere. They had to learn how to survive at work which was unfamiliar, and all the while in the control of people – their owners and employers – who were alien and often dangerous. Africans found themselves in an utterly unknown world, at the beck and call of people whose languages they could not understand, corralled into strange dwellings and communities, and marshalled – in gangs, teams or individually – to labour at unfamiliar tasks. They soon learned that failure to comply, to be slow on the uptake or even not to understand, was to provoke reprimand. Africans had to adapt – and quickly.

Adapting to life as an American slave was never easy and there were many Africans who simply could not adapt – or would not. Some ran away, even en route from the slave ships to their new, as yet unknown, homes. Others ran away time and again from slave settlements. Planters' records, local laws and newspaper advertisements all offer revealing testimony to the continuing story of slave runaways: slaves escaping to distant relatives and loved ones, others headed to the bush, with some forlornly hoping to find their way back 'home'. Many came together to create free communities of runaways. These 'maroon' settlements of escaped Africans became dynamic communities hidden away in inaccessible or distant redoubts of hills and forest and often posed a danger and irritant to planters and colonial authorities. Impossible to destroy or capture, the maroons were, at once, a threat to the very idea of slave society and a beacon for new runaways seeking to escape from slavery.[1]

The great majority of slaves, however, did not run away, though doubtless many more would have liked to flee. Most remained bound to their owner and to the land they worked, and it was there, in the myriad slave communities dotted around the Americas, that Africans developed their own means of coping with slavery. On plantations and in towns, slaves who had stepped ashore alone developed ties of family and kinship, of friendship and community, creating personal and communal networks which formed the life-blood of slave life and society. Forged against the odds, such bonds formed the bedrock of slave life across the Americas. Yet all this could be (and was) destroyed by sudden and unexpected removal, by onward sale and dispatch to another property (often in the far, unimaginable distance).

Slaves everywhere learned how to avoid or minimize life's risks, trying to make their lives tolerable while, at the same time, doing as they were told. But there was always a fine line between bending to owner's demands and maintaining their self-respect. Much depended on the work they did. Slave labour differed enormously from one crop to another – between sugar and tobacco, for instance – between town and country work, between field and domestic labour. Much too depended on a slave's age, though all were set to work at appropriate tasks from their early childhood years through to old age or physical decline.

Quite apart from the rhythms and rigours of their labouring day, slaves everywhere found themselves subject to the unpredictable and capricious moods of their masters and mistresses. They had to cope with anger and spite, frustration and malice – often for no apparent reason. This was perhaps most common and widespread in the impulsive sexual advances suffered by female slaves. Some fought off unwelcome advances, while others simply succumbed to the inevitable, allowing themselves to become a regular lover or partner and to take material advantage from the sexual services they provided. Across the Americas, slaves were largely defenceless in the face of the anger or lust of the people who owned them, all made worse by its unpredictability. It flared up without warning, fuelled by frustration, drink, by a moment of passion or unfathomable fury.

Such moments were not the daily experience of every slave, but the *threat* of such encounters was inescapable. No slave could ever be certain, from one day to another, what might happen to them. They knew that each day entailed its own regime of strenuous toil, but they also realized that their labours might be compounded by other, more personal sufferings, and they had to learn how to cope with all this – and more. They needed, for their own sake and for the well-being of loved ones who depended on them, to be able to accommodate themselves to the rigours and the blows of life at large, adjusting in ways which allowed them to survive in a hostile environment, learning what was possible and what was not, how far they could go – and which boundaries they could not cross.

Slave owners, on the other hand, could rarely trust their slaves completely. At worst, they feared them, never sure what they might do, and were generally prepared to believe the worst of them. From one slave society to another, slave owners complained, loud and regularly, about their slaves and especially about their laziness, claiming that slaves seemed unwilling to work unless compelled, that they were incorrigibly lazy and hence in need of rigorous enforcement. It was a rare slave owner who expected slaves to work readily of their own accord. The slave owners' philosophy was rooted in the belief that force alone could secure the necessary labour.

To their owners – indeed to the outside world at large – many slaves intentionally presented a demeanour of ignorance, feigning stupidity and incomprehension (though language conflicts were often real enough between Africans and European colonists). In common with other (notably classical) slave societies, slaves were thought to be stupid and in need of constant supervision and coaxing. The dim-witted, lazy slave was a perennial figure from one slave society to another. Of course, it suited the slave to appear like this. Why be intelligent and industrious when it might simply bring more work and responsibility?

Chaîne d'esclaves venant de l'intérieure.

R. G. Villeneuve, engraving of African slaves in chains led by guards, 1814.

145

Why be trustworthy when failure at responsible tasks brought retribution and punishment? Better by far to be cunning and to appear dim. Such behaviour carried its own dangers, of course, but a slave's life was hemmed in, *defined* even, by risks, and slaves clearly opted to live with risks of their own making.

Slaves everywhere needed to know how much tolerance they could expect from those in authority, whether it be a mistress in the house or a driver in the field. Such tolerance, however, varied enormously: behaviour that would go unnoticed by one master might provoke rage in another. Slaves learned by trial and error and by gauging how a particular owner would react to their behaviour. In their turn, slave owners tried their best to gauge their slaves: how much work to expect, how much back-chat to tolerate. Knowing what was possible and what was risky became part of slave folklore, within slave families and in the broader slave community, and was passed on to the young. Slaves taught their children the lessons of life which were vital for navigating the dangers of slavery. Most thus learned to adapt, to accommodate themselves, to being a slave. Many, however, simply refused to accept this, and sought to escape completely; some even challenged slavery itself. But theirs was a much more dangerous route.

Slavery in the Americas was characterized by violence. Africans had been enslaved violently, transported across the Atlantic in the most violent of fashions, and kept in place by draconian regimes which were themselves lubricated by violence. Not surprisingly, Africans often responded with violence of their own. Many of them must have felt that this offered the only way out of a system which heaped indignity upon physical suffering. They all had good reason to hesitate: slaves needed only to consider the fate of Africans who fought back – and failed. On the African coast, at sea, and then in the Americas, defeated rebel slaves faced death and suffering – on a terrible scale. Though never close to the suppression of the Spartacus rebellion (in 73 BCE the Romans lined the Appian Way with the crucified bodies of 6,000 rebellious slaves), slave revolt – even the *fear* of revolt – provoked gory reprisals in all slave societies. Slaves knew what to expect if they failed, or even if they were suspected of plotting. Many Africans who had survived the Atlantic crossing had witnessed the ghastly fate of failed rebels on the slave ships. It was a horrifying prologue to similar upheavals in the Americas. Despite that, rebellion 'punctuated the history of African American slavery from its beginnings'.[2]

Slave revolts periodically flared across the Americas. Some were small-scale, with limited, local impact; others were widespread and ambitious – a few aimed at toppling the entire slave system. In the Caribbean and Brazil, where numbers seemed to favour the slaves, they could see with their own eyes that small bands of white people lived in isolated places, surrounded by a sea of slaves. Yet despite this imbalance, on only one occasion, and that late in the history of slavery, did rebel slaves overthrow the system: in St-Domingue, called Haiti after 1791. Other slave revolts came close to success: some caused massive damage and destruction, attracting thousands of slaves in a tumult of revenge and liberation, before being bloodily crushed. When slave owners regained control, town centres and crossroads near plantations became a via dolorosa, with slave corpses and body parts left to rot in the tropical heat – a nauseating reminder of the fate of failed rebellions.

Though slave holders were most apprehensive about revolt where Africans lived in large concentrations, even in North America, where local-born slaves soon outnumbered Africans and where rebellions were less common and less savage, slave rebellion never seemed far away. Slave owners everywhere suspected slaves of plotting and scheming and were easily persuaded of plans for revolt, and also generally willing to believe the most alarming rumours. At times it was (and remains) difficult to distinguish between rumour and reality in the world of slave revolts. Slaves were rounded up and tortured, when they usually confessed, of course, to plotting rebellion where often none existed. There were many more rumours and fears of rebellion than there were actual revolts, itself a reflection of the slave owners' innermost anxieties. They prided themselves on knowing their slaves well, understanding what made them tick and appreciating what was needed to get the best out of them. In many places they even claimed a paternalistic fondness towards their slaves; some believed that the feeling was reciprocated. At the same time they also distrusted slaves and remained vigilant for tell-tale signs of trouble and danger. The reality of relations between slave owners and their slaves was its apprehensive uncertainty. They could never be sure what their slaves might do – and they generally feared the worst.

Slavery in North America seemed different from elsewhere in the hemisphere. There were, it is true, plenty of revolts and conspiracies, though there were more rumours of plots which failed to materialize.[3] Some upheavals were not restricted to slaves, but were popular outbursts that attracted support from other marginal groups. Trouble in early colonial Virginia, for instance, erupted in the wake of rebellious white labourers and friction with native Indians: an illustration of just how volatile were the pioneering days of settlement, with their unpredictable social mix of native peoples, African slaves, indentured Europeans – and free people. The emergence of sizeable communities of Africans, even when they were outnumbered by local whites, created an entirely different set of problems.

As slavery embedded itself as the foundation of economic life (in tobacco and rice cultivation), slave unrest became a taxing issue. South Carolina's ricefields were especially brutal. There, in 1730, the Stono rebellion, lead by an Angolan, was an attempt by a band of Africans (who possibly had had military experience in their African homelands) to escape to freedom by crossing into Spanish Florida. More than twenty white people died in the conflict. The rebels' defeat was followed by a savage revenge inflicted by local militia, with some forty slaves killed. It set a pattern which was to be repeated time and again elsewhere. Two years later, when an African slave named Caesar Varick planned to burn down New York City, he and twelve others were burned alive, and a further eighteen slaves were hanged. Exemplary revenge quickly became the blueprint for dealing with defeated rebels. When, in 1800, Gabriel Prosser marched on Richmond, Virginia, with a small band of rebels under a banner, 'Death or Liberty', local slave holders assumed that they had been influenced by news of revolutionary upheavals in the Caribbean. The rebels were routed and Prosser and 25 others were executed. The slave owners' concerns were heightened by the presence among insurgents – in this and subsequent revolts – of slaves who had landed from the Caribbean: people who had fled in terror with their owners from the uprising in St-Domingue and other French islands, before resettling in North America. But all were easily stopped and suppressed.[4]

The revolutions in France in 1789, and in St-Domingue in 1791, cast a long and unsettling shadow across all contemporary slave societies. In the immediate aftermath of those revolutions, slave holders throughout the Americas were quick to detect the influence of revolutionary influences wherever they saw local slave unrest, not surprisingly, perhaps, where slaves had been relocated from the French Caribbean. Numbers of them had settled in South Carolina and Louisiana, for example. In 1795, a slave conspiracy at Pointe Coupe in Louisiana was crushed and 23 slaves were executed. More serious still, the German Coast rising of 1811, again in Louisiana, proved to be the most extensive slave conspiracy in North America. Hundreds of slaves, some of whom had fled from the French Caribbean, joined an insurgent march along the Mississippi towards New Orleans, destroying a number of plantations en route. Although they killed only two white people, about ninety slaves were killed or executed in the fighting with militia and in the subsequent trials: hanged, beheaded, bodies burned, heads displayed in New Orleans and body parts posted on local plantations. This reprise of the punishments meted out on the slave ships was, again, a warning to other slaves to take note of what happened to unsuccessful rebels.[5]

For all this ferocity, the uprising had been suppressed in a matter of days. Here, and on countless other occasions, the levels of slaughter and the ritual dismembering of the dead, seem out of all proportion to the damage inflicted by rebels. Such outbursts of bloodletting against slaves erupted in all slave societies. Rebels did not have to be numerous or to have inflicted widespread death and destruction. Even when small bands roamed over a limited area, for a very short time, they constituted the slave owners' ultimate nightmare: a corrosive threat to the fabric of society at large. Unless they were stopped, quickly and totally, the dangers they posed would spread far and wide. Revenge – swift, exemplary and terrifying – was designed not only to punish the offenders but to leave horrified survivors in no doubt about the fate of all rebels. Punishment also destroyed and tore apart the African body. As on the slave ships, here was punishment which was intended to defile the African body and destroy any possibility that the dead might be able to make their way to their own spiritual afterlife.

The ferocity of planters' revenge was played out time and again. In 1822, Denmark Vesey, an African in South Carolina who also had previously lived in the Caribbean, seemed an unlikely candidate to be a rebel. He had bought his freedom via lottery winnings, was an active member of a local Christian church and, like many others, had been greatly influenced by news of the slave upheaval in St-Domingue. Though historians have disputed the importance of Vesey's plans to raise an insurrection among Charleston's slaves, the aftermath of the revolt once again raises the problem, not so much of slave rebellion, but of the outlook of besieged slave owners. It seems that Vesey wanted to kill the whites in Charleston, seize money from the banks and sail to Haiti. Though the plot was leaked before anything took place, the subsequent revenge was savage and exemplary. A total of 35 slaves were hanged, including Vesey.

The most famous of all North American slave revolts was that led by Nat Turner in 1831. Turner had been a regular runaway and, like Vesey, was a devout, educated man who was convinced that he was destined to lead. This, again in Virginia, was a revolt which lasted only a few days but spread panic among local whites, as the insurgents moved from one homestead to the next, attacking white families (killing 57 people in all) and seizing whatever arms they could find. Turner's rebel band was halted and destroyed after only four days by hastily rallied white forces, including federal artillery and sailors from warships in the Chesapeake. Turner found himself alone and on the run in the woods. The outcome was inevitable.

Turner had wanted to be free from the oppression of slavery, but unlike other rebel leaders in North America, he expressed no great plans or ambitions – of escape to the Caribbean, for example, or claiming the rights afforded other Americans by the Constitution. He seems to have been guided by the belief that the Lord would protect him and his followers.[6] He was to be brutally disappointed. Twenty-seven slaves were tried and seventeen executed, though the full death toll was much higher, with upwards of forty dying at the hands of vengeful white mobs. Merely trying and executing Turner was not enough to satisfy white demands for revenge. After being hanged in November 1831, Turner's corpse was melted down to fat. The survivors (that is, the slaves who had nothing to do with the rebellion) paid their own price, as local slave laws and restrictions were tightened further. Failed rebellion once more ensured that life for the survivors was made even harsher.

There was undoubted hysteria surrounding both the Vesey plot and the Nat Turner revolt, with local slave owners and politicians using and exaggerating the event for their own sectional interests. In essence, this was true, in differing degrees, of *all* slave plots and revolts. The *threat* of servile rebellion, the imagined dangers posed to life and property, accentuated slave owners' worst fears. Slave sympathizers found their arguments challenged by others' recitations of the gory details of what rebellious slaves typically planned to do. In turn, the growing band of anti-slavery activists, who were keen to end slavery, were able to throw the same evidence back at the planters: continue to treat men as slaves and they will inevitably seek to end their bondage in the only way open to them. Whenever slave revolt threatened, each side, pro- and anti-slavery, found support for their own position. Slave owners saw revolt and plots as proof that slavery could only be maintained by unflinching resolve. Their opponents, looking at the same events, saw further evidence that only an end to slavery itself could stop the cycle of violence and suffering. The slaves, meanwhile, caught in the middle, found themselves squeezed still further by the inevitable tightening of laws and practices governing local slavery. Although defeated rebels paid the most terrible price for failure, slaves throughout the affected region felt the slave owners' wrath, though admittedly in a much less brutal fashion.

Wherever we look in the wake of slave unrest, the punishments, killings and reprisals invariably outnumbered the casualties caused by slave rebellion. Unforgiving retaliation was generally a much bloodier affair than revolt itself. Despite the callous brutality of such vengeance, the history of slave rebellion in North America, even in the 'age of revolutions' which shook the Western world after 1789, is relatively small-scale compared to what happened in other slave societies. Only one North American rebellion – in Louisiana in 1811 – involved more than 100 slaves. In the Caribbean and Guianas we know of nine rebellions which involved more than 1,000 slaves.[7] It is not to deny the sufferings of North American slaves, nor to diminish the bravery of rebels and their leaders, to suggest that there was a qualitative difference between what happened in North America and elsewhere in the Americas. Indeed, the story of rebellion there is more a story of plots and frustrated insurgency than it is of open rebellion, though that was to change with the coming of the Civil War in 1860. The contrast between slave rebellions in North America and the Caribbean is stark. The early history of Caribbean slavery was marked by a string of major slave rebellions. Until the last years of slavery, those upheavals were primarily the work of Africans, though this is not surprising given the huge numbers of Africans which continued to pour into the islands until 1807.

The geography of the Caribbean islands and of South America were important factors in slave revolts. On the bigger Caribbean islands, and especially in Brazil, Europeans had barely a toehold on the land, and some colonial outposts were difficult to control. Inaccessible mountainous terrain, in Cuba and Jamaica, for example, and vast rivers reaching deep into jungle and disappearing into an apparently never-ending interior such as in Brazil, provided slaves with ample scope for flight and concealment, either for a permanent escape or as a base to launch attacks on slave settlements. It was in precisely such locations that colonial officials and settlers were thin on the ground and where military help was both distant and limited. Though slave owners and colonial soldiers in the Caribbean and Brazil usually had superior firepower, they were invariably greatly outnumbered by Africans. Furthermore, slaves on rural properties could quickly arm themselves with an array of tools: cutlasses, axes, hoes, machetes, bills and spades – all the basic hardware of agricultural labour, and all easily used as weapons in violent clashes.

The British had persistent trouble controlling their most important Caribbean possession – Jamaica. From the early days of settlement, the island's densely wooded and mountainous interior afforded escape for runaway slaves. The resulting maroon communities, like similar communities of freed slaves in South America, were to prove a serious problem for Jamaican planters and for British colonial authorities throughout the era of slavery. More threatening still were the periodic outbursts of slave violence which harassed isolated planters and at times threatened to topple the entire slave system. It is easy to imagine the fears of isolated planters, cut off in remote plantations and dependent for safety on their own strength and the support of neighbours – but nervously alert to dangers posed by the Africans living close by. Suspects paid dearly for plotting – real or imaginary. On 21 June 1760,

> Three rebellious negroes [from Worthy Park] have been this week executed near Spanishtown. Two of them had endeavoured to ferment an Insurrection at Lluidas but were happily discovered and on July 5th Captain Webley with a detachment of black grenadier's Company marched to St Thomas in the Vale to keep things quiet there.

Sir Charles Price, owner of Worthy Park, had been tipped off by other slaves – who 'were rewarded with their liberty'.[8] The history of Caribbean slavery is littered with such incidents, and with accounts of their brutal conclusion. Slave owners rarely hesitated to display their power of life and death over the slaves. In 1675, for example, of the seventeen slaves found guilty of plotting in Barbados, eleven were beheaded and six burned alive. And so it continued, whenever a plot was uncovered on that small island, with slaves slaughtered by gibbeting, beheading and burning, with their mortal remains left on public display to allow witnesses to draw their own conclusion.

This litany of terrible stories unfolded from one slave island to another. On Antigua, in 1735–6, a planned slave revolt was lead by an African named Tacky (a man thought to be 'artful, and ambitious, very proud, and of few words'). The aim was to kill all the whites in a general uprising of slaves, beginning with an explosion to kill the Governor and the island's leading planters at a social event celebrating the coronation of George II. Although local-born slaves were involved, Antigua's whites were terrified by what they considered to be the African nature of the plot – the swearing of African oaths, *Obeah* (slave religion), war dances and the drinking of slaughtered cocks' blood. The plot was betrayed and torture inevitably widened the number of African suspects and victims. In all, 88 slaves were executed – 77 of them burned alive.[9] A generation later, a much greater and more violent upheaval rocked Jamaica.

There had been a number of revolts in Jamaica in the first half of the eighteenth century, in 1739, 1742 and 1745, but the revolt of 1760 was altogether more serious. Africans had been landed on the island in huge numbers, to develop the expansive properties which flourished in previously undeveloped reaches of the island. The Jamaican revolt in 1760, led by another African named Tacky, erupted in the eastern parish of St Mary at Easter time, with a rapidly growing band of slaves descending on Port Maria. There they seized arms before spreading out, gathering support, destroying and killing as they swept through local plantations. Revolts flared across the island, with local planters, militia and the military struggling to maintain control. Planters everywhere noted troubling signs among their slaves – shaved heads, oaths, unexplained visits by slaves – and, finally, the sudden arrival of terrified neighbours anxious to alert friends to the dangers. There were desperate, violent clashes across Jamaica, with the Royal Navy rushing ships and men around the island to provide military aid – and to imprison rebel slaves on board. Africans again found themselves incarcerated on board a British prison ship.

Finally, in October 1761, a full nineteen months after the initial outburst, the island's Lieutenant Governor announced 'the total suppression of the rebellion'. The cost of the damage and destruction of property was enormous, but, of course, the highest price was paid by the slaves: 400 had been killed, 500 more transported (to the Bay of Honduras) and 100 executed. Prominent rebels were burned or starved to death in public. In the words of Edward Long, the pre-eminent contemporary historian of the island (and himself a major planter), Tacky's revolt of 1760 had been 'more formidable than any hitherto known in the West Indies'.[10] The cycle of bloody events seemed endless: slavery begat slave violence, which in its turn inspired 'plantocratic' (that is, planters as a ruling class) and colonial revenge on an even greater scale.

Throughout the eighteenth century, the Caribbean became a diplomatic chessboard as European warfare and peace treaties saw control of the islands change from one European power to another. Slaves were central to this, though they were not the only subject people involved. In places, surviving native peoples, Caribs in Dominica for example, proved as troublesome to colonial authority as imported Africans (though in many places, indigenous Americans had simply died out). Moreover, when the British acquired a 'new' island, via military victory or diplomatic agreement, they also inherited the local European settlers, notably French and Spanish, who did not always welcome the transfer of allegiance to the British Crown. This complex human mix – of African slaves, native peoples and disgruntled European colonists – made for unstable colonies. The whole brew was rendered even more volatile by the impact of revolutionary ideas after 1789.

In the half-century after the French Revolution there was an unprecedented wave of slave revolts and plots. We know of about 180 revolts or slave plots in that period, among them 'the largest, the best known, and most frequent'. There was an epidemic of rebellions across the region, most spectacularly, of course, in St-Domingue/Haiti. There, the seismic rebellion dwarfed all other slave revolts 'in magnitude, duration, and outcome'.[11]

The roots of the age of revolution were American. In the course of the American war against the British in 1776–83, thousands of slaves were freed, or freed themselves, though many found that freedom brought hardship of a different order when they were transported to Nova Scotia, Britain and Sierra Leone.[12] Most influential, however, was the spread of news and ideas about freedom. Slaves in the Caribbean, for example, heard that their counterparts in the northern colonies had secured their freedom. They also picked up the language of change which rippled through the Atlantic world in newspaper reports and, more potently perhaps, via table talk throughout the Caribbean. Slaves could not remain deaf to what they heard about events in North America and even further afield, from other slaves, from slave masters in their infamously careless table talk, and via the ebb and flow of people between North America and the islands.

The upheavals in North America, however, were as nothing compared to the turmoil triggered by the French Revolution in 1789. As the revolution in France veered into violence, it created social and ethnic tensions in the French slave islands. More broadly it raised the universal aspirations of oppressed people everywhere: the universal principles of 'liberty, equality and fraternity' could not easily be restricted to white people. It was no accident, for instance, that large numbers of democrats in Europe, inspired by events in France, also turned against the slave trade and slavery. But the principles of 1789 had their most electrifying impact on slaves in the Caribbean, with the political and social turmoil in France after 1789 being replicated by local variations throughout the French slave islands. Political and ultimately military struggles erupted between colonial and metropolitan groups and between whites, freed people of colour – and slaves. By the time the French Republic abolished slavery in February 1794, the slaves had unleashed their own war for liberation in Martinique, Guadeloupe and especially in St-Domingue.

Africans had been arriving in St-Domingue in unprecedented numbers from 1725: almost three-quarters of a million had arrived in 75 years.[13] Even by the harsh standards of Caribbean slavery, the lot of African slaves in St-Domingue was miserable in the extreme. From 1789, rebellion spluttered across the colony, but between August and November 1791 a massive uprising in the north, involving an estimated 100,000 slaves, swept away slavery, decimating life and properties en route, in a wave of fiery and bloody destruction. Slave revolt engulfed the entire colony, destroying (with the aid of disease) French and then British and Spanish armies. The British, keen to add St-Domingue to their own collection of Caribbean possessions, lost upwards of 20,000 soldiers and sailors. But the independent Republic of Haiti (as of 1804) was forged at an enormous cost.[14] The once massive sugar industry – a real threat to the dominance of British sugar before 1789 – and much of the coffee industry lay in ruins. The irony was that the collapse of

'Revenge taken by the Black Army for the Cruelties practised on them by the French'.

'Revenge taken by the Black Army for the Cruelties Practised on them by the French'. The uprising in St-Domingue, 1780s, engraved by Inigo Barlow, from *An Historic Account of the Black Empire of Haiti* (1805).

the Haitian economy provided opportunities for other sugar and coffee producers, notably in Brazil, who continued to use slave labour.

The pattern of bloodshed in St-Domingue had taken a familiar path at first, with rebels and plotters killed by French planters and colonial officials. But this time the revenge of the enslaved was massive and brutal. For once, slave holders had no need to exaggerate the physical dangers posed by slaves: the reality of what happened in St-Domingue confirmed their worst nightmares. Slave holders everywhere were terrified by what they learned of the slaughter in St-Domingue, with eyewitness accounts racing around the Atlantic, in print and in gossip – and all confirmed by slaves who escaped the upheavals and who fled to other islands, New Orleans and Charleston. As similar, though less traumatic and devastating, revolutions swamped other French islands, the world of slavery seemed on the brink of revolutionary disaster.

Slave rebellions could not be confined to the French islands and slave holders elsewhere were ready to blame the example of St-Domingue for their local troubles. They also blamed the rise of British abolitionists. After 1787, the British campaign against the slave trade had become a major, popular campaign, generating public support across Britain and establishing an influential voice in Parliament itself. The criticism of the slave trade (and less directly, at first, of slavery) was increasingly fierce. To the surprise even of the founding abolitionists, the campaign had quickly seized the moral and political high ground, which they were not to relinquish until abolition was passed by the British in 1807. The once mighty slave lobby in London, a powerful pressure group of merchants, traders and, above all, planters, was henceforth outmanoeuvred and on the defensive.

News of what was happening in France and Britain became a topic of heated discussion in all the slave colonies – and inevitably in the slave quarters. Slaves believed that they had *already* been freed, but that freedom was being denied by local authorities and planters. These rumoured myths of freedom prompted slaves to rebel in a number of colonies, but, more than that, the stories from London and Paris added to a surge of information – some true, some false – which lapped across slave communities everywhere. It is impossible to minimize the significance of this flow of ideas and half-truths. It was, obviously, reflected in print, it appeared in graphic satire, cropped up in gossip and whispers – and even in song – as people in all corners of the Americas became engrossed by the startling events taking place on both sides of the Atlantic. The effects were unpredictable and some-times surprising. Nowhere seemed immune from the contagion of slave unrest.

Slave revolt burst out even on the tiny island of Curaçao, the Dutch possession which flourished in its role as an entrepôt, mainly for slaves shipped onward to Spanish colonies and North America. Its popula-tion in 1789 was only 20,988 – 12,864 of whom were slaves. There, and throughout the Dutch slave colonies, slave revolt had flickered throughout the eighteenth century but the events of August 1795 were on a different scale. What began as a slave strike escalated to a revolt involving 2,000 of the island's slaves. It was suppressed, with the usual story of on-the-spot killings and subsequent executions, and the death of two whites was revenged by the killing of 100 slaves. The leaders were broken on the rack, burned and dismembered. The leader, Tula or Rigaud, now a national hero, clearly knew about events in St-Domingue and elsewhere and spoke the language of Christian freedom and secu-lar rights. Though the rebels were defeated, the urge for freedom lived on and was encouraged by the political turmoil on the island as it passed from Dutch to French and then British control, reflecting the changing patterns of conflict in Europe itself. Other, less well-known slave risings erupted in Curaçao in 1799–1800.[15]

Slave upheavals blazed like bush fires across the Caribbean, espe-cially in 1795, all serving to shake and threaten slavery as never before. In places, slave discontent emerged on the back of other local frictions. Across the islands, the arrival of terrified refugees and their slaves, fleeing the nightmare in St-Domingue, added to the hazardous mix. In Dominica, slave unrest was put down using local maroons and the black West India Regiment. But soldiers also rebelled (led by Africans) and were put down only after 100 deaths. On St Vincent, the British were not able to quell the violence until 1796, when they promptly shipped 5,000 black Caribs off the island to Honduras. Wherever we look, local people – slaves and Caribs – had obviously heeded the noises from St-Domingue.[16]

Recently acquired colonies posed special difficulties for the British, who clearly hoped that by seizing French islands they would enhance their own colonial riches. Instead, in the short term, they inherited a combined hostility of French settlers and officials and the violence of rebellious slaves. Grenada, which became British at the Peace of Paris in 1763, taxed them to the limits. Two-thirds of the colony's free residents were French – and half of them were people of colour. The revolutionary arguments which flowed into the Caribbean from Paris via St-Domingue had a clear resonance in Grenada, and the revolt there in 1795 was a mix of many of the social, political and ethnic tensions already seen in St-Domingue. Perhaps half of the island's 25,000 slaves were involved in an uprising which forced the British to retreat to their coastal defences and cede control of most of the island to the rebels for two years, but for the British the Royal Navy's supremacy in the Caribbean was critical. Military support poured into Grenada, and when vengeance came it was, again, extreme. Fifty rebels were executed and others sent to Honduras, though the leader, Fedon, escaped and was never found.[17]

It sometimes took thousands of troops to force back slave rebellion. In 1796, slave rebellion in St Lucia was only quashed by the arrival of 5,000 troops, and even they took more than a year to reimpose order. By 1796, the British had effectively staunched slave unrest in her slave colonies. But other colonial powers in the region were less successful. Spain, for example, like other colonial powers, had long struggled with the problems of slave resistance, made worse by the sheer size of Spain's possessions. Slaves had periodically joined rebellions of indigenous peoples in Peru and Bolivia, and in New Grenada. But the era of revolution heralded a totally different set of problems. Efforts to promote the interests of free people of colour, and the withdrawal in 1794 of the *Código Negro* in the Spanish colonies,[18] sparked slave resistance which stretched from Buenos Aires to Louisiana, which was in Spanish hands between 1763 and 1800. In addition, in 1795, slave rebels in Venezuela demanded freedom and social equality, clearly echoing the language of St-Domingue. Later, slave unrest in the Spanish Caribbean was stimulated by news of the debates in Spain about ending slavery itself. Similar trouble broke out, much later, in Puerto Rico and Cuba when rumour spread that help for the slaves was on hand from foreign abolitionists.

The revolutionary and Napoleonic wars and political turmoil in mainland Europe between 1791 and 1815 convulsed the slave empires of both Spain and Portugal. The French invasion of the Iberian Peninsular in 1808 and the subsequent war led to the collapse of Spanish order, both at home and in her colonies, and in the ensuing struggle for colonial independence, slaves found themselves wooed by both sides in the colonial conflicts: loyalists and patriots both wanted slaves as soldiers. In the confusion of fighting and revolt, it proved ever more difficult to maintain slavery, and Spanish slavery was fatally weakened by 'liberal and republican aspirations, the breakdown of traditional forms of order, and the spread of the language of liberation'. Across the vast stretches of Spain's South American empire, slaves naturally flocked to the armies fighting for colonial independence, uniting with people of colour to secure their own freedom – and that meant independence from an imperial Spain. As Spanish colonial rule crumbled in the 1820s, slavery was fatally damaged, though full emancipation was delayed as slave holders and political compromise stalled the process of freedom until mid-century.[19] The struggle for black freedom in the nineteenth century, in both Cuba and Brazil, was to be an epic of slave resistance, and, as we shall see, was to continue until the last quarter of the nineteenth century.

In the political and military turmoil of the era of revolution, all the major colonial powers sought both to secure their own colonies against unrest whilst trying to destabilize their enemies. But they were all at risk from inescapable problems of slave unrest. The spark for rebellion differed from place to place – a new law, a tightening of old slave controls, a dispute with the metropolitan authority – but the outcome was similar, with political turbulence followed by slave unrest. Everywhere, news and gossip about outside affairs could also fan the embers of slave unrest. Stories about the progress of abolition in Europe sometimes served to convince slaves that they were being denied their rights. That slaves were now able to argue about their 'rights' reveals how deeply the principles at the heart of revolution had seeped into colonial life.

Though Britain itself had lived under the shadow of revolution after 1789, and had wrestled with its impact on her American colonies, she had remained relatively secure from revolution at home. The cost, however, of fighting revolutionary and Napoleonic France, and the loss of manpower in the Caribbean, was enormous. Despite the eventual French defeat in 1815, the years of revolutionary turmoil had consequences for slave societies which could not be eradicated. Indeed, slave unrest continued to flare in British colonies long after the tide of war and revolution had been pushed back. The simple truth was that the revolutionary upheavals after 1789 had uncorked the genie of black freedom – and there was no way of putting it back.

Events in Britain, notably the speed with which the British campaign for abolition became a major political force, also had profound ramifications for slavery in the Americas. The rapid rise of the abolition campaign after 1787 was, however, arrested by the very events which, initially, had offered so much promise, namely the rise of black resistance and revolution in St-Domingue and elsewhere. Fear of slave revolt, the continuing wars on both sides of the Atlantic, and concerns for domestic political stability delayed the progress of abolition in Britain. When the Abolition Act was finally passed in 1807 the British approach promptly underwent a remarkable transformation. Henceforth they became the scourge of the Atlantic trade, and ending the slave trade became both a guiding principle of British diplomacy and a strategic matter for the Royal Navy. Notwithstanding the fact that the Anglo-American Atlantic naval patrols were readily evaded, British and diplomatic debates about abolition had major unsettling effects in the Americas, fuelling febrile rumours among slaves. Though slaves knew little about the details of those debates, they grasped the broader gist: that outsiders were discussing black rights and freedom. More directly, the slaves also knew that their owners, in the colonies, were deeply resistant to any concession towards abolition. The resulting tensions in the slave colonies were made worse by the demographic changes produced by the ending of the British slave trade. Although the slave population in North America had long been growing rapidly of its own accord, the British colonies, long dominated by Africans but after 1807 denied new arrivals, now experienced a population change over the course of one generation. At the same time, Christian (notably Non-conformist) missionaries brought new organizations (chapels), new leaders (preachers) and a new message (the Bible) to the slave colonies. It proved a potent mix in helping to ferment slave demands. Black Christian preachers, steeped in the rhetoric of the Old Testament, demanded to lead their people to the promised land – of freedom. The consequences of all this were to prove catastrophic for the slave holders and the system they tried to defend. The year 1807 ended the British slave trade, but colonial slavery lived on until 1834.

Three major upheavals shook the British slave system to its foundation. In Bussa's Rebellion (named after the rebel leader) in Barbados in 1816, one white civilian and one black soldier had been killed, but fifty slaves were killed in the fighting and seventy promptly put to death in the field. Of the 300 slaves later put on trial, 144 were executed and 132 deported. The executions were spread out across the island 'for the sake of example to the slaves' and body parts scattered on the slaves' home plantations. For all its savagery, this repression diminished neither the slaves' unrest ('They are sullen and sulky and seem to cherish feelings of deep revenge') nor the planters' worries ('It behoves us to be upon guard').[20] Five years later another major rebellion erupted, further south in the relatively new British settlement of Demerara (modern Guyana).

Demerara was a region renowned for its harsh environment and for its tradition of slave unrest under a variety of colonial rulers (who had responded with cruelties which were barbaric even by the standards of the enslaved Americas). Here, too, slaves had begun to succumb to the attractions of British missionaries, adopting biblical vernacular to express their grievances. In 1822, upwards of 12,000 were involved in a revolt which rolled along a 40-km coastal strip, where an intensification of labour had compounded the natural hardships of local labour. The deaths of three whites were revenged by the killing of 250 slaves. The bodies of the dead leaders were – again – allowed to rot in the tropical sun for all to see. An English missionary, Revd John Smith, accused of fomenting the uprising, was sentenced to death (with a resulting outcry in Britain) – but he died of consumption before he could be executed.[21]

The ramifications of the Demerara rebellion were far-reaching, especially in Britain itself, where a revived abolition movement, now aiming for total emancipation of slaves, made great political capital out of the continuing violence at the heart of colonial slavery. British abolitionists, now numbered in their tens of thousands, and expressing their opposition to slavery in churches and chapels across the land, denounced colonial slavery for generating an endless spiral of violence. Viewed from Britain, it appeared that slaves were forced to rebel to secure their freedom, while planters and colonial officials seemed able to respond only by acts of ever more calculated brutality. A growing body of British opponents asked: what possible justification could now be offered for such an endless saga of suffering?

Just when the British Parliament seemed poised to end slavery in the colonies, it was challenged by the biggest and most violent of all British slave revolts, in Jamaica. In December 1831, a massive slave uprising in Jamaica – known significantly as 'the Baptist War' – wrought death and destruction on a vast scale. Upwards of 60,000 slaves were involved in an upheaval which destroyed huge numbers of plantations and properties. Violence and destruction raced across the

northern and western parishes – destroying property to the value of
£1 million. In all, eighteen whites died, with 540 slaves killed or executed. Though inspired (and today symbolized) by Sam Sharpe, the
enslaved charismatic Baptist preacher who wielded great influence
over his congregations in the north and west of the island, the revolt
flared from a complex mix: of early Christian ideals, of chapel-based
organization, and from the widespread frustration among slaves
who felt that, though Britain talked of freedom, conditions for the
enslaved in Jamaica remained as harsh as ever. Jamaica's powerful
planters, and the colonial authorities, were shaken to the core by the
extent and speed of the escalating violence. Their response was predictably gory. Thirty slaves died for every white person. This time,
however, the end was in sight. Jamaica's Baptist War of 1831–2 was,
in effect, the *coup de grâce* for British slavery. Around 8,000 km away,
the British Parliament, but especially the British people, had had
enough of colonial slavery: enough of the centuries-old plantocratic
plea that only violence and retribution could keep slavery in place. A
week after Sharpe was executed, Parliament formed a committee to
study ways of ending slavery. Emancipation – black freedom – was
enacted partially in 1834, fully in 1838.

It seems ironic that the British Empire experienced its worst slave
rebellions in the years *after* the British slave trade had been abolished
– years when the tide was actually running *against* slavery. These were
years of inevitable demographic change, as each of the enslaved islands
adjusted itself to slavery without regular arrivals of Africans and to
the inescapable numerical decline of the local African population. But
they were also years which illustrate the power of ideas, of popular
(and to a degree) democratic debate, with political arguments about
rights and about freedom flowing in unpredictable patterns from
Europe to the slave islands – and back again. Once people began to
assert their commitment to liberty, equality and fraternity there could
be no turning back to the old days of slave owners' unquestioned dominance. (This was precisely what Napoleon discovered when he tried
to reintroduce slavery into the French colonies in 1802.) Clearly, specific
conditions in each particular colony formed the stuff of local rebellion,
but the heightened awareness of the discussions about rights – for
black and white, men and women, and for colony versus Europe – all
served to weaken the grip of the old order, both in the colonies and in
Europe. Slave owners would never again have their unquestioned way

The 'Baptist War' of 1832, the biggest and most violent of all British slave revolts in Jamaica. It saw the Roehampton Estate go up in flames. Engraving by A. Duperly, 1832.

in Europe, and their hold over colonial power was itself fatally damaged. Slave resistance and rebellion formed the immediate prelude to the ending of the British slave system.

Although the British emancipated three-quarters of a million slaves in 1838, millions of people remained enslaved elsewhere in the Americas, notably in the USA and Brazil. There were, for example, 4 million slaves in the USA on the eve of the Civil War and, despite the British and U.S. abolitionist navies, in the half-century after 1801, almost 2 million Africans were shipped into Brazil.[22] Like their contemporaries in other slave colonies, Brazilian slave holders had long complained that their slaves were slow and lazy, feigned ignorance and were stupid – in fact that they showed all the personal and communal failings alleged of slaves throughout the Americas. Similarly, Brazilian slaves periodically reared up in anger, in moments of dire frustration and despair, striking back at their tormentors. But, like slaves elsewhere, most found mundane, unobtrusive ways of coping with life as slaves.

Brazil offered huge possibilities for slaves who simply wanted to flee. Individual runaways could find refuge – albeit a harsh and often dangerous one – in the varied geography of the immensity that was Brazil. More striking, perhaps, were the development of maroon communities of freed slaves (known locally as *mocambos*, later *quilombos*), some of which grew to a substantial size. Brazilian slave holders were permanently worried about those communities, but efforts to bring them to heel using the military and local indigenous people failed, and runaways and their communities continued to display astonishing outbursts of bravado and truculence, taunting both planters and colonial officials. Slave owners came to accept, however, that it was perhaps better to have troublesome slaves escape and to live far away from the plantations. For all the trouble they caused and the threats they posed, better that than having to cope with their rebellious instincts on the plantations themselves.[23] In common with other regions of the Americas, all that changed at the end of the eighteenth century.

In the half-century after 1789, Brazilian slavery was convulsed as never before. At one level, the collapse of the Haitian economy created opportunities for Brazil, which found itself ideally placed to expand its sugar and coffee production. Though land was abundant, labour was not. The expansion of Brazilian sugar and coffee required more Africans, and hence Brazil embarked on ever more massive African importations. The numbers of Africans shipped to Brazil had been growing throughout the eighteenth century, but the flow after 1800 was concentrated in new areas of economic growth, especially in the southeast (centred on Rio) where, between 1776 and 1850, an astonishing 1,546,000 Africans were landed. An estimated 2,343,000 Africans arrived in Brazil as a whole between 1791 and 1856.[24] Such huge numbers, in such concentrations, laid the basis for Brazilian economic growth but also for slave unrest.

Other Brazilian groups had their own grievances, of course, a fact reflected in the Brazilian rebellion of 1798 (the 'Tailors' Revolt'), which was prompted by a mixture of concerns about class, colour and freedom – all aggravated by news from France and St-Domingue. But non-slave rebels were understandably wary of aligning themselves with slaves. Events in St-Domingue offered a cautionary tale, though Brazilians did not need to look so far afield to see the risks. Whatever their complaints, free people in Brazil – white and freed people of colour –

realized they were swamped by a sea of African slaves, and they were anxious not to unleash or encourage an unpredictable wave of slave unrest. Thus slaves tended to nurse their grievances alone, without alliances or support from other groups.

Africans, however, had other sources of strength and unity. Among the armada of slave ships bringing Africans to Brazil, many were filled with Africans brought from regions of West Africa beset by warfare and upheaval, and many of Brazil's new slaves were bound together by African kinship ties, by bonds of community and mutual organizations which were forged in Africa but now transferred to the enslaved communities of Brazil.[25] Many also had military experience in Africa. There were, in addition, large numbers of Muslim Africans. Thus, many of the new African arrivals shared important bonds which were to provide rudimentary networks which could be used, for example, in promoting slave volatility.

Such unrest was most severe in Bahia. In 1809 a string of risings took place among Africans on plantations, with other Africans escaping to join freed slaves in the city of Salvador. Another rebellion, this time north of Salvador, led to killings and destruction, before it was suppressed and savage punishments doled out to the guilty. Despite the violent punishments, slave plots and outbursts continued to proliferate, erupting in 1813, 1814 and December 1815, notably among Hausa slaves. Throughout, there was persistent friction between slave-owning colonists and the Portuguese imperial government, with slaveholders in Bahia feeling that colonial powers did not handle slave unrest firmly enough. More significantly, however, some Bahia slaveholders had begun to change their mind. Faced by the obvious evidence of unending slave troubles, overwhelmed by huge numbers of Africans, and under political pressure from British abolition, some began to think the unthinkable: that slavery was doomed. Perhaps slavery ought to be ended and a policy of European immigration to Brazil encouraged? This confusion in Brazil was made worse by the upheaval in Portuguese politics, with the post-war return of the Royal Court from Rio to Lisbon in 1821 and the emergence of demands for Brazilian independence from Portugal (finally secured by 1824).

Throughout, the slaves' resentments festered, but were kept in check. That ended in the 1820s, however, with a string of slave revolts. One was led by an African 'king' and with a specific African group, the Yoruba-Nagos, prominent in a battle fought outside Salvador itself.

Slave rebellions broke out in other parts of the country, and unrest even erupted in urban areas. In Salvador, dockside workers rebelled and were joined by Africans fresh from the slave ships. Pitched battles were invariably won by government forces, though sometimes only just, with the defeated slaves fleeing into the bush or being tried, executed or flogged. In the face of continuing and massive African arrivals, the danger of slave revolt seemed so real and so widespread that slave owners worried that *any* kind of local grievance, any political dispute, and even conventional celebration (notably Christmas), might become the occasion for slave revolt. By the 1830s, the heartlands of Brazilian slavery were in a feverish state, and the ultimate test came in January 1835, with the uprising of Muslim slaves in Salvador known as the Male rebellion.[26]

This was a planned, urban uprising, which attracted slaves from outside the city intent on destroying local political and military powers. Three hundred slaves threw Salvador into turmoil for two days, but suppression and the killing of fifty rebels was followed by the familiar story of executions, floggings and transportations (back to Africa).[27] Thereafter, serious efforts were made to curb Islam, and to woo slaves to Catholicism, all part of a broader determination to maintain a firm grip over the slaves. Both sides – slaves and slave owners – had learned a lesson. For their part, the slaves had, once again, been shown that they were permanently outgunned, outmanoeuvred and outflanked. Revolt seemed only to provoke terrible retribution and suffering. But there was also a growing number of Brazilians – including some slave owners – who began to think that some way other than slavery might be found of exploiting the riches of Brazil. Even so, Brazilian slavery was to survive for another fifty years: the country which had been the effective birthplace of slavery in the Americas was to be the last country to abolish slavery, in 1888.

Even though rebellions and plots had formed an irrepressible feature of the history of slavery throughout the Americas, slave resistance had, with the exception of Haiti, failed to bring an end to slavery. Most slaves learned to resist in more everyday, commonplace fashions, and time and again, from one enslaved corner of the Americas to another, rebellious slaves were beaten back and savagely crushed. Defeated rebels, on the ships and in plantation societies, were cruelly punished, yet even these periodic bloodlettings failed to snuff out the instinct to resist. Slaves everywhere showed their hatred of bondage and eagerly seized opportunities to free themselves, escape, or simply to make their lives less onerous.

By the mid-nineteenth century there was a perplexing contrast at the heart of the story. While there was a growing resolve throughout the West to end slavery, at the very same time, two major, prospering nations, the USA and Brazil, continued to sustain, and benefit from, slave systems which had been introduced centuries before for the early exploitation of land in the Americas. Through it all, slavery continued to prove itself to be not so much a peculiar, but a durable, institution.

EIGHT

Chasing the Slave Ships:
Abolition and After

For centuries, all the major European maritime nations, and, increasingly, North America and Brazil, had profited hugely by shipping Africans to the Americas. Few raised ethical or religious objections to slave trading or indeed to slavery itself, and those who complained found their voices drowned out by the clatter of profitable business. There had been, it is true, critics from the earliest days, but they formed a tiny, virtually unnoticed irritant to what became a massive industry. Supporters of the trade had simply to point to the material benefits flowing from the Atlantic ships to squash objections. The economics of slave trading and slavery trumped ethical or religious criticism.

All that quickly changed in the last quarter of the eighteenth century, at the very same time that one of the Atlantic's major slaving nations – the British – were shipping ever more Africans across the Atlantic. Here lies the key paradox. Just when the slave trade seemed more attractive and lucrative than ever, the nation which had perfected the system decided that the slave trade was wrong. In the space of a quarter of a century, the British turned their back on the slave trade and thereafter embarked on complex diplomatic and naval policies to prevent other nations from transporting African slaves by sea. The USA, for its own internal political reasons, followed with abolition of their own in 1808. By 1822, the British Foreign Office was seized with the idea that the Atlantic slave trade was the 'scandal of the civilized world'.[1] A mere twenty years earlier, the British had been at the forefront: the dominant slave trader. Here, then, was a transformation of a remarkable, and in many respects bewildering, order.

What makes the story even more curious is not merely the British volte-face in the face both of their own history and of the continuing demand in the Americas for more Africans, but the brutal fact that, despite Anglo–American efforts to blockade the Atlantic trade, 3 million slaves were landed in the Americas, primarily in Brazil and Cuba. Almost as many were landed in the Americas in the sixty years *after* abolition as in the sixty years *before* 1807.

The British abolitionist campaign was instituted by a small band of Quakers. This band of radical dissenters, conceived in the turmoil of seventeenth-century England, were, by the mid-eighteenth century, scattered in small communities across Britain and the American colonies. Plain and honest, they applied a strict egalitarian philosophy to the world at large and from an early date were opponents of slavery. The Society of Friends, as the Quakers are also known, had long railed against slavery, on both sides of the Atlantic, their criticisms given a sharper edge by the American War (1776–83). Slavery became a major strategic and political issue during that war, notably in the form of thousands of loyalist slaves who deserted their American owners to join the British. In the event, they joined the losing side and their subsequent relocation (to Nova Scotia, London and Sierra Leone) proved a small illustration of the wider human problem spawned by African slavery in the Atlantic. At the end of the war, in 1783, Quakers doubled their efforts against the slave trade. A group in London began to study the slave trade, and to discuss how best to press for its abolition, sponsoring publications, essays and articles in the press to promote the case. In late 1783, London Quakers took a public stand against the slave trade, sending an abolitionist tract to MPs, government ministers and the royal family. There followed a flood of inexpensive Quaker literature, disseminated nationwide via the Quakers' remarkable national network of meetings and local committees. Those publications raised not merely the morality of slave trading, but also questioned the economics of the trade. Would it not be better (that is, more profitable) to trade with Africa in a 'normal' fashion – rather than trading for humanity? This appeal, and its proposed alternative to the slave trade, struck a chord with a growing band of people uneasy with the practice.

London Quakers found an ally in the quirky person of Granville Sharp, an Anglican and general reforming gadfly, who had for twenty years waged a lone battle against the problem of slavery in England itself. He had campaigned about the issue with lawyers, with clerics and government ministers, and his efforts were given a grotesquely brutal twist between 1781 and 1783 by news of the murder of 133 Africans on the Liverpool slave ship, the *Zong*. In the subsequent legal case, the Lord Chief Justice, Lord Mansfield, heard the ship owners' claim for insurance on the value of the Africans murdered on the *Zong*; Sharp (and others) launched themselves into a fury of abolitionist activity.

Sharp angrily brought the question of the *Zong*, and of the slave trade in general, to the attention of politicians, the Admiralty, legal experts, senior clerics in the Church of England, a string of reformers, and major figures at Oxford and Cambridge universities. Many agreed with him that the slave trade was an outrage, and all were horrified to learn of the cold-blooded *Zong* killings, followed by the equally chilling application for insurance costs from the ship's owners.[2] None were more distressed by news of the *Zong* than the band of Africans living in London. One of their spokesmen, Ottobah Cugoano, denounced the *Zong*'s owners as 'inhuman connivers of robbery, slavery, murder and fraud'.[3] John Newton – the ex-slaving captain, now Anglican preacher and abolitionist – thought it 'a melancholy story'. Even by the debased standards of the slave trade, it was a story which almost defied belief, and people of sensibility were incensed. Yet the killings – a mass murder – were not an isolated affair. For a start, the thriving English insurance industry, based in London, did a flourishing business insuring the lives of Africans on board the slave ships, and it was commonplace for ship owners to be compensated by their insurers for the loss of Africans who had been killed in shipboard rebellions. Nor was it a secret that death and suffering, often on an epic scale, were common on board the slave ships. All this could easily be confirmed by merely asking any of the thousands of sailors who had served on a slave ship. The evidence for what happened as a matter of course on every slave ship was readily available. It was this realization, and the dissemination of this evidence, which was to fuel the rise of abolition sentiment across Britain.

The man who used that evidence to spectacular political effect was Thomas Clarkson. Clarkson, a brilliant Cambridge undergraduate, was won over by an abolitionist sermon delivered in Cambridge by one of Sharp's associates – Dr Peter Peckard, Master of Magdalene College and Vice Chancellor of Cambridge, and an early abolitionist – before establishing his name by winning a university prize for his essay on slavery. His research for the essay launched him into his lifetime's work. Clarkson was to become the valiant foot soldier of the abolition campaign, travelling thousands of kilometres to lecture against the slave trade and to uncover damning evidence about the slave ships. He was soon familiar with the early literature about the slave trade and friendly with abolitionist Quakers in London. They, in turn, realized that they had chanced upon the ideal man to promote the abolition cause. Clarkson was young and energetic, a good researcher, writer and lecturer. With Quaker backing after 1787, Clarkson embarked on a nationwide lecture tour promoting the abolition of the slave trade, initially using Quaker networks and contacts around Britain. When he began his research into the slave trade, Clarkson had been unaware of the existing abolitionist literature, his breakthrough coming with his discovery of the pioneering abolitionist tract *Historical Account of Guinea* (1771), written by Anthony Benezet, one of North America's most prominent Quakers, and published by London Quakers. It proved a revelation. 'In this precious book I found almost all I wanted.'[4]

Benezet's *Historical Account* was based on detailed research and sought to cast aside the deeply entrenched racial prejudices about Africa and Africans, illustrating instead the equality of Africans and doing so by the careful use of primary data. It was, at once, both a pioneering – almost anthropological – study and a bold and exceptional assertion of African equality. Benezet also scrutinized published data about the slave ships in order to calculate the true size of the trade.[5] His findings – but more important, perhaps, his *method* – were to enter the abolitionist campaign. Benezet had provided, admittedly in a simple form, a methodological blueprint for research. His was a book informed and shaped by hard, empirical data, by looking at Africa and Africans though the eyes of men who had been *personally* involved: men who had been to Africa, who had lived and worked there, and men who had worked on the slave ships.

Here was a template which Thomas Clarkson adopted and was to make his own. By chance, he had hit upon a critical and revealing approach: a means of discussing the slave trade, not by the traditional ping-pong of moral assertions, but by the use of primary evidence. He now set out to unearth and arrange hard statistics from the slave ships and to collect verbatim accounts from men who sailed those ships. He quickly learned how to acquire, process and use evidence from a first-hand source.

Other Quakers also encouraged Clarkson to look closely at the slave ships. William Rathbone, a prominent Liverpool Quaker merchant, and himself familiar with that city's slave ships, urged Clarkson to study the slave ships' muster rolls in order to unearth the factual evidence of life and death on the slave ships.[6] When he did, Clarkson's work quickly revealed some stunning facts. Of 5,000 men who sailed from Britain on slave ships in 1785, only 2,320 returned home. Clarkson wrote that 'every vessel, that sails from the port of Liverpool in this trade loses more than seven of her crew, and . . . if we refer it to the number of seamen employed, more than a fifth perish.'[7]

Here was potent and irrefutable evidence, scooped from the very heart of the slave ships themselves, which lifted the arguments about the trade to an entirely new level. (We now know, for example, that in the last generation of British slave trading, before 1807, about 20,000 sailors died on British slave ships.[8]) The slave trade was a brutal, killing affair, and not only for Africans.

Thomas Clarkson was also deeply influenced by the way Quakers lived and worked. He was, for example, impressed by the attention they paid to accountancy and paperwork, both in the meetings of the Society of Friends and in their commercial businesses. This 'Looking over the papers', the beady-eyed bookkeeping which was a vital ingredient in Quaker commercial success, generated a culture of arithmetical and statistical scrutiny which was to be a feature of the subsequent analysis of the slave trade. Regular and meticulous accountancy – and external supervision of that data – was basic to Quaker life (both at work and in the Meeting House). This commitment to statistical analysis encouraged Clarkson to adopt a similar concentration on the paperwork spawned by the slave trade.[9]

Thomas Clarkson had, via Benezet and through his work with Quakers, quite unconsciously alighted upon a methodology which he was to perfect and develop with great success over the next few years. It soon yielded rich returns, providing first-hand statistical material which was incontrovertible and which became the shank of abolition activity well into the nineteenth century. Indeed, this is the very system employed by modern students of the slave trade: accumulating and analysing the primary data which was generated in profusion by the vast industry that was the Atlantic slave trade.

When the Society for Effecting the Abolition of the Slave Trade (SEAST) was formally launched in 1787, the founding committee consisted mainly of Quakers, who were already primed to launch their own offensive against the slave trade. Via tracts, inexpensive publications and articles in the press across the country, and also through lectures – delivered most famously by the young Clarkson (he had covered 56,300 km by 1794) and rising parliamentary agitation led by British politician William Wilberforce, the abolition cause blossomed beyond the wildest dreams of its founders. Petitions demanding an end to the slave trade attracted tens of thousands of names (60,000 in 1787) and descended on Parliament in their hundreds from across the nation. Lecture halls were packed wherever abolitionist lecturers spoke. And throughout, an increasingly literate nation was bombarded with tens of thousands of abolitionist publications. In 1787–8, the Abolition Society issued 51,432 pamphlets and books, 26,525 reports and papers. Those publications, and the abolitionist lecturers, presented the *details* of the horrors of the slave ships. In all this, Thomas Clarkson emerged as the central figure. As he travelled the country, Clarkson researched busily, garnering overwhelming evidence about the ships, about the sailors, and about the potential for normal trade with Africa. He presented factual information which the supporters of the slave trade simply could not deny or refute. Within a year of the launch of the Abolition Society, it was admitted in the Lords that 'It was a matter of public notoriety, that the question of the Slave Trade had engrossed the attention of every part of the kingdom for above these past twelve months.'[10]

Arguments about the slave trade before 1783 had been largely assertions of economic facts – statements of the obvious benefits which flowed from the slave system – in addition to ethical and religious claims, though the established Church of England had, by and large, turned a blind eye to slavery and had even connived in the slavery business. (It benefited financially, for example, from slave plantations, and had made no real attempt to preach to or convert the slaves.) Now, analysis of the evidence yielded a new critique of the trade. Here was statistical eye-witness and first-hand evidence which could be used to dislodge the previously unquestioned dominance of the slave lobby. Moreover, it was evidence which had an *immediacy*, a resonance, which had been absent before. Most famously of course, abolition took root in Parliament, under the often indecisive leadership of Wilberforce. But the parliamentary abolition campaign faced the unpredictable vagaries of political moods and upheavals, especially after the outbreak of Revolution in France and St-Domingue, and the impact of the wars with France. Slave holders everywhere were terrified of what might happen. It seemed as if enslaved peoples across the Americas were likely to rise up. The government received word from Jamaica in 1791 that 'The ideas of liberty have sunk so deep in the minds of all Negroes, that wherever the greatest precautions are not taken they will rise.'[11]

The mounting tide of alarm about revolution and war inhibited abolition, and by the mid-1790s even staunch abolitionists felt obliged to keep their heads down. 'I keep myself as quiet as I can in my own habitation', said Joseph Woods, one of the founding Quaker abolitionists.[12] The changed political and military climate of the new century, however, the emergence of new ministers and governments sympathetic to abolition, enabled Parliament finally to pass the Abolition Act. Even the traditionally resistant Lords eventually agreed. The Act was passed in the Commons by 175 votes to seventeen. Wilberforce, tears streaming down his face, was given a standing ovation. From 1807 the British were no longer allowed to engage in the Atlantic slave trade.

The ecstatic celebrations following the Abolition Act (described as 'the triumph of virtuous principle' by – of all places – the Liverpool abolition society[13]) tended to obscure a number of key issues. First, the British had, before 1807, shipped more Africans across the North Atlantic than anyone else: in the last years of the British trade, one African in five crossed the Atlantic in a ship from Liverpool. Parliament, now basking in its new-found role as abolitionist legislature, had spent long periods over the previous two centuries facilitating and promoting the slave trade: it had been a slave-trading legislature long before it became abolitionist. More pressing, however, was the fact that, for all the abolitionist zeal displayed by the British and Americans, there was a powerful and in some places growing demand for African slaves in the Americas.

The most immediate taxing problem was this: how was abolition to be enforced? The British solved the problem in their Caribbean slave colonies (where slavery itself survived until 1838) by the gradual introduction of 'Slave Registration'. This, a census of local slaves, would enable officials to tabulate the changes in the enslaved population, and any unexplained rise in a slave population could thus be traced to illegal imports of Africans.[14] This was, of course, in keeping with the introduction of the new census in England and Wales and was also, like the initial research led by Thomas Clarkson, an example of the rising importance of statistical analysis to the study and explanation of contemporary social and political questions.

Enforcing abolition in the wider Atlantic, however, posed enormous difficulties. Given the geographic immensity of the West African coastline, of the Atlantic, and of Brazil, how could the new abolitionist powers even hope to staunch the flow of Africans across the Atlantic? Passing an Abolition Act had been achieved by overcoming extraordinary political problems in Britain: *enforcing* abolition now seemed even more daunting. The first step was to persuade other maritime powers of the need to abolish the Atlantic slave trade. After 1815, the British launched a diplomatic effort at the post-1815 Congress meetings designed to restore order to war-torn Europe, and again with Thomas Clarkson in a starring role, scurrying from one Congress and capital to another. It was immediately obvious that not all European powers shared the British enthusiasm for ending the slave trade. Some, notably France, Spain and Portugal, had an interest in *maintaining* the slave trade to their colonies, while others remained cynical of British motives. The sceptical view was that the British were demanding an end to a trade which they had perfected, and from which they had derived enormous bounty, but which they no longer needed. Suspicious observers, none more so than the French and the French maritime industry, felt that now, with her economic self-interest diverted elsewhere, notably into the rise of new British industries, Britain wanted to prevent others from benefiting from the slave trade.

After 1815, the British faced two distinct problems. The first, to get other maritime nations to commit to abolition; the second, to enforce abolition in the teeth of what was obviously continuing commercial demand for slaves in the Americas. The legislative story of abolition was straightforward. (The Danes had been the first, abolishing their slave trade in 1803; the last was Portugal, in 1836.) But legislating for abolition was only part of the problem. Even after Portuguese abolition in 1836, 1 million Africans were shipped across the Atlantic. The last African slaves were landed in Cuba in 1866. Clearly, naval enforcement of abolition laws and international treaties remained the major problem.[15] Though there was no doubting the rising power of the British and the Americans, and their related naval strength, they were confronted by a major international issue, with complex ramifications, which could not be easily solved by a muscular approach. In addition they had no clear international guidelines to help them. They could and did try to impose their will by force, but that was often counter-productive, not least when the British Royal Navy tried to stop and search ships flying American and French flags.

For thirty years after the French wars, the British pressed on, signing a plethora of treaties, conventions and bilateral agreements with other major maritime powers, all seeking to limit and penalize slave trading from Africa. But these diplomatic agreements frequently foundered on humdrum practical difficulties of enforcement, often in the face of the simple refusal by officials and by slave traders to comply. Even though the British and the Americans agreed to 'use their best endeavours' to staunch the flow of Africans, they too fell out, primarily over the issue of the right to board and detain American ships and citizens (a matter not fully resolved until 1842). The French were especially suspicious of British intentions, notably when the British began to strike separate deals with African leaders to secure favourable trading rights on the African coast. It seemed to the French that the much-trumpeted British display of abolition morality was a mere smokescreen for British economic self-interest.

International courts – Courts of Mixed Commission – were established, largely consisting of representatives from the major powers and set up to sit in judgement of offending ships, captains and their human cargoes seized by the abolitionist navies. By necessity, the Courts were as far-flung as the slave trade itself, sitting eventually in Freetown, Luanda, Cape Town, Rio de Janeiro, Surinam, Kingston, Havana and New York. The physical, human and diplomatic complexities involved were enormous. All this was made worse by the fact that both France and the USA expected the courts to hand over their nationals for trial in their own courts.[16] For the Africans involved, the legal proceedings merely prolonged their agonies. When HMS *Cherub* seized the slave ship *Joseph* in 1818, the vessel, which had departed from Cape Mesurado (Liberia) with 45 Africans, was taken to Jamaica and then to Sierra Leone, where the Africans were freed – having crossed the Atlantic twice.[17]

Until the last enslaved Africans crossed the Atlantic in the 1860s, the key players in all this were the British. They were the initiators and driving force behind international abolition, but their zeal, roused at times by evangelical fervour at home, raised serious doubts among other parties involved. How could they explain this recently found British passion for preventing what they, the British, had refined. Despite those doubts, the evidence was clear enough. Anti-slavery petitions were signed by tens of thousands of people, abolition gatherings attracted packed audiences, and politicians felt under persistent pressure from their electorate to act on the matter of the slave trade. All agreed that British public opinion was doggedly against it.

The first British efforts to bring other maritime nations in line via diplomacy was led by Lord Castlereagh in Vienna (1814–15), then Wellington at Verona in 1822. Thereafter, the diplomatic momentum from London for abolition grew ever more powerful, despite periodic questions about the cost and about the meagre results. (Between 1839 and 1890 more than 300 international abolition treaties were signed – but most of them ineffective.[18]) By 1842, Lord Aberdeen claimed that slave-trade diplomacy had become 'a new and vast branch of international relations'.[19] Castlereagh, himself no great lover of abolition, felt that public opinion at home obliged British governments to press ahead with abolition diplomacy, and he used Wilberforce for advice and information to help the cause. They all believed France to be the key. If France could be won over, Spain and Portugal would follow. But after the wars ended in 1815, all three nations wanted to renew the slave trade. The restoration to France of her slave colonies, and the continuing expansion of the slave economies in Brazil and Cuba, provided an obvious market for African slaves. Notwithstanding the efforts of the Royal Navy, the years immediately following peace in 1815 seemed to offer enormous opportunities for slave traders in the South Atlantic.[20]

Slave traders became adept at circumventing the laws and treaties, their favourite ruse being to use false flags and papers to evade seizure. Even those governments which had signed up to abolition sometimes ignored the agreements. British Foreign Office officials accepted that the Atlantic seemed to be dotted with ships using flags of convenience. Traders used whatever flag was required – American, Portuguese, Spanish, French – to circumvent the current state of diplomatic agreement.[21] The British were infuriated by governments simply turning a blind eye to the deceptions of their nationals: the British drive for international abolition seemed to be foundering on the national self-interest of other maritime powers.

In addition to the huge logistical difficulties, there were, then, enormous hurdles facing international abolition. How could Britain's Royal Navy hope to patrol the immensity of the Atlantic routes with an initial anti-slave trade squadron of only six vessels? From the first, reports from naval officers told of desperate shipboard conditions for the enslaved Africans. Gradually, it became apparent that conditions had possibly worsened *because* of abolition. The efforts of the abolitionists, and the unflagging ingenuity of Atlantic slave traders to avoid seizure, had produced a deterioration of conditions on board the slave ships. The commercial imperative was to fill ships quickly, to crowd as many Africans on board as possible, and to make a quick escape from the loading point. Africans were kept on shore until the last possible moment. Then, when the ocean or river seemed clear of naval patrols, the Africans were hurriedly packed on board. One sailor, from a ship carrying 943 Africans, testified: 'in half an hour after the slaves, or negroes, were brought on board, we went to sea.'[22] Africans were corralled in large numbers at African loading points, waiting for a slave ship, and were then loaded 'in less than one third of the time vessels were formerly detained'. It was claimed in 1826 that a slave ship could take on 381 Africans in a matter of a few hours. Observers agreed that the 'packing' was much worse than it had been when the slave trade was legal. A Royal Navy officer on HMS *Tartar* told of intercepting a 'Margate Hoy' (a vessel of roughly 60 tons) loaded with 400 Africans.[23]

Chronic overcrowding, and lack of adequate provisions for the huge numbers taken on board, inevitably led to high levels of mortality. But even heavy death tolls were recorded with an icy dismissal. One crew member reported that 'Nothing particular occurred during the voyage, excepting that a great many died.' Reports regularly surfaced both in the U.S. and Britain of staggering numbers of Africans loaded on ships destined for Brazil, with the inevitable heavy loss of life. An American sailor on a U.S. ship – technically a whaler from New Bedford – claimed that they carried 1,150 Africans on three voyages to Brazil. The losses were sometimes horrific. A Brazilian ship in 1846 was reported to have lost 373 out of 943 Africans crammed on board. There was not enough water for all on board, and Africans soon began to die – 74 in the first night. One sailor on board admitted that many deaths occurred 'because the ship was too full'.[24] The British Dolben Act of 1788 had restricted the number of Africans to be carried on British ships to a ratio of three Africans for every 2 tons. The illegal trade of the nineteenth century was restrained by no such limits, and evidence spilled forth about the intensity of crowding. A ship of 180 tons, which would have permitted 270 Africans under Dolben, took on board 530 Africans; one of 270 tons, permitted 410 under Dolben, carried 642 Africans. The death rates were correspondingly high. One ship carrying 530 Africans lost 120. Another, loaded with 642 Africans, lost 140. Worse still, a ship packed with 600 Africans lost 200. Ships on the long haul from Mozambique to Brazil suffered exceptionally high mortality. In 1818, *The Protector*, carrying 807 Africans, lost 339.[25]

In trying to make a swift crossing of the South Atlantic, the slave traders made efforts to conceal Africans from abolitionist scrutiny. This, in the words of George Canning, British Foreign Secretary in 1822, caused 'the most dreadful suffering'.[26] Worse still, chilling evidence emerged from the British Royal Naval patrols in the 1820s and 1830s that slave traders were willing to butcher their African captives rather than be caught by the Navy and have the ship confiscated. Some slave captains had no hesitation, when a naval patrol approached, in pitching Africans overboard to avoid detection. It became apparent that mass killings, reminiscent of the *Zong* murders in 1781, had returned to haunt the Atlantic slave trade.

Royal Navy officers began to send back regular reports of mass killings from the decks of slave ships, both at African loading points and at sea. Those reports quickly found their way into abolition publications and into *The Times*. For example, readers learned that 80 Africans had been killed on the *Carlos* in 1814. In that same year, the crew on another French vessel, the *Jeune Estelle*, loaded young Africans into barrels and pitched them overboard to avoid detection. When the boarding of Africans was disturbed at African locations, slaves were thrown overboard into the massive African rivers. Upwards of 180 were killed in this way from two Spanish ships in 1831 in the Bonny River (Nigeria). Four years later, another Spanish vessel jettisoned 97 Africans to avoid the Royal Navy. When mass sickness or epidemics struck, the crew, again, had no hesitation in throwing sick Africans overboard. Africans on the French ship *Rodeur*, sailing from Bonny and Calabar in 1819, were afflicted by an outbreak of eye disease: thirty blind Africans were thrown overboard. A similar number were killed in this way on a voyage hit by smallpox between Mozambique and Brazil in 1838.[27] In 1824, the captain of a French slaver, the *Louise*, having taken on board more Africans 'than he could accommodate . . . had thrown the odd 65 into the sea'.[28] Details of the killings carried out by the *Rodeur*, a ship from Le Havre, were harrowing in the extreme. Captain Boucher (a grotesquely suitable name) decided to kill those blinded by disease and claim for their loss on the ship's insurance. Delivering blind slaves to the destination in Guadeloupe would have involved an economic loss. It was a remarkably similar story to the killings on the *Zong* forty years earlier, but unlike the *Zong*, the owners of the *Rodeur* were compensated by the insurers for the murdered Africans.

How many other mass killings took place which have simply remained undiscovered? Such callous wholesale slaughter did not seem to trouble the slave traders. Captain Boucher, for example, was rewarded for his work by command of another voyage on the *Rodeur*, to ship more Africans to the Caribbean:

> Persons who make a trade of human misery are not likely to trouble themselves much about human life. They throw the bodies overboard, whether alive or dead, with much more apparent indifference than they would the sum they have given for them.[29]

These atrocities were not secret. They were widely reported and became well known. Eyewitness accounts were sent to London in naval and diplomatic messages, were repeated in the London press, and were publicized and denounced in abolitionist publications and at public meetings throughout the 1820s and '30s. Mass killings were formally reported in Washington and were censured in outraged popular petitions in both the U.S. and Britain. It was widely accepted that they were not unusual, but 'are the staple of this trade'.[30]

Such grotesque accounts naturally fuelled public outrage, which surfaced in the press, public meetings and parliamentary discussions, but the slave trade nonetheless rolled on, feeding millions of Africans into the belly of the Brazilian and Cuban beast, each new abolitionist naval tactic or treaty outflanked or outwitted by resourceful slave traders willing to run the risks involved. They acquired speedy new ships, the best being the fast-running Baltimore Clippers, which could outrun naval vessels and which were openly sold in Havana for the purpose.[31] Ships were constructed in U.S. shipyards specifically for fast Atlantic crossings:

> constructed with a view principally, to their rapidity of sailing, whereby to escape the pursuit of cruisers, and without the least regard to the health, comfort or even lives, of the throng of wretched beings who are destined to embark in them.[32]

One abolitionist complained that 'Few of our men of war (even if they were in the neighbourhood) have any chance of coming up with them.'[33]

The ingenuity of slave traders was boundless. An American officer, fresh from patrols in the Canaries and Cape Verde islands, reported to the Secretary of the Navy in 1822 that small ships regularly arrived in those islands, with Africans from French and Portuguese trading posts on the African coast. The Africans were brought on shore, baptized and detained before being shipped on to Brazil as Portuguese citizens.[34] Some of the ships involved were tiny – especially on the short voyages from Africa to the offshore islands. One vessel of just 7 tons carried 30 Africans (ten of whom died) from Calabar to Príncipe.[35] The *Nova Felicidade*, a mere 11 tons, captured by the Royal Navy in 1819, was carrying 71 Africans.[36]

Traders became adept at juggling flags and papers. Canny merchants simply exchanged ships' manifests and logbooks, and swapped ships' ownerships and flags, as easily as any card-sharp. Slave captains combined a slippery commercial awareness with an inhuman brutality towards the Africans, all working together to spin a web of international maritime intrigue which, time and again, outfoxed the U.S. and Royal navies and the courts. In 1820, HMS *Myrmidon* captured a schooner which had been bought in Baltimore by a merchant from the Cape Verde Islands and had loaded its cargo in Bristol, Rhode Island, and sailed to Cape Verde with a crew that consisted of Americans, Portuguese, Italians and French. There it intended to load slaves for Havana.[37]

The complexity of nineteenth-century slave trading was contributed to by commercial interests from both the USA and even Britain. Money was to be made from feeding Africans into Brazil and Cuba, and there were plenty of investors available, though their support often came in a complex, roundabout way. Even innocent, unexceptional business could serve 'to favour the slave trade'. The U.S. representative in Rio in the 1840s, Henry A. Wise (later a Confederate General and Virginian politician), took great pains to calculate and spell out to Washington the degree to which British capital and businessmen lay behind Brazil's slave trade: the very trade under attack by British governments and the Royal Navy. British merchants, for example, sold goods to Brazil which were then used to purchase slaves in Africa, and in return the British took Brazilian coffee, which they sold in the USA. Wise reported: 'Any candid person can attest the truth of what I have said in respect to the employment of British capital, credit and goods in the slave trade.'

The correspondence from the U.S. representative in Rio (his letters were published in Washington in 1848) was emphatic about the bulk of the Brazilian slave trade being 'paid for by the produce of British growth, and goods of British manufacture'. Lord Aberdeen simply batted back this accusation by citing the evidence of American ships, sailors and merchants active in the Brazilian trade.[38] American ships and American crew sailed, for instance, to Cuba, where they took on Spanish identity before heading to Africa, complete with a variety of misleading papers. If stopped by the British, they showed American papers; if stopped by the Americans, they produced Spanish papers. Not unlike the story of the British economy in the eighteenth century, it was virtually impossible to trade with Brazil, or to invest in Brazil before the mid-nineteenth century, without becoming entangled in that country's all-pervasive slaving system.

For all that, for nearly thirty years after the Napoleonic Wars, it was the French who offered the most persistent and devious obstructions to British abolition. They infuriated successive British governments and ministers by asserting their ethical and diplomatic aversion to the slave trade while turning a blind eye to French commercial and maritime involvement in the trade. One abolitionist reported from Paris in 1822 that 'No Member of the Ministry cares a fig for the abolition of the slave carrying trade while many are really interested in its continuance.'[39]

The main problem, however, remained the *demand* for slaves in the Americas. Brazil's appetite for Africans seemed boundless, and Africans fuelled the country's economic growth and the urban development of Rio, Salvador and Pernambuco. Slaves worked in mines, on plantations and even on the slave ships. Africans were everywhere, in large and growing numbers. In the half-century after 1800, more than 3 million Africans landed as slaves in Brazil, all shipped across the Atlantic by European (and, increasingly, Brazilian) traders. Other places in the Americas also wanted African slaves. Though French vessels (many from Nantes) transported large numbers of Africans to the French colonies in the years 1800 to 1850, many were then sold on to other regions.

The early naval successes after 1815 had taken place against the slave trade in the North Atlantic, against vessels leaving Sierra Leone and the Bights of Benin and Biafra, but that changed after 1839 when the naval patrols were extended to the South Atlantic, to target ships departing from the Congo and Angola regions.[40] From there, it was a relatively direct and swift crossing to Brazil, and the great bulk of that trade was conducted by Portuguese vessels trading from Portuguese possessions in Africa. Authorities in Lisbon, Angola and Mozambique did little to stop the trade, despite rising British pressure throughout the 1830s and '40s. Faced by the obviously robust slave trade to Brazil, successive British governments found themselves under pressure from London's powerful abolitionist lobby and the press. Finally, in 1838, Lord Palmerston, the Foreign Secretary, convinced Parliament to pass an Act allowing the Royal Navy to detain suspected Portuguese slave ships. Resented in Lisbon as interference in Portuguese affairs, the Act was nonetheless effective, enabling the Royal Navy to harass the Portuguese slave traders as never before. Finally, in 1842, a new treaty between Britain and Portugal confirmed the right of search south of the equator, with new courts established to adjudicate on seized vessels. Henceforth the Royal Navy enjoyed rich pickings – seizing more than 150 ships bound for Brazil and others heading for Cuba.

In truth, this increased aggressiveness of the Royal Navy derived not so much from legal treaties or agreements, but from a new, flinty political determination. British foreign secretaries, notably Palmerston and Lord Aberdeen (who between them held the office from 1830 to 1851) resolved to tackle the Atlantic slave trade, whatever other Europeans might feel or say. They deployed a high-handed imperiousness which suitably reflected Britain's global power at its most arrogant. Moreover, even when new abolitionist treaties were signed (with Spain in 1835, for example), they often derived ultimately from Britain's power to coerce and bribe European partners into agreement.[41] In this, Lord Palmerston was the key figure. For more than twenty years he dominated the Foreign Office, employing a caustic style at home and abroad and using every means at his disposal to promote British interests. He used ruthless measures to secure abolition, bribing Brazilian politicians and Brazilian newspapers and employing spies in all corners of the Atlantic world to keep abreast of the slave trade.[42] He (and other British Foreign Secretaries) regularly browbeat their European counterparts in diplomatic meetings and aggressively used the Royal Navy to attack slave ships. Bit by bit, this assertion of British diplomatic and naval power had the desired effect.

One major problem, however, lay in the very courts designed to adjudicate on impounded slave traders. The Courts of Mixed Commission sometimes simply refused to accept this British *force majeure*, and rejected the claims of seizure. The Brazilians – independent after 1824 – were reluctant to bend to British abolitionist policies, not least because there was money to be made both from the slave trade and from slavery at home. When Brazil revoked the right of search in 1844, the British Parliament passed an Act declaring Brazilian slave traders pirates, and thus liable to prosecution in British Vice-Admiralty courts. Brazilians were not alone in disliking the powers claimed by the British. Even British merchants and manufacturers, involved in trade to and from Brazil, felt penalized by the Act. Nonetheless, the Royal Navy now had what it had wanted for years: parliamentary authority to wage war on Atlantic slave ships in any corner of the Atlantic, though concentrated essentially on the African coast. The abolition patrols began to have a greater effect also because the number of vessels had increased substantially. By the 1840s there were more than sixty abolitionist vessels patrolling the African coast, the lion's share of the work falling to the Royal Navy, which handled 90 per cent of all captured slave ships. Between 1845 and 1850, the Royal Navy seized almost 400 slave ships trading to Brazil.[43]

Despite all this diplomatic and naval effort, and thanks to the continuing boom in Brazilian and Cuban sugar, tobacco and coffee, the Atlantic slave trade continued. After forty years of abolitionist efforts, it seemed obvious that the Atlantic slave trade would survive as long as slavery itself thrived in the Americas.

There were signs, at mid-century, that British resolve was beginning to flag, largely because of the heavy cost of the abolitionist patrols. At the same time, however, there was growing alarm in Brazil about the massive increase in the numbers of Africans in the Brazilian population – and all this at a time of increased Royal Naval aggression. In 1850 the Royal Navy even attacked slave ships lying in Brazilian ports, raids which were themselves piratical. Finally, Brazil succumbed. Although Brazil had agreed to ban the slave trade as long ago as 1826, a law was not passed until 1831 – and even then little action was taken. But in 1850, seriously bruised by Royal Naval attacks on its ports, Brazil expelled the slave traders. Legislation followed which effectively put an end to the slave trade to Brazil.[44] Despite all this abolitionist effort, 1 million African slaves had landed in the Americas after the various agreements to end the trade.[45]

The end of the slave trade in Brazil left the outstanding problem of Cuba. That island's slave-based sugar plantations had boomed in recent years, greatly helped by the rapid decline of British Caribbean sugar after 1846, and by mid-century Cuba was producing a quarter of the world's sugar. But Cuba needed more labour, and between 1837 and 1867 more than one-third of a million Africans were landed in the island.[46] The British Consul General in Havana sent regular dispatches to London identifying the ships and their cargoes of Africans. Indeed, consular reports from both Brazil and Cuba provided details of the actual numbers of Africans being landed. Tabulating the scale of the Atlantic trade had, in the mode of Thomas Clarkson, become part of abolitionist policy: statistics now went hand-in-hand with moral outrage.[47] The Cuban trade was greatly helped by U.S. finance, especially from New York City, and by vessels sailing under American flags.

It was also assisted by Cuban officials accepting bribes and by the Spanish government (Cuba was still a Spanish colony) simply ignoring British demands for suppression. There was a growing volume of U.S. investment in the expanding Cuban economy,[48] and the U.S. reacted sharply to any infringement of what they regarded as their citizens' right to trade and do business freely; the British had no legal right to board or seize American ships. (There were a number of ugly confrontations between the two navies in Cuban waters, and the issue teetered on open conflict at one point.[49]) Moreover, there had been a general decline in American interest in enforcing abolition off the African coast, and by 1859 a solitary American warship was all that remained. The British persisted, though now trying to staunch the flow of Africans by tackling the problem at source, by mounting aggressive diplomatic and naval policies against West African slave trading states.[50]

Throughout this complex story, the position of the USA as an abolitionist power looks anomalous. Although the Republic had ended its own slave trade in 1808, slavery expanded in the southern cotton industry. In addition, and despite the U.S. commitment to international abolition, American finance and shipbuilders greatly assisted the illicit Atlantic slave trade, especially to Cuba. That ended, however, with the election of Abraham Lincoln in 1860 and the outbreak of the Civil War, which, eventually, put paid both to slavery in the U.S. and to the vital American commercial support for the Cuban trade. The Union was anxious to maintain British support in the war, and the consequent change in U.S. political atmosphere was grimly confirmed in the hanging, for piracy, of Capt. Nathaniel Gordon, a U.S. slave trader, in New York in 1862.

In 1862 a new agreement was signed between the U.S. and Britain, allowing the Royal Navy to stop and search vessels suspected of flying

U.S. flags of convenience. The blockade of Cuba was tightened, and by 1862 New York had effectively ceased to be a major source of money and ships for transporting Africans to Cuba. Without this vital economic backing, and harassed by the Royal Navy, the Cuban slave trade went into sharp decline. When the British finally persuaded Spain itself to abide by abolition in 1865, the trade was effectively dead.[51]

In their abolitionist zeal, the British took many actions, on both sides of the Atlantic, against foreign slave ships and nations which were legally dubious – and some were clearly illegal, even piratical. When it suited them, and when they could get away with it (though rarely against the Americans), the British allowed their sense of moral superiority to ride roughshod over legal and diplomatic niceties. On the issue of the slave trade, the British simply assumed that they were in the right and were rarely prepared to let fine legal points get in the way. The British were possessed of a potent combination – moral certainty allied to diplomatic and military clout – and were generally ready to use the latter to enforce the former. And therein lay the genesis of a new attitude towards Africa which was to become influential later in the nineteenth century – the urge to be imperialist. Abolitionists were convinced that they knew what was best for Africa and insisted on policies that were said to be in Africa's best interests. It was a small step from demanding an end to the African slave trade to imposing abolition on Africa by force of arms, even by occupation. The British, and later other European powers, came to accept that they had a responsibility and a duty to decide what was best for Africa and Africans.[52]

This policy effectively began during the abolitionist campaign, via treaties with African rulers. As early as 1838, a treaty with the Sultan of Zanzibar secured not only an end to the local slave trade but a beneficial trade agreement for the British. However, if Africans resisted the blandishments of such treaties, the British simply resorted to tougher measures. London's powerful abolition lobby had long pressed for a vigorous response to the slave trade on the African coast, urging instead the encouragement of 'normal' trade in the region (an idea which was mooted as far back as the 1780s by Equiano and Thomas Clarkson). From the 1840s, African rulers and states who persisted in trading in slaves could expect a physical response from the Royal Navy. In 1840, for example, there was a naval blockade and the destruction of slave barracoons on the Gallinas River. The action was repeated in 1849 and local rulers quickly agreed to an abolition treaty. The Kingdom of

Dahomey (today's Benin) – and its territorial waters – were next in the firing line. Following failed discussion with the King of Dahomey, a blockade was imposed, later stretching to include all the ports along the Bight of Benin. Lagos, another centre of persistent slave trading, was attacked and occupied in 1851–2, and an abolitionist treaty imposed on the local monarch. (The British thus laid the foundations for what was to become, in the form of Nigeria, Britain's biggest African colony.[53])

Blockading key African outlets had now become the Royal Navy's major tactic, and by mid-century the stretches of African coast available to slave traders had been greatly reduced. Slaving posts along Africa's major rivers, notably the Congo, were destroyed or, in the case of Lagos, occupied. All this dramatically reduced the opportunities for slave traders to acquire African slaves and, by the mid-1860s, profitable slave trading on the West African coast had become virtually impossible. This, however, was imposed with barely a hint of legitimacy on the British side, and though doubts were expressed in London about the legality of these actions, military might prevailed. When African rulers resisted British demands for abolition, or when British citizens were harmed, the instinct was to impose abolition by force. In the process, legal issues were simply overlooked: the ends – stopping the slave trade – justified the means.

At the heart of this thicket of abolitionist intentions and policy there was a weighty principle at stake. From the 1840s onwards there was a pronounced drift in London towards denying African states the protection of international law. The British began to talk not of 'treaties' with Africans but of 'agreements'. Henceforth there was to be a formal distinction 'between Agreements with barbarous Chiefs and the international Compacts of Civilized States'. This distinction – treaties for the civilized, agreements for the barbarous – paved the way for hostile actions against recalcitrant African states whenever there was a need to impose British will (in this case, on the question of abolition of the slave trade).[54] This policy was, in essence, an assumption that the morality of abolition took precedence over legal considerations.

Throughout the sixty years between the abolition of the British slave trade in 1807 and the final demise of the Atlantic slave trade to Cuba, the British had been the driving force behind abolition. They had provided most of the naval muscle and had, throughout, generated the main diplomatic and political energy. In the process, abolition had become a guiding principle of British foreign policy, largely in the Atlantic but, increasingly, in other corners of the globe. Moreover, the commitment to abolition lasted long after the Atlantic slave trade had ended and was to leave a deeply influential legacy in British dealings with Africa south of the Sahara in the second half of the nineteenth century. It was one of the astonishing ironies of British abolition that it was to be transmuted into an important reinforcement for British imperial policy towards Africa. There had been an imperialist tone to much of Britain's abolition diplomacy in the first half of the nineteenth century, *despite* fierce opposition – in government, in Parliament and within the abolitionist movement itself – to the idea of securing imperial African possessions. During the era of the Atlantic slave trade, occasional proposals for British expansion into West and Central Africa were fiercely resisted, though the most potent objection had been the brutal impact of tropical disease. Such settlements (Sierra Leone after 1787) or military intrusions (the Niger Expedition in 1841) were effectively shattered by the devastation caused by tropical disease. Why, asked *The Times*, as late as 1873, should Britain even contemplate any form of control 'over this pestiferous coast?'[55]

By the mid-1860s, after more than three centuries of African misery, the Atlantic slave trade had died away. In the words of an official in the British Foreign Office, in July 1866, 'the exportation of Slaves from the West coast of Africa has been almost entirely suppressed'. In the previous two years a mere four slave ships had been tracked, and only one had crossed the Atlantic successfully.[56] Like many modern historians, this Foreign Office official puzzled over the simple question: what had really brought this once-mighty industry to an end? A century earlier the slave trade was ascendant. Now, in the 1860s, it was the object of almost universal abhorrence. True, a demand for African slaves survived in places, but even some dyed-in-the-wool slave holders, in Brazil, for example, had come to accept that the Atlantic slave trade had long since run its course. The Western world had not only turned its back on slave trading, but had come to regard it as anathema: an ethical and religious outrage which affronted the Christian world's most precious values.

The switch from support for the slave trade to strident and aggressive abolition represents a profound change in cultural attitude and policy. No one was affected by this transformation more profoundly than the British themselves. A dominant Atlantic slave trader of the eighteenth century strained every diplomatic and naval muscle in the nineteenth century to destroy the very same trade. Ships of the Royal Navy which had once secured and safeguarded the Atlantic and Caribbean sea routes for British slave ships were now stationed off Africa to intercept and seize slave ships, which were no longer British.

The British revelled in this new role: to be the world's leading abolitionist was to display the nation's great virtues and moral standing, especially when set against those who did not share Britain's revulsion. Eventually, even those who persisted with the slave trade – and who bore the brunt of diplomatic and naval assault – were won over, or worn down, coming to accept that the Atlantic slave trade was doomed. That abolition was a major theme in British foreign and naval policy was, in essence, an expression of British power. Thanks to Nelson's defeat of the French at Trafalgar, the Royal Navy had no serious rival after 1815 (until the rise of Germany and the USA). At the same time, British diplomats dominated European international gatherings. But behind this naval and diplomatic drive for abolition there lay something that was even more astonishing – the power and influence of the abolition movement in Britain itself.

Led for many years by the indefatigable Thomas Clarkson (if we need to find heroes in this story, Clarkson surely has the pre-eminent claim), the campaign against the slave trade emerged from tiny, mainly Quaker, origins to become a political movement which commanded the support of millions. It had almost universal approval in Parliament and, at times, enjoyed unique access to the highest levels of British diplomacy. But the Atlantic slave trade, as we have seen, was a complex international trading system which bound together three continents and, not surprisingly, attacking this system created knotty strategic and diplomatic complications. Equally, as long as there was profit to be made from selling Africans across the Atlantic, there would be sectional or national interests which were willing and able to continue the trade, whatever obstacles the British placed in the way. The greatest difficulty was a conflict of national interests and the reluctance of some nations to relegate their self-interest to an aggressive morality promoted by abolitionist nations, especially by the British.

It took sixty years to bring all the major maritime nations to accept abolition. In that time, the British Foreign Office and the Admiralty spent ever more time, resources and effort tackling the slave trade. By the 1830s, for example, the 'Slave Trade Department' was the largest section within the Foreign Office and fully 10 per cent of the Royal Navy was employed against Atlantic slave traders by the 1840s. Of all the slave ships seized, 90 per cent were the work of the Royal Navy. In the process, 200,000 Africans had been freed – but almost 3 million Africans were shipped into slavery in the Americas.[57] The Royal Navy seized 1,575 ships, a large proportion of them in 1847–8, when their presence on the African coast was at its peak. Naval success came from blockading the African slave ports and loading points.[58]

Residual problems caused by the Atlantic slave trade survived in the mid-1860s, but they were minor compared to the mountainous difficulties faced by abolitionists a mere generation earlier. They were, in effect, details which needed to be tidied up. Brazil, for example, remained reluctant to free completely some of the freed slaves handed over by the British from impounded slave ships. And France, despite diplomatic agreements, continued to resist demands that the Royal Navy could stop and inspect her ships. For half a century the French had been generally reluctant to succumb to what was essentially a British demand for abolition. In any event, the trade was now virtually extinct. The obstacles from Portugal took the form of corrupt officials in Africa who turned a blind eye to small-scale slave trading (notably between Angola and the Portuguese islands of São Tomé and Príncipe). However, Spain – the last real resistant piece in the entire Atlantic system – was ready and willing by 1865 to prevent any further African importations into Cuba. The British could feel their efforts had worked.

The fate of 200,000 Africans freed from the slave ships was not always a happy one. They were released into various possessions and colonies, living out their days as peasants or indentured workers, in Sierra Leone or the Caribbean. Some became (unpaid) workers in Brazilian cities, while others ended up on Cuban plantations. Most bizarre of all, some, having been returned to Sierra Leone, were later enslaved once more and found themselves back on a slave ship.[59]

Those most intimately involved in the British abolition campaign – in the Foreign Office, but especially the men on board British warships, plus those who recorded in some outrage and despair the conditions of enslaved Africans on the slave ships – felt that they had done good work and that their efforts had been worthwhile. Even so, throughout the entire campaign between 1815 and 1866, and notably among those who remained resistant to abolition, there remained a persistent feeling that this show of British zeal was a smokescreen for more dishonourable, self-interested motives. Britain's abolitionist treaties with various African states and rulers, granting favourable trading or strategic benefits to the British, appeared to confirm that view. The American representative in Rio in the late 1840s was convinced that British abolitionist patrols on the African coast were really designed 'to monopolize the African commerce'.[60] But the development of 'normal' trade with Africa had been an abolitionist aim since 1787. For years, part of Thomas Clarkson's message had taken the form of his famous chest of drawers, packed with African goods and commodities, which he hauled to all corners of Britain to demonstrate the potential benefits of normal trade with Africa.

The spirit of abolitionism had securely embedded itself within both the Foreign Office and the Admiralty. By the late nineteenth century, Britain's anti-slavery sentiment had become what Seymour Drescher called the 'gold standard of "civilization"'.[61] It could easily be directed at other corners of the globe. Even as the Atlantic slave trade faded away, there was abundant evidence that there were other slave trades, most notably from East Africa to Arabia and the Ottoman Empire, which were actively transporting huge numbers of people by land and sea. It was to take little effort to switch attention from the Atlantic to East Africa, the Indian Ocean – and beyond. It seemed only logical for British foreign and imperial policy to maintain its commitment to the ethical and religious spirit of the well-oiled abolitionist movement. Yet this extraordinary cultural impulse had begun in the most unlikely of circumstances, in 1787, among an unassuming group of high-minded Quakers.

NINE

The Durable Institution: Slavery after Abolition

For the best part of three centuries, slavery in North and South America, and in the Caribbean islands, had proved itself a remarkably durable and adaptable institution. But it had always been able to rely upon, and refresh itself with, the human cargoes delivered by the slave ships. What would happen to slavery once the Atlantic slave trade had ended? Some hoped that abolition would naturally lead to the end of slavery itself, but in the event the Anglo-American abolitions of 1807–08 provided yet another opportunity for slavery to reveal its remarkable resilience. It was to be another eighty years before slavery was finally ended (in Brazil).

To modern eyes it may seem contradictory that campaigns to abolish the slave trade nonetheless left millions in bondage, yet both the British Caribbean colonies and the U.S. South continued to reap great material benefits from their enslaved peoples long after abolition. Though those two acts of abolition took place in quick succession, they derived from entirely different circumstances. The British abolished their trade when their colonies cried out for still more Africans. The U.S. abolished their trade when they no longer needed imported Africans. The British Act of 1807 was the culmination of a campaign which reached back twenty years – but had been delayed by revolution and war abroad and by political uncertainties at home. To add to the confusions, British abolition evolved in the years when Caribbean planters were demanding, and British slave ships were delivering, unprecedented numbers of Africans to the islands. Though warfare and revolution had caused massive upheavals in the generation before 1807, demand for Africans bounced back from each successive disruption. In the 25 years to 1810, almost three-quarters of a million Africans were landed in the British Caribbean, especially in the new 'frontier' colonies acquired by the British in the wars.[1] These massive numbers do not suggest an industry in decline.

The slave-trade figures for North America tell a different tale. In the same period, 108,970 Africans were shipped into North America, including people who were uprooted and scattered from the French colonies during the revolutionary upheavals of the 1790s.[2] As large as these numbers are, they are relatively small compared to the massive African arrivals in the Caribbean and Brazil. American independence in 1776 had effectively ended African imports into North America, with only Georgia and South Carolina (1804–07) receiving significant numbers of Africans thereafter.[3] The newly created USA quite simply did not need more Africans because the enslaved population of the USA grew naturally. In fact, the natural rise in slave numbers in North America was remarkable. The 1.1 million slaves in the USA in 1810 had grown to almost 4 million in 1860. The growth of slave populations elsewhere, especially in the Caribbean and Brazil, derived overwhelmingly from massive African imports.

At American independence there was reason to believe that slavery in the USA would simply fade away. The future of the traditional slave crop, tobacco, seemed bleak, largely because of soil exhaustion. In the event, slavery in the new Republic was to be revitalized by the success of a new variant of an old crop – cotton – in the expansive frontier lands of the South and West. Here, once again, slavery proved its remarkable adaptability. It could be transferred to new locations, and to new forms of cultivation, and could be adapted to any number of labouring tasks. Once slavery became the dominant form of labour in cotton cultivation, it quickly seeped out into every aspect of local life, and slaves were soon to be found in all pockets of society across the South: from the street corners of major towns and ports, to the dockside and on the ships, to homes, even of humble people, and, of course, working in large concentrations on plantations. Cotton revitalized and extended the North American addiction to slavery, with slave-ownership filtering down to all levels of society. Slave-ownership in the South was not a monopoly of planters or of the prosperous. And all this was made possible by the massive increase in the slave population, not from Africa, but from the slave states of Maryland, Virginia and the Carolinas. The world of 'Cotton Kingdom' was populated initially by American slaves, transported overland from the east.

British abolitionists had realized from the earliest days that, however much they disliked colonial slavery, and however much they wished to see slaves emancipated, to embark on a campaign for black freedom was a hopelessly over-ambitious task. British abolition began, then, with the single aim of ending the slave trade, in itself a monumentally massive task. Indeed abolitionists frequently denied, especially in times of international turmoil, ambitions for black emancipation. In 1807 Wilberforce himself denied wanting to free the slaves: 'Can it be necessary to declare that the Abolitionists are full as much as any other man convinced, that insanity alone would dictate such a project?'[4]

Even so, they nurtured a hope that, with the end of the slave trade, planters, now unable to buy new Africans, would be forced to treat their slaves better, and thus, in some indefinable fashion (which was never really explained by abolitionists) slavery would simply wither away. Better treatment would undermine slavery itself. Slavery would be killed off by planters' kindness. Unsurprisingly, this did not happen.

There was an immediate problem after 1807: how could anyone *know*, precisely, what was taking place in the slave quarters of the colonies? In the campaign for abolition, the data and horror stories from the slave ships had been critical in winning over public support. Henceforth, comparable evidence was needed – but this time from the slave plantations. Thus, after 1807, attention switched from slave ships to plantations. The initial emphasis was again on collecting data. The census of slave colonies, the 'Registration returns', first used in Trinidad in 1812 then applied generally through the islands after 1820, were bitterly opposed by the planters. Despite their obstructions, the slave returns began to provide an abundance of factual information about the slave populations of the British Caribbean. Empirical evidence once again became available to help the abolitionists – but this time to press for black freedom.

British debates about slave emancipation (should it be immediate or gradual?), especially after 1820, were affected by the succession of slave revolts in the British islands. Throughout, planters and the West Indian lobby angrily resisted suggestions of black freedom. Indeed they resented any interference in the slave colonies, but by the mid-1820s planters were caught between two powerful forces: slave resistance and general truculence in the islands and a rising demand in Britain for black freedom. That demand in Britain was informed by evidence from the registration returns and, equally important, by eyewitness accounts from a new generation of Christian missionaries who were busy converting huge numbers of slaves. Nonconformist chapels sprang up across the slave colonies, much as they did in Britain in the same years, the two networks linked by messages and by peripatetic ministers passing to and fro. Planters, of course, were obstructive while British congregations were outraged by what they deemed to be the persecution of fellow worshippers in the slave colonies. The inroads of Christianity proved corrosive of slavery: black congregations, black (enslaved) preachers, a Bible which impressed with its stories of salvation and the Promised Land – all worked to create an intoxicating climate. As ever more British colonial slaves become Christian, they and their friends in Britain demanded freedom and their rights as God-fearing Christians. Their supporters among the armies of British Nonconformists (there were a quarter of a million Methodists in Britain in the 1820s) campaigned and petitioned on their behalf.

Planters now faced a host of problems, especially when slave numbers began to decline after 1807 and did so until the 1820s, when a new generation of slaves entered their childbearing years. Planters were forced to reorganize their slave-labour force, and they also expected more of the slaves: skilled men were drafted into labouring roles, and women and children especially found their working lives more burdensome. Many slaves must have felt that the end of the slave trade had made their working lives more, not less, oppressive. At the same time, planters found their labour force increasingly troublesome, though they had hoped that, as the Africans died out, local-born slaves would prove more biddable and manageable. In the event, slave dissent – expressed in a Christian vernacular and, worst of all, through open revolt – proved the exact opposite.

All this took place at a time when the British slave colonies were under intense scrutiny, inside and outside Parliament. It revealed a depressing story: of rising slave expectations and powerful Christianity among the slaves, with each episode of slave resistance suppressed with extreme violence. To ever more people, the slave colonies looked like a throwback to a bygone age. Viewed from a rapidly changing Britain, increasingly proud of its modernization and attachment to 'progress', slavery seemed more barbaric and intolerable than ever. And all for what? Cheap sugar to sweeten the British palette? But sugar, as a new generation of free-marketeers pointed out, could be bought more cheaply when produced by free labour – elsewhere. From the mid-1820s, then, a revived British campaign for emancipation was launched. Black freedom was now seen to be ethically imperative *and* commercially sensible. Once again the campaign was led by the peripatetic Thomas Clarkson and reprised the tactics of earlier campaigns: Parliament was besieged by petitions demanding black freedom, and the country at large was periodically awash with mass demonstrations of support for full emancipation (with women very vocal at the fore of the campaign).

The campaign fluctuated, but peaked in 1831–2 when news of the Jamaican revolt coincided with the British debate about the Reform Act of 1832. That Act proved the last straw for British slavery, and the newly reformed Parliament made emancipation inevitable. The Abolition of Slavery Bill of 1833 partially ended colonial slavery in August 1834, by creating an interim period of 'Apprenticeship' which shielded planters from full black freedom, a full three decades after the ending of the slave trade. Full freedom finally came on 1 August 1838. Planters could have no complaints because Parliament raised £20 million to compensate them for the loss of their slaves. In effect, the slaves were bought from the planter, though no compensation was offered to the three-quarters of a million slaves who now found them-selves free people.[5]

As the date approached, British colonial society fretted about what emancipation might herald. Fearful rumours and alarms swirled through the islands, amid anxiety that the about-to-be-freed slaves might take their revenge, as in Haiti, for years of violent injustice. In the event, what happened was remarkable. People who had been violated since time out of mind celebrated their freedom in huge, peaceful crowds, but above all they went to church to give thanks for freedom. British slavery – conceived and nurtured in violence – ended in astonishing displays of peaceable celebrations by freed slaves. Only forty years before, freedom had come to the people of Haiti in a con-vulsion of revolutionary and military violence, and it was to come to the slaves of the USA via the calamity of the Civil War. The slaves of the British colonies entered freedom peacefully.

The ending of the slave trade had no effective impact on the USA. Indeed, in the years after abolition in 1808, slavery in the USA thrived as never before. Just as at the apogee of Britain's eighteenth-century slave empire, economics in the USA during the early nineteenth century prevailed over ethical doubts. Slavery in the North American colonies had attracted its share of ethical and religious criticism, notably from Quakers. The creation of a Republic founded on democratic principles and rights was naturally accompanied by a tortuous debate about the role of slavery. Revolutionary leaders – many of them slave holders – saw little conflict between the way they denounced Britain, and George III in particular, for trying to impose slavery on the colonies and the actual existence of African slavery in North America.

The new nation had to make compromises with slavery. Though it slowly faded in the north, led by legislation in Vermont and ending when New Jersey banned slavery in 1804, slave ownership lingered on throughout the years before the Civil War. But in the north slavery effectively died out and the Republic became sharply divided between North and South, creating the two nations which were to be so bitterly polarized by war after 1860. The fault line was geographic, but the seismic origin of the divide was slavery.

Slavery blossomed in the cotton plantations of the South. Indeed, cotton was the major driving force in the wider U.S. economy until the 1830s. Thanks to Eli Whitney's cotton gin, which made possible the cultivation and processing of short-staple cotton in new, inland and upland locations, U.S. cotton production soared. The figures are astonishing. At the end of the eighteenth century, the U.S. produced 2,300,000 kg of cotton; twenty years later, the figure had risen to over 77,000,000 kg. By 1850, the South was producing 2.5 million bales of cotton – each of 181 kg. After another decade, that figure had doubled.[6] Cotton cultivation spread west and south, creating a cotton belt that eventually stretched from South Carolina through Georgia, Alabama, Mississippi, Louisiana, Arkansas and into Texas. It attracted armies of settlers to land from which indigenous peoples had been expelled, but the settlers needed labourers – and they were to be had in abundance, not from Africa, but from the slave states of the Old South. Slaves – and slave trading – once again became big business.

Before the Civil War, some three-quarters of a million African-American slaves were driven towards the cotton frontier, some travelling with their settler-owners but most under the control of highly organized slave traders, walking and sailing their gangs of slaves to the auction blocks in the cotton states. In popular mythology, the American people's surge westward has traditionally evoked the quest for freedom, but for African-Americans it involved a brutal transfer to a new form of slavery.

Slavery quickly permeated life in the South. There were, it is true, many large slave-owning plantations, but slave owning became commonplace at most levels of society. To own a slave became a way of life in the South, and northern objections to slavery were bitterly resented as a threat, not merely to southern material well-being, but to an entire way of life. It was, however, a new way of life which also depended on the complex economic and social links to the North, for investment and commercial assistance, and also down the rivers, to the Gulf of Mexico and thence to the expanding markets of Britain and the wider world. Cotton flowed through Mobile and New Orleans, across the Atlantic, through the former slave port of Liverpool and on to the cotton mills of Lancashire. Cheap cotton goods clothed the growing population of Britain – and eventually of the wider world. Fittingly, the new coat of arms of the city of Manchester in 1842 contained an image of a sailing ship. But who even thought that it was a ship which linked that city to the slaves and the cotton plantations of the U.S. South?

Some of the most familiar and popular images of American slavery derive from the years of U.S. cotton slavery. Yet slavery had evolved in North America from the earliest days of European settlement, and Africans had helped to shape the course of American history in many of the early colonies. But the nineteenth-century cotton revolution transformed everything, and slavery quickly established itself as a seminal institution. The South became the epicentre of U.S. slavery and was itself utterly transformed in the process, notably by the patchwork of cotton plantations which emerged on newly settled lands. New Orleans and Mobile swiftly grew into major urban areas – entrepôts for massive movements of people and goods, especially for the enormous volumes of cotton heading to Europe. The rivers, especially the Mississippi, became (as it remains to this day) the lifeline into the heart of North America, its massive waters teeming with rivercraft linking distant inland communities to the Gulf and beyond. The slaves working the rich land of the Mississippi Delta created new wealth, to be seen today in the elegant former homes of merchants and planters in local towns and on ex-plantations, in New Orleans and on the bluffs at Natchez. Settlers swarmed into the region, following the prosperity and prospects generated by cotton. In 1810 the population of Louisiana stood at 77,000: forty years later it was more than half a million. Alabama – a mere 9,000 in 1810 – had 772,000 people in 1850.[7] A majority of those people were enslaved. The emergence of cotton had created a new phenomenon for North America: localities and regions where the great majority of inhabitants were black.[8] Slave-owning was now the distinguishing social characteristic of life across the South: some quarter of a million people owned fewer than ten slaves each.

The benefits of southern slavery to the North – through banking and commerce – were enormous (but are often overlooked). Southern slavery also had major international consequences. Who in Britain, when considering the massive economic benefits which flowed from the textile revolution, bothered to point to the slaves of the U.S. South? Yet the fruits of slave labour substantially underpinned Lancashire's rise as the world's leading cotton manufacturer. From Friedrich Engels onwards, historians and critics of British nineteenth-century industrial change regularly point to the hardships of Lancashire's textile workers as evidence of the immiseration of working people caused by the Industrial Revolution. Yet those conditions were also linked to the fate of people who cultivated the cotton. If we bring together the slaves in the cotton fields of the South with the lives of early cotton workers in Lancashire, the story of King Cotton becomes even bleaker.

Nothing, however, remotely approached the grief inflicted on legions of American slaves by the upheavals and family break-ups caused by the migration westward to the cotton frontier. These were the years of slaves 'sold down the river', of legions of people marched, sold and resold, inherited and bequeathed and separated from family, friends and loved ones. It was a heart-breaking wrench, multiplied endlessly across the USA. The death or poverty of a slave owner, the prospects of profit by the sale of a slave, the growth, marriage and re-settlement of slave owners' children and their slaves travelling with them to their new homes – all of these incidents regularly tore at the fabric of slave family and social life. The essence of slavery was the status as a *thing* – a piece of property – which could be shuffled around the immense land mass of the USA. Such upheavals formed the ultimate threat which slave holders held over their slaves: behave, work, do as we say – or you, or a loved one, will be removed, sold and dispatched. Though slaves devised their own means of keeping in touch, and of passing on news, even across great distances, the sale and removal of a loved one was often the last that was heard or seen of the departed slave. They literally disappeared over the horizon.

Every African landing in the Americas had been removed from their own African families and societies, but within a generation, the slave family had been reconstituted and became the foundation for slave culture and society, the focus and core of their values and attachments. Now, the slave family was threatened by the rise of King Cotton and the massive migrations of slaves from the east. The slave traders who sold slaves to the cotton region paid no heed to their emotional ties. Though mothers were often sold with their young, the auction block took little notice of family links and affection. What mattered was the price each slave could fetch at sale. It is hard to exaggerate the personal and communal grief which these family break-ups brought to the slave quarters. They haunt the literature, became a powerful theme in abolitionist attacks on southern slavery and served to remind outsiders of the essential heartlessness of the slave system.[9] In 1858, a Georgian slave wrote to his wife:

> to inform you that I am sold. Give my love to my father and mother and tell them good bye for me, and if we shall not meet in this world I hope to meet in heaven. My dear wife for you and my children my pen cannot express the grief I feel to be parted from you all.[10]

Yet such scenes had *always* been true of Atlantic slavery. Every single one of the 11 plus million Africans who stepped ashore from the slave ships had been wrenched from their families and homes. But that had taken place in Africa, unseen by the Western world. Now, in the U.S. South, such family upheavals were close to hand: under the very nose of critics who sought evidence for arguments against slavery – whatever material wealth King Cotton generated. It was the start and the essence of Harriet Beecher Stowe's story *Uncle Tom's Cabin* (1852), which became an astonishing bestseller – with 1 million copies sold in the first two years, outstripped only by the Bible – and which had such a dramatic impact on the campaign against slavery in the USA and abroad.

Despite the growing power of abolition sentiment in the U.S. North, and abroad, notably in Britain, southern slavery showed no signs of weakening. It was not unlike the world of British colonial slavery before 1787: its material rewards were its own justification. The alternative, black freedom, would produce a free black majority across great swathes of the South. And that threatened to destroy everything. In the South, supporting the slave system was transmuted into a powerful sense of racial superiority (again, much the same had been true of plantocratic arguments in Britain in the late eighteenth century). In both cases, the pro-slavery arguments were complex: part 'racial', part biblical and part social, though at the heart of the Southern pro-slavery ideology lay self-interest. Slavery had made possible material well-being of a kind, and on a scale, never experienced before in the USA. To undermine slavery would destroy both that well-being and the culture that went with it. But in the thirty years before the Civil War, new voices supporting slavery were heard in the South, notably from southern clerics leafing through the Bible for pro-slavery evidence.[11] These were often voices which repudiated the very philosophy of equality which lay at the heart of the American Republic. Long before the fissure in 1860, the South had been boxed into a corner by its own political and philosophic defenders, who, though making heavy use of the Bible, had veered away from the democratic principles of the Great Republic. The USA became starkly divided, and the main source of that division was slavery. It was to take the Civil War to end southern slavery. As in Haiti seventy years before, slaves in the USA were freed in a violent turmoil.

The two leading abolitionist powers of the nineteenth century, Great Britain and the USA, had, then, their own distinctive experiences of slavery after abolishing the slave trade. At first, neither turned their back on the institution of slavery, both managing to maintain thriving slave systems without those mass importations of Africans which had traditionally nurtured slavery. Other slave-owning societies, however, wanted more African slaves, *and* to be able to ship Africans into the Americas, whatever the British and Americans might say or do. The difficulty they faced lay not merely in the threat of naval patrols but in belonging to a post-1815 diplomatic culture, effectively dictated by Britain, which demanded that all Europe's maritime and colonial nations abide by abolition.

France in particular posed a major obstacle to British plans for international abolition. Smarting from her defeat in the recent wars, France was anxious to revive her own colonial empire – which had effectively been destroyed in the French Revolution and wars – and was reluctant to succumb to Britain's persistent diplomatic demands.

In 1794, France had outlawed slavery, and though Napoleon restored slavery and the slave trade in his efforts to revive France's colonial system in 1802, both were again outlawed in 1815. For the next thirty years France paid lip service to abolition yet tolerated both slavery in her colonies and slave trading from her major Atlantic ports.

The early British abolitionists had tried to encourage support from France in the 1780s and '90s, but French abolition consistently lacked the popular roots it enjoyed both in Britain and in the U.S. North. France did not have the kind of Nonconformist movement so vital in the English-speaking world, and the Catholic Church remained largely indifferent to the appeal of abolition. Even when abolition became an issue of considerable diplomatic importance after 1815, and when French government ministers simply could not ignore it, the pressure to restore French maritime commerce, and French colonial prosperity, remained a pre-eminent concern. Thus, after their wars, the French quickly fell back on the tried-and-tested movement of African slave labour to the colonies, primarily for sugar cultivation.

After the loss of Haiti (independent in 1804), France had hoped to revive sugar cultivation in her other slave colonies. Although the French had agreed with the British to outlaw the slave trade in 1818, the economic need to revitalize the sugar industry, especially in Martinique, Guadeloupe and Réunion, in the Indian Ocean, was given priority over diplomatic niceties. Notwithstanding British pressure, and treaties to the contrary, French merchant houses, and ships from her Atlantic ports, overwhelmingly from Nantes, continued to ferry Africans across the Atlantic. Vessels from Bordeaux carried 11,700 Africans between 1808 and 1837, but much greater numbers – 102,000 – left Africa on ships from Nantes in the years 1813–41, many of them bound for Cuba.[12] This trade to Cuba confirmed that French slave traders were not simply promoting French colonial interests. Wherever there was a market for slaves, the merchant houses of Nantes were happy to oblige – in defiance of diplomatic agreements. France did not enforce abolition until 1831, and even then, French colonial slavery lingered on until it was finally ended by the revolutionary French government, in 1848.

From the 1830s, however, the global sugar market was changing dramatically. New areas of the world, notably Cuba, were being turned over to sugar cultivation, though the major future challenge to tropical sugar cane emerged from within Europe itself, with the development of the sugar beet industry. Germany and France pioneered the process and by 1840 France dominated Europe's sugar-beet production. Cheap sugar was henceforth available from a non-slave source.

By the mid-nineteenth century, it was Cuba – a Spanish territory until 1898 – which had become the pre-eminent cane-sugar producer. African slaves had been shipped to the island from the early days of Spanish settlement and had been used in most forms of labour. Africans and their descendants toiled in mining and in the heavy construction of Havana's fortress and harbour: in 1600, one-third of Havana's population was African. Slave-grown foodstuffs supplied the Spanish fleets which used Cuba as a way-station en route between Spain and Central America. Until the eighteenth century, however, Cuban plantations were small (compared to neighbouring Jamaica, for example), but in the course of that century Cuba began to receive significant numbers of Africans, and by 1800 perhaps one-third of Cuba's population consisted of slaves.[13]

The slave trade to the major Spanish-American ports, originally licensed by *Asiento* agreements, was thrown open by the Spanish Crown in 1789, creating what was, in effect, a free trade in slaves, with later royal decrees encouraging greater expansion of the Spanish slave trade. The dramatic collapse of the French slave economy after 1791 left Cuba ideally positioned for a major expansion of tropical agriculture, though the island was desperate for labourers. Africa again beckoned. The paradox was that Cuba's growing hunger for African slaves coincided with the initial Anglo-American abolitionist campaigns after 1808. As Cuba scrambled to capitalize on the Haitian economic collapse, British diplomats were trying to force Spain to agree to abolition. The end result, as with France and Brazil, was that Spain signed diplomatic agreements while turning a blind eye to the thriving slave trade to Cuba. In the event, most of the slaves shipped into the Caribbean after 1808 were landed in Cuba.[14] Slave traders to Cuba had little trouble evading hostile patrols and diplomacy, and huge numbers of Africans arrived in the island, sometimes upwards of 20,000 a year, from West-central Africa and the Bight of Biafra. African imports into Cuba and Puerto Rico were higher in the years 1831–40 than in any comparable decade. Over the entire history of the slave trade, 779,000 Africans were landed in Cuba out of 890,000 embarked in Africa, twice the number of Africans imported into North America. More than half of Cuba's Africans stepped ashore in Havana.[15]

Traders to and from Cuba adopted the successful evasions used elsewhere: flying false flags and shuffling a variety of ship's papers to satisfy any hostile naval patrol. At the same time, Spanish officials effectively blocked the work of the Courts of Mixed Commission operating in Havana. Viewed from London, it seemed supremely ironic that, just when abolition pressure was at its strongest, Cuba's economy was booming, thanks to a massive influx of African slaves. Strengthened by their armies of Africans, Cuban planters now launched into a period of unprecedented growth and prosperity. Sugar plantations grew bigger and many were highly modernized: they adopted railways and steam power even before they were widely used in Spain. Tobacco parallelled sugar as a major export crop, though often cultivated on smaller holdings and employing smaller numbers of slaves. There was a major expansion in Cuban coffee production, which lasted until Brazilian coffee made serious inroads, from the 1840s onwards. Thereafter, the Cuban coffee industry declined, its land and slaves often bought up by sugar planters. Sugar, however, was king, and in the thirty years to 1860, Cuban sugar dominated the island's economy and quickly established itself as one of the world's leading sugar industries.[16]

Then, in 1840, Cuban debates about the slave trade and slavery were sharpened by the arrival in Havana of an assertive Scottish abolitionist, David Turnbull, as British consul. Openly anti-slavery, Turnbull clashed with Cuban politicians, with the Captain-General, and with Cuban planters. His Cuban enemies believed that, underneath his humanitarianism, Turnbull was really the agent behind a British design to help the flagging British colonies in the region. In the short-term, his words seemed to give support to Cuban slave resistance and discontent, but eventually, he was removed from his post.

Turnbull stood out not only because he was a trenchant critic of slavery, but also because Cuba had no real abolitionist tradition or voice. Spain itself was effectively devoid of abolitionist spokespeople and organizations, and Cuban critics of the slave trade were, like their counterparts in Brazil, worried about the impact of African immigration on the balance of the island's population. They were fearful that the island was becoming ever more African, and concerned about the effect that any local criticism might have.

Despite such concerns, Cuba boomed. The removal of the sugar duties on British Caribbean sugar in 1846 led not simply to a further collapse of British sugar but a corresponding upsurge in Cuban production, a related increase in African slave imports and a massive rise in slave prices. Slave prices doubled between 1820 and 1860.[17] The Cuban slave trade was now delivering 30,000 Africans a year to the island's planters,[18] with the British apparently powerless to stop it. Though this was largely because of Spanish and Cuban obstruction, the role of the USA was an additional factor. North American commercial and maritime interests were closely involved in the Cuban trade, and in Cuba at large, and Britain was unwilling to alienate the USA – even for abolition – by trespassing in their friend's backyard at a time when American power was on the rise and Anglo–American economic ties were vital.

At mid-century, Cuba was one of the world's wealthiest colonies, but was ever more isolated. Most other (newly formed) Latin American nations had abolished slavery or were preparing to do so; the USA was embroiled in its own divisive political conflict, which would culminate in the Civil War; and even Brazil offered little comfort to resistant Cuban slave owners. Gradually, outside pressure made an impact in Cuba. The founding of the Spanish Abolitionist Society in 1865, for example, created an alliance of Spaniards, Cubans and Puerto Ricans, and their pressure helped to persuade Cuban planters to end the Cuban slave trade, in 1867.[19] The struggle for full freedom for Cuba's slaves was linked to the complex fight for Cuban independence from Spain. Cuban slaves naturally gravitated to the independence movement, and slaves were freed – or freed themselves – to join in the political demands and military activity for that cause. Slaves and ex-slaves appreciated that cutting the Spanish links meant ending slavery itself. From its original base in the east of the island, the independence movement spread, spawning 'The Ten Years War' for independence, which ended in 1878. The war witnessed a dramatic reduction in the number of Cuban slaves from 363,288 to 199,094. Under pressure of events in Cuba, especially from the slaves, the Spanish Cortes passed a number of laws which began to qualify and ultimately to undermine slavery itself. Finally, in 1880, a new law, mirroring the Apprenticeship scheme that had briefly followed British slavery between 1833 and 1838, established a new relationship between the enslaved and their masters. It specified that groups of slaves would be progressively freed until, by 1888, slavery would finally be abolished. The slaves, however, were not prepared to wait, even a few short years, and began to leave the plantations in droves. Planters gave up trying to staunch the flow. Many cut their losses by striking new labour bargains with their labour force, offering freedom in return for a pledge from the ex-slaves to remain on the property to work. Cuban slavery effectively died on its feet, and on 7 October 1886, it was finally abolished by Royal Decree. By then, of the 779,000 Africans landed in Cuba, the very great majority – some 711,000 – had arrived *after* the British and Americans had abolished their slave trade. Throughout eighty years of aggres-sive Anglo-American abolition, Cuba had thrived as never before on imported African slaves.

The huge numbers of Africans shipped to the French and Span-ish colonies after 1808 simply pale when we consider the numbers transported to Brazil in the same period. Between 1810 and 1866, 1,691,405 Africans stepped onto Brazilian and Portuguese slave ships: 1,525,352 survived to landfall.[20] The Portuguese-Brazilian slave-trading system in the South Atlantic shipped twice as many Africans as the trade to Cuba: ten times as many Africans went to Brazil as to the French colonies in the nineteenth century. The reason was obvious. The immensity and physical diversity of Brazil afforded a huge variety of economic prospects, all of which cried out for labour. Slavery seemed the answer – if only because slavery had been a fea-ture of Brazilian life from the early days of European settlement. Brazil had effectively been the first American settlement to develop a viable African slave system, and she was to be the last to abolish it.

Brazil and Portugal (Brazil's European colonial master until 1824) created an astonishing trading nexus in the South Atlantic. Beginning in the sixteenth century, the Portuguese Crown had developed a dis-tinctive form of colonial settlement, by granting parcels of coastal Brazil to Portuguese nobles for development. Early trading and log-ging, using local indigenous peoples, had given way by the last thirty years of that century to sugar cultivation using African slaves, some of them accustomed to sugar cultivation in the Atlantic islands. As Brazil-ian sugar thrived, helping to create an apparently insatiable European appetite for sweet drinks and food, local plantations demanded ever more Africans. The early Portuguese trading posts in Africa, notably Senegambia, obliged, but by the seventeenth century other kinds of Africans – from the Congo-Angola region – were being shipped across the South Atlantic in growing numbers.[21]

The opening of new regions of Brazil, notably Minas Gerais (for gold, initially) and the developing agricultural plantations of

Amazonia, was followed by a massive expansion of slave labour in the eighteenth century. Again, the figures are staggering. By the time of British abolition, slave ships had delivered 1,940,950 Africans to Brazil from 2,195,150 taken on board in Africa. There were separate flows of Africans into Brazil – from Upper Guinea into Amazonia and from the Bights of Benin and Biafra, for instance. African communities in Brazil, with their pronounced links to particular regions of Africa, developed their own distinctive cultures – reflected in religions, language and foodways. They also became images, in exile, of their African homelands. It was, however, the transportation of Africans from the Congo-Angola region which accounted for the largest movement of African peoples to Brazil. It also lasted longer than any other. It was essentially a two-way, not a triangular, trading system. Though Portuguese ships had initiated the trade (helped briefly by the Dutch when they controlled Brazil and key African trading points between 1630 and 1654), the slave trade across the South Atlantic became increasingly Brazilian. Ships from major Brazilian and Portuguese, not northern European, ports dominated the South Atlantic trade, their task made easier not only by the emergence of Brazilian finance and commerce but also by the winds and currents of the South Atlantic. As early as the mid-seventeenth century, Brazilian ports had dispatched ships which returned with more than one-third of a million Africans, but the numbers for the period between 1642 and 1807 were extraordinary. Vessels from Recife imported 460,000 Africans, ships from Rio carried 658,000 – while more than 1 million Africans arrived on ships from Salvador.[22] The Brazilian slave population grew enormously, but like the major colonies of the Caribbean, the slave communities of Brazil expanded because of African imports. Brazil's prosperity, and its African population, depended on the Atlantic slave ships.

The economies of Brazil and the Congo-Angola region became closely linked. Merchant houses emerged with bases both in Rio and Luanda, for example, with family members living either side of the Atlantic to supervise the family's local trading business and to keep in touch with relatives and colleagues on the other side of the ocean. This trading nexus across the South Atlantic survived as long as the slave trade survived, its most abiding and visible feature being the human and cultural ties forged between Brazil and Angola.

British and American abolition seemed to do little, at first, to reduce Brazil's appetite for Africans. The early abolitionist patrols operated north of the equator, leaving Brazilian ships, trading in the South Atlantic, an effectively clear run east and west. Recife's ships brought back more than 200,000 Africans between 1808 and 1851. Salvador's ships, which had traditionally traded north of the Equator, and therefore ran foul of an Anglo–Portuguese treaty of 1810, still managed to import 388,000 Africans – via much deceptive juggling of paperwork. Ships from Rio imported an amazing 1,047,000 up to 1856.[23]

The huge numbers of Africans destined for Rio headed to the thriving coffee and sugar plantations and were purchased through a trade operating in areas of the African coast which were largely untroubled by British patrols. Increasingly, Rio's ships also made the much longer voyages, which were therefore more perilous for the Africans, to and from Portuguese ports in southeast Africa.[24] That region had traditionally supplied slaves for the markets of Arabia and the Indian Ocean islands, but from 1781 Atlantic slave traders, especially Brazilians and the Portuguese, made their way there for slaves. Along a coastline which stretched from Zanzibar in the north to Lourenço Marques in the south (though concentrated largely at the main Portuguese trading posts on the coast), slave traders were able to load 488,000 Africans onto their ships. Many of the Africans had been enslaved deep in the interior, as far inland as the great lakes. These were the slave routes which Dr Livingstone denounced and hoped to end on his expeditions across the continent in the twenty years after 1854.

For the African captives, the journeys round the southern tip of Africa, and thence across the Atlantic, were crowded, protracted – and deadly. Africans from southeast Africa were at sea for substantially longer periods, as already noted, than the Africans destined for Brazil from the major points of departure on the West African coast. In about 1800, it took an average of 71 days from southeast Africa compared to 41 days from West-central Africa. Though journey times fell in the nineteenth century, this basic difference remained. Between 1825 and 1850, the sailing time from southeast Africa averaged 63 days, but 35 from West-central Africa.[25] It was on these protracted voyages that some of the worst stories and statistics of overcrowding and high mortality rates were recorded. The irony was that, in the very years when abolitionists were trying to end the Atlantic slave trade, conditions for many of the enslaved had clearly taken a turn for the worse. It may well be that the last days of the Atlantic slave trade saw a return to some of the worst levels of African suffering endured in the earlier, slower and less well-organized days of the Atlantic trade.

Wherever they traded, and however they circumvented patrols and treaties (even avoiding the gaze of Brazilian officials by landing at small, less noticeable locations away from major ports), Brazilian slave traders delivered massive numbers of Africans right up to the mid-nineteenth century. Between 1791 and 1856 an estimated 2,343,000 Africans landed in Brazil.

The Atlantic crossing was only the most obvious of the traumas facing Brazilian slaves in the nineteenth century. As in the U.S. South, there were major *internal* Brazilian slave trades which saw large numbers of slaves trekking and sailing from the old slave holding regions (Pernambuco, Bahia and Amazonia) to the expansive economies in the south of Brazil.[26] The distances were enormous – and accompanied by all the personal distress of family break-up and upheaval.

The armies of people shipped across the Atlantic to Brazil, and those shunted around within Brazil, were directed primarily to major areas of new economic growth, but slavery invariably slipped its original moorings in those major industries and prospered in all corners of Brazilian life. Slaves laboured in sugar and cotton fields and at higher altitudes in coffee; they worked as agricultural labourers on and off the plantations and as cowboys in the country's ranches; and they were used extensively in the artisan trades. Slaves were vital in the brute labour of gold mining. And, of course, they populated the homes of the prosperous and not so prosperous as domestic workers, catering for their owners' every need, from cooking to child-care, from nursing to sexual services. They were inescapable in towns and ports across the country, as casual labourers and as workers on quaysides and in shipping. Charles Darwin, visiting Brazil on board the *Beagle*, was incensed by the sight of Africans being unloaded from the slave ships and was astonished by the ubiquity of slaves wherever he went.[27] Visitors to Brazil were taken aback by the sheer numbers of slaves and by the casual brutality doled out to them. They were on hand at their owners' beck and call and their presence seemed to encourage laziness and fecklessness among slave owners, even to the point where they were carried in public by slaves. Slave ownership became a status symbol as much as an economic necessity. Brazil and the U.S. South had much in common in the early nineteenth century.

Brazilian slavery was periodically reinvigorated by new economic developments – the discovery of diamonds in Bahia, for example. But sugar, the effective origin of and inspiration behind Brazilian slavery, remained one of Brazil's leading crops. Between 1821 and 1825, Brazil produced 632,000 tons of sugar. Thirty years later, from 1851 to 1855, the figure stood at 3,895,000 tons.[28]

The real boom in nineteenth-century Brazilian slavery, however, took place in coffee cultivation. Coffee exports from Brazil, which stood at 125,000 tons in 1821–5, had grown to 1,553,000 tons in 1851–5 – a leap made possible by the enormous numbers of Africans imported, largely through Rio. In the thirty years to 1850, more Africans were landed along a 644-km coastal stretch close to Rio 'than in the rest of the Americas put together'. Coffee had become the regional heart of Brazilian slavery.[29] By mid-century, Brazil was producing half the world's coffee. Fifty years later it produced five times as much as the rest of the world *combined*. This explosion in Brazilian coffee derived from the rapid growth in the world economy, but especially from the explosive growth of the U.S. coffee market. For many years coffee was imported duty-free into the U.S., where the huge demand for coffee among a rapidly expanding population created coffee-drinking on an unprecedented scale: U.S. coffee consumption increased 2,400 per cent in the course of the nineteenth century.[30]

When we consider the history of slavery in the Americas, but especially in Brazil and the USA in the nineteenth century, it throws into sharp relief the achievements and impact of the campaign against the Atlantic slave trade. Half a century *after* the abolitions of 1807–08, the two major exporting economies of the Americas – the USA and Brazil – were producing highly successful major export crops with slave labour. Moreover, their slave systems thrived alongside the rapid *modernization* of economic life. Indeed, modern technology greatly assisted Brazilian slave production: railways and steam power were introduced to facilitate the movement of slave-grown produce, notably coffee. There was little sense, in Brazil and Cuba, that technology and modernization (industrialization, urbanization and growing European immigration) would serve to undermine slavery. Yet slavery was a labour system forged for the pre-industrial, pre-modern world, but now eagerly adopted and harnessed to modern technology. Brazil, however, was exceptional in one particular respect. Unlike in the USA, or earlier, in the case of the British Caribbean, there was no effective or audible political campaign against slavery – except, of course, among the slaves themselves.

It was not surprising, then, when Brazil formally ended the slave trade in 1831, that Brazilian planters were confident that their slave system would survive. They had the ear of government and politicians, their critics in the press were powerless and generally ignored, technology had emerged as an ally of slavery, and slave-grown produce continued to deliver handsome returns.[31]

External pressures increased, however, and became a major problem for Brazilian slave owners. The threat of British naval incursions continued, British diplomatic pressure persisted, and the American Civil War afforded its own cautionary tale. Details of the destruction involved in the war, regularly transmitted to Rio in graphic detail from Brazilian officials in Washington, confirmed the terrible prospects of what might befall Brazil unless the problem of slavery was tackled. At the end of that war, and following the Thirteenth Amendment and U.S. emancipation, Brazil stood out as the major exception in a Western world that had distanced itself from slavery. People of African descent – free and enslaved – hugely outnumbered all other groups, and to those of a nervous disposition, Brazil seemed like a human tinderbox, a combustible and unpredictable human mix. In the teeth of slavery's brutalities, how could Brazilians continue to claim that their nation was a cultured outpost in the Americas?

Ironically, one major initiative and driving force for ending Brazilian slavery came from the country's emperor, but even he found it hard to rally political support for emancipation. Finally, the Rio Branco law of 1871 offered a framework: a complex and slow-moving process towards emancipation. Children born to slave mothers were freed, but might work for their master until aged 21. The whole process was hedged around by convoluted provisos, designed to provide the planters with a labour force by leaving slaves only partly free. Yet even this modest law lacked the popular support for black freedom which had characterized emancipation movements in Europe and North America. In both the USA and in British colonies, slavery had ended to a background political sound of widespread denunciation. Brazilian planters, however, continued to be optimistic that their case would prevail, not least because they sensed no popular mood running against them.

That began to change in the 1870s, however, with the gradual rise of a popular abolitionist movement, strengthened by mounting evidence of the sufferings endured by slaves on their overland travels to regions still demanding slave labour. As slaves were moved south, for example from Bahia to the coffee-growing regions, family break-up, and the general physical and social distress, reminded people of the horrors endured on the slave ships and helped fuel slave resentment. As slave disturbances predictably erupted in the 1870s and '80s, ever more people – including, reluctantly, slave holders – began to recognize that slavery was not the long-term answer to Brazil's labour needs.

Support for black freedom in Brazil evolved in a piecemeal fashion, taking root in localities and towns, with planters' power contested by new urban political groups which were committed to black freedom. By 1880, support for slave emancipation had developed a genuine popular dimension. As it grew in strength, it took over towns and regions throughout the 1880s. It also developed a distinctively Brazilian form on the streets, capturing the popular voice in carnival displays which involved women as well as men. Not surprisingly, the slaves took heart at these massive displays of public support. Slaves began to flee from the plantations in growing numbers; they plotted and displayed that communal defiance towards their owners which was the curse of slave holders everywhere. But, most important, many of them simply fled, walking along the railway tracks which led away from plantations and slavery to Rio – and freedom.

Black and white abolitionists demonstrated against the most infamous and violent of planters, encouraging and helping slaves to quit the plantation there and then. By the mid-1880s, soldiers and police were refusing to hunt down runaway slaves. Brazilian slaves voted with their feet, fleeing the plantations in droves, with authorities powerless to resist their flight to freedom. When planters stamped down, their violence shocked and alienated outsiders. Violent corporal punishments – an essential and traditional ingredient in the slave holder's management guidebook – disgusted the impartial and infuriated the slaves. Brazilian planters of the mid-1880s looked on as 'the institution dissolved before their eyes'. Planters were engaged in damage limitation, and henceforth political arguments revolved around how best to terminate slavery: how to secure black freedom whilst guaranteeing some form of labour for the planters. Planters could do little to stop the haemorrhage of slaves, and they finally came to see that their future as successful agriculturalists lay in employing free, not enslaved, labour. They took some comfort from the growing numbers

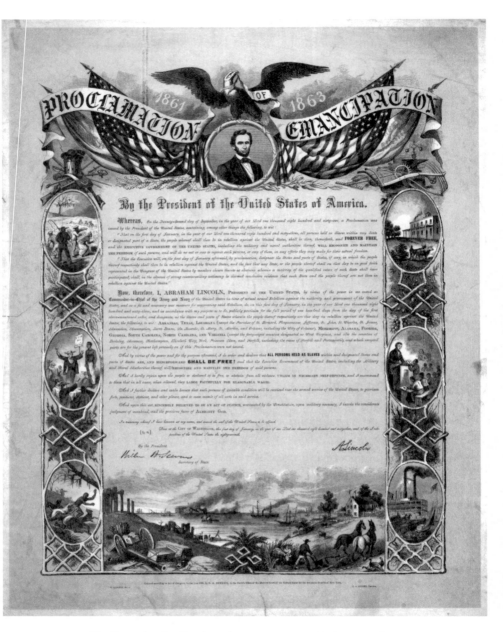

The Emancipation Proclamation, engraving by W. Roberts, 1864.

of European immigrants settling in Brazil. Finally, in May 1888, Brazil's remaining slaves were freed.[32] Eighty years after the Anglo-American abolition of the Atlantic slave trade, the trade which had sustained Brazilian slavery for centuries, Brazil was the last country in the Americas to free its slaves.

TEN

Then and Now: Slavery and the Modern World

T he slave system which had linked Africa to the Americas for more than three centuries was effectively brought to an end with the emancipation of slaves in Brazil in 1888. What survived, of course, were the myriad African cultures transplanted across the Atlantic, but now transformed by the Americas.[1] Optimistic opponents of slavery must have thought that the history of slavery was finally over. A century had passed since that small band of Quakers and a few sympathizers had gathered in London in 1787 with the intention of ending the British slave trade. In that time, the largest enforced transportation of people to date (the Atlantic slave trade) had been ended, and the slave societies, which had proliferated and thrived throughout the tropical and semi-tropical Americas, and beyond, had become communities of free people. Freedom did not always bring material prosperity or even betterment. Indeed, from the first days of black freedom, right down to the present day, black society was to be scarred by levels of poverty and deprivation which were out of kilter with the material well-being in society at large. Slavery, in its heyday, may well have created wealth for many, but it scattered in its wake widespread poverty among freed slaves and their descendants.[2] Freed slaves were not always materially better off. But for now, they simply wanted freedom.

The end of slavery in the Americas looks like a triumph for that anti-slavery sentiment which had become so powerful in Western societies in the nineteenth century. The British had been at the forefront of the campaigns, first, to stop the slave trade, then to end slavery. Abolitionist organizations, publications, speakers and parliamentarians had come to constitute one of the most powerful and successful pressure groups in nineteenth-century Britain. They rallied more support, evoked more communal passion, generated more religious and ethical outrage, than any comparable campaign. It was easy to dismiss all this as 'telescopic philanthropy' – Dickens's brilliant evocation in *Bleak House* of Mrs Jellyby's passion for Africans while ignoring domestic problems under her nose – but it was a mighty force for all that.

Throughout the nineteenth century, abolitionists also dominated the diplomatic high ground, leading the charge to make slavery both an international cause célèbre and an international crime. Between 1815 and 1850, British foreign secretaries and their officials popped up at regular diplomatic gatherings to demand treaties – and actions – against the slave trade and slavery. If the number of abolitionist treaties indicates success, then abolition swept all before it: between 1839 and 1890 more than 300 international treaties were signed against the slave trade. Such a huge number, however, is more an indication of ineffectiveness than triumph. All were aimed at preventing oceanic slave trading, but in 1885 the first measures against slave trading *by land*, and against slavery itself, were agreed in Berlin, and were completed by a treaty of more than 100 clauses in 1890 at Brussels. The main aim henceforth, using an organization operating from offices in Brussels and Zanzibar, was preventing the enslavement of Africans. This was reconfirmed by yet another agreement in 1919, this time including a much more thorough denunciation of slavery itself. The campaign against slavery took a different direction in 1920 with the founding of the League of Nations. Slavery now became part of the League's general mandate to maintain peace.[3] Peace was to prove illusory, but in 1926 the League established a Slavery Convention which formally outlawed slavery and slave trading globally. Though it lacked means of enforcement, the Slavery Convention was an important step towards rendering slavery illegal at an international level *and* establishing the principle that slavery was a crime against humanity.[4] These principles were absorbed into the mandate of the United Nations in 1956, and thereafter all member states had to adopt measures against specified forms of slavery, bondage and slave trading. Needless to say, there were many ways of avoiding these UN prohibitions, and many of the specific illegalities – debt bondage, serfdom, forced marriages and child slavery – survive to this day.[5] In the twenty-first century, as in the nineteenth, countries often turned a blind eye to the very international principles they had formally accepted.

Through all this, slavery itself proved remarkably resilient, even in the face of strenuous efforts to eradicate it. Nonetheless, in the early twentieth century, the emergence of an international consensus against slavery, notably in diplomatic circles, gave grounds for believing that slavery was a fading memory – an institution from the past rather than the present. Such optimism was utterly dispelled by events in Europe in the 1930s and '40s. The Second World War provided depressing evidence both of the return of slavery and of the transportation of millions of people huge distances to work as slaves. Germany, whose litany of terror and organized killings in the war were on an unprecedented scale, was also held to account, when the war ended, for the slave labour which had helped to sustain its massive war machine. As the war progressed, and finally engulfed Germany itself, slave labour became ever more important to the German war effort.

One of the major embarrassments in 1945, however, was that one of the victors (and therefore a lead prosecutor of Nazi war criminals) – the Soviet Union – had itself used slave labour on a massive scale, and continued to do so *after* 1945. For very different ideological and practical reasons, both those tyrannical regimes used slave labour to an extent not seen since the height of Atlantic slavery. It was, on the whole, not the same form of ethnic slavery which had dominated the Atlantic for centuries. Nonetheless, the War Crimes Courts after 1945 and subsequent scholarship accepted it as *slavery*. Slavery had returned, with a brutal vengeance, to haunt, not Africa or European colonies, but the European heartlands.

A taste of what was to come during the war had already been exhibited in the Soviet Union in the 1930s. Often disguised as 'penal labour', Soviet slave labour emerged from a variety of Soviet economic and penal experiments, notably the 'Five Year Plans', with the most brutal form – and the most destructive of human life – scattered in camps across Russia's harshest regions. Where colonial powers had once used African slaves to tap the resources of tropical settlements, the Soviet Union now used its own citizens as slave labour, to open up the vast prospects and resources of Russia's immense wilderness. The now infamous Gulag began to swallow people by the millions.[6] Two small examples: some 1.5 million Muslims and upwards of 5 million peasants were simply removed and relocated over immense distances.[7] Such terrors provoked outside denunciation, but criticism was effectively silenced after the German attack on Russia in 1941. Henceforth, and despite serious reservations among the Western allies, the Soviet Union was a wartime partner, and criticism of Soviet internal politics had to be relegated to the need to work and fight together. Inevitably, wartime also saw a further tightening of control over Russian labour, as indeed it did in all the wartime nations, enhancing still further state domination over everyone's lives. What happened in Russia, however, was amazing. Anne Applebaum's study shows that the 179,000 Gulag prisoners of 1930 had increased to 1,929,729 by 1941 and 2,468,524 as late as 1953. What these figures do not show is the high turnover in the camps: during the war, for example, almost 1 million people left the camps to join the Red Army.[8] The economic benefits of this vast labour system are debatable: there was a string of unsuccessful and abandoned camps and there were immense inefficiencies and irrationalities within the system. But as long as Stalin lived, the Gulag would thrive. His death, in March 1953, opened the camp gates, and prisoners were released in their droves: within three months, 60 per cent of the Gulag's inmates – 1.5 million people – had been freed.[9] Thereafter, the camps contracted and emptied and the Stalinist experiment with slave labour was laid to rest. But for twenty years, in peacetime and throughout years of ferocious warfare, slave labour had been a basic feature of the Soviet economy.

The major fighting in Europe had been primarily between Germany and Russia, and the irony remains that *both* regimes used slave labour. What emerged in Nazi Germany was, however, very different from Russian slave labour. Although Nazi Germany has remained infamous for its death camps and its genocidal killing, the Nazi regime also made extensive use of slave labour, much of it transported from distant, conquered territories to labour in war industries in Germany. German-conquered territories, from France to Russia, yielded a vast bounty of enslaved labour and prisoners of war, to be marshalled for the Nazi war effort. This, along with the long-term plans to depopulate the East to make room for German settlement, and the genocidal policies towards Jews and others, saw massive enforced removal of peoples from their homes.

The 'General Plan for the East' – the blueprint to create *Lebensraum* and German resettlement across swathes of Eastern Europe, specified that 14 million inhabitants would be made slaves. But things did not go to plan.[10] The tide of war turned, and as German military casualties mounted under the Russian onslaught, and as the German population was drained for military service, foreign captives were transported into the German labour market. By the last year of the war, 13 million foreigners were working in Germany. This was not normal labour: the Nazi leaders were quite open that the expansive war machine they had created required *slave labour* at home.[11] Many of those victims survived the war to press their legal claims for compensation against Germany and against the industries which had employed them as slave labour.[12]

Through this unparalleled human devastation, all unfolding in a very brief period of time, there was little public outrage expressed in the German heartland about the widespread employment of slave labour at home. But how could there be? African slavery had ended to general denunciation and loathing, but that was not true of slave labour in Nazi Germany. The apparatus of the German state ensured that the war, and the imported slave labour necessary to keep the war effort functioning, were pursued with a brutal efficiency which brooked no objections. War and slave labour were part of the universal misery which continued right to the bitter end – courtesy of a violently intrusive state, even in its shattered form – until the last days of the regime in May 1945.[13]

Peace in Europe revealed a wrecked continent, with millions of displaced people stranded great distances from their former homelands. The subsequent post-war recovery saw not merely the emergence of a reformed and revitalized Western Europe, but a drive to call Germany to account for its manifold crimes against humanity. The War Crimes Trials in Allied occupied Germany saw 5,000 people convicted of war crimes. Almost 800 were sentenced to death and 486 eventually executed.[14] The claims for compensation for the survivors of slave labour proved much more protracted, continuing long after the war had ended, even though German enslavement and forced transportation of slave labour were clear contraventions of treaties which Germany had itself signed up to, notably under the terms of the Brussels Act of 1890 and the Slavery Convention of 1926.[15] As late as 1999 there were an estimated 2.3 million survivors of Nazi slave labour, and their campaign for compensation from Germany continued into the twenty-first century. Many only began to receive compensation for their sufferings a full half a century after the war had ended.

The Second World War had witnessed a startling revival of slavery. A parallel story could be repeated for Japan's sacking and rape of countries across Asia in the same conflict – 290,000 Asians died working as slave labour for the Japanese during the war.[16] When writing of the innocent victims of the Second World War, Max Hastings coined the phrase 'Masters and Slaves'.[17] It was as if he were writing about eighteenth-century Brazil. In Europe and in Asia, millions of people had been enslaved in the course of the Second World War, and though there was punishment for many of the perpetrators, even the horrors of that global war failed to put an end to slavery. Slavery lived on.

Despite everything, despite prohibitions and agreements at the highest levels of diplomacy, despite post-war punishment and execution for wartime perpetrators, slavery bounced back. In fact, it had never gone away. Today, slavery continues to pose serious problems for governments and humanitarian campaigners. Anti-Slavery International, a major campaigning group based in London, conducts a vigorous trade in exposing and challenging slavery wherever it exists in the modern world. Founded in 1839, it is the direct descendant of the original British anti-slavery campaign and rightly prides itself on being 'the world's oldest international human rights organisation', which 'works to eliminate all forms of slavery around the world'.[18] Anti-Slavery International targets particular abuses – bonded labour, forced marriage, slavery by descent, child labour and human trafficking – which flourish in different parts of today's world, *despite* formal outlawing by the UN. The forms of bondage survive regardless of unremitting campaigns against them by an alliance of international governmental and independent agencies. And all this despite widespread public hostility to slavery and the lingering nightmares about wartime slavery.

Ironically, the recent debate about trafficking began in the early twentieth century, with the alarm about the '*white* slave trade' – of women trafficked into prostitution. That too was a debate with British roots (in the campaign against prostitution led by Josephine Butler). Beginning in 1904, a string of international agreements tried to prevent the movement of women and children into prostitution, and both the League of Nations, and more recently the UN, adopted the cause. By the end of the twentieth century, similar moves against systematized trafficking for prostitution had been made by the European Union, with concern prompted by the rise of organized criminal gangs controlling large-scale trafficking of women into prostitution within Europe. At the same time, a new international social problem intruded into the debate: the large-scale, international trafficking of people by gangs. A major industry developed for trafficking people from poor or war-torn regions to employment and security in Western countries. The victims paid large sums to be smuggled, by complex and often dangerous routes, to employment and safety in the West, where they worked for little or nothing to pay off the enormous debts owed to the trafficking gangs who controlled them.[19]

Many of the resulting political and diplomatic debates in New York and Europe about prostitution and trafficking descended into political and philosophical confusion about definitions of freedom and slavery (could a woman voluntarily agree to be a prostitute?). Arguments would spin off into the realms of unreality and often seemed totally removed from the very victims under discussion. Even so, they had the effect of raising public awareness about trafficking and enslavement in general. But it was all far removed from the forms of slavery and slave trading familiar to historians of the Americas and Africa.

Through this confused welter of detail about different forms of slavery and trafficking, it is hard to know, precisely, how many people are actually enslaved in the modern world. Estimates range from 2 million to 27 million, much depending, as always, on the exact definition of slavery.[20] However we define slavery, few serious critics doubt that modern slaves are to be counted in their millions. Most seem to have been enslaved via poverty, and many have been trafficked long distances from their homelands. Not surprisingly, the topic surfaces regularly in the media. In May 1992, for example, *Newsweek* carried a major report about worldwide slavery under the front page headline: 'Around the World, Millions of People Are Still Held in Bondage.'[21] Eleven years later, it was the turn of *National Geographic*, which ran a lead article – accompanied by dramatic photographs of '21st-century Slaves' – estimating there were 27 million people enslaved in different parts of the world. Some were even trafficked into the heartlands of Western society.[22] Then, in 2007, the BBC reported the trial of 29 men in China for their role in using slave labour in north China brick factories. One man was sentenced to death.[23] Finally, as I was writing this book, in the summer of 2012 *The Guardian* carried a report of slavery in India centred on Bihar (the poorest Indian state), where 200,000 children *a year* fall into the hands of slave traders. Some were sold for as little as £11.[24] In October 2012, the BBC continued a similar debate: 'There are, shockingly, more people in slavery today than at any time in human history.'[25] Slavery and slave trading continue to catch the public eye, and major media outlets frequently reveal the depressing details, while stressing the links to slavery's long, historical past.

Through all these arguments about modern slavery there was a clear line of descent between modern-day discussions and their historical antecedents. Debates in the press reflected the revelations in the nineteenth-century press, and discussions in the Council of Europe and the UN were directly descended from those early diplomatic arguments about the slave trade beginning with Lord Castlereagh in Vienna in 1815, even though the focus of attention had shifted. Although some modern debates looked at the problems of the continuation of slavery and slave trading in Africa, the discussions about the nature of modern slavery, and about human trafficking in their broadest definitions, would have puzzled nineteenth-century abolitionists. Theirs was a narrowly focused and specific problem even when, in the event, the diplomacy and naval attacks on the slave trade spawned unexpected complexities.

Through this late twentieth-century interest and legislation, one basic issue remains clear beyond doubt: 'Traditional slavery and the related Atlantic slave trade are surely abolished by international law.'[26] While this may seem obvious – a cliché, even – it speaks to a seismic shift in attitude. For centuries, very few people in the West so much as questioned slavery. Today it is universally denounced both as a crime and as a moral outrage. That slavery manages to survive, even in forms which would have been recognized by our eighteenth-century forebears, does not detract from the argument that slavery, today, is anathema. In the protracted campaign to bring about that change of attitude, the British had occupied centre-stage. It is no surprise, then, that the British seem to have a special place in their public memory for anniversaries of abolition and periodically mark the campaigns against slavery with major commemorations. Here were events – ending the slave trade and freeing the slaves – which the British could feel proud of.

In fact, ever since the apogee of their own slave empire, the British have taken particular pride in their abolitionist efforts. They have, however, been much *less* enthusiastic about owning up to their history as architects and creators of the Atlantic slave system. Over the past century, the British have recalled the various highlights of their abolitionist past with celebratory commemorations.[27] Each commemoration, however, was more revealing about the cultural values of Britain at the time of the celebration than about abolition itself. In 1907, it was thought that the abolition of a century before had been 'an event of the highest importance', and the anniversary was marked by a thanksgiving service in Westminster Abbey – the burial place of William Wilberforce.[28] A generation later, British slave emancipation was marked, in 1933, with more elaborate ceremonies. In Hull – birthplace of William Wilberforce – tens of thousands of spectators enjoyed a civic procession, in the company of the Archbishop of York, and all to the music of a black and a white choir on what *The Times* called the 'Centenary of Wilberforce'.[29] These commemorations were, however, as nothing compared to what unfolded in Britain in 2007 on the bicentenary of the abolition of the slave trade.

Perhaps the most striking fact of 2007 was the enthusiastic engagement of Tony Blair's Labour government. The Department of Culture, Media and Sport issued a publication about abolition with the title *Reflecting on the Past and Looking forward to the Future*. A number of glossy government publications were produced, marked 1807–2007 and offering a calendar of forthcoming events, potted histories of the major turning points in abolition, and a supporting letter from the Prime Minister explaining why abolition remains important for modern Britain.[30] The Deputy Prime Minister, John Prescott, chaired a committee in the build-up to 2007 to monitor the course of events. There was even a debate in Parliament to mark the anniversary of abolition.[31] The political timing seemed right for all this interest. In March 2007, the British government signed the latest European Convention against human trafficking.[32]

There were exhibitions galore in 2007. Parliament itself hosted a major exhibition about the passing of the Abolition Act, in Westminster Hall, which attracted more than 100,000 visitors.[33] An exhibition in Birmingham, devoted to Equiano and abolition, drew 30,000 visitors. The Heritage Lottery Fund allocated an estimated £15 million to 270 different projects marking 1807–2007.[34] Most of the country's major cultural institutions responded – galleries, museums, libraries, churches, archives – alongside village schools and tiny local libraries, and all sought to say something interesting about the abolition of the slave trade.[35] The Royal Mint launched a special abolition coin, and the Royal Mail issued six new stamps bearing the images of prominent abolitionists – two of them African.[36]

The BBC was especially vigorous in remembering abolition, both on radio and TV,[37] and the media in general, along with major publishers, all responded. So too did academics, at a series of scholarly gatherings round the country. There was also a genuine groundswell of popular interest, especially in urban black communities, which felt the most personal and pressing need to have a say in the discussions. Black churches were especially prominent in the commemorations.[38]

There was, then, a veritable cornucopia of commemorations in 2007, with large numbers of visitors, viewers and audiences joining in what became a broad cultural debate about the ending of the slave trade in 1807. It formed an exceptional display of national interest in what had been, only a few years earlier, a rather arcane area of historical research. Nor was it a mere passing fancy. It left behind major projects which continue to reveal the significance of British involvement in the Atlantic slave trade, especially at unexplored local levels.[39] Most important, perhaps, the events of 2007 managed to establish slavery and the slave trade at the heart of wider debate about the school curriculum and became a theme in the cultural discussions about the historical foundations of British identity itself.[40]

Along with other historians who had been interested in abolition for years, I could hardly believe what happened in the course of 2007. I was just one of a small band of British scholars who, having talked to ourselves for years, now found ourselves working on a public stage with great public interest and participation. The upsurge in interest was as unpredictable as it was exciting. But it was also slightly bewildering. How had the history of the Atlantic slave trade become a topic of such widespread public interest in Britain, from Westminster's political elite to poor immigrant church communities?

After a fashion, it was a topic which had come of age. Even among academic historians, the slave trade and its consequences were no longer viewed as a fringe topic, existing on the margin of mainstream historical investigation. There had been an accumulating scholarship, developing slowly in the 1950s and '60s but growing in profusion in the following thirty years, which established Atlantic slavery as a major historical concern for anyone interested in the history of the West since, say, the sixteenth century. Much of the impetus for that intellectual change came from the USA, where the scholarship of slavery had a long and distinguished pedigree. In addition, the political upheavals of the 1960s served to generate growing and often acrimonious interest in the role of slavery in the shaping of the USA.

At much the same time, the face of Britain had changed fundamentally. British life, especially its major urban centres, had been transformed, most markedly by the process of post-war immigration. There were, quite simply, huge numbers of younger Britons, born to immigrant parents, for whom the slave trade had a deeply troubling personal, family resonance. Here was one of those historical subjects – apparently dead and gone – which had a painful *relevance* for large numbers of people, many of whom were already searching for an explanation of their own historical identities. Much of what they had learned in school, and much of what they heard in the wider cultural debate in Britain, simply did not speak to or reflect their own experience. Their historical roots lay elsewhere. For many people, but above all those of Caribbean descent, those roots were to be found in the history of Atlantic slavery and the slave trade.

For large numbers of black Britons, the real story of 2007 was not about abolition but about what had happened *before* abolition: the cruel and distressing story of the Atlantic slave trade itself. Indeed, there was an underlying rumble of complaint – expressed in scholarly and community circles – that the elaborate abolitionist commemorations in 2007 were little more than a smokescreen which hid a history of brutal exploitation. In the event, the most fruitful discussions in that year – in exhibitions, publications and broad cultural debate – tried to confront that issue head-on. How could you possibly consider the abolition of the slave trade without addressing the slave trade itself? It was important to remember that, for a century and a half before the Abolition Act of 1807, Parliament had passed dozens of Acts helping and encouraging the Atlantic slave trade. Thus 2007 saw a rolling national debate which quickly moved beyond abolition in 1807 to embrace a wider study of British history itself. It became clearer, to ever more people as the year and the commemorations progressed, that Atlantic slavery, with all its complex ramifications for Africa, the Americas and Europe, was a seminal force in shaping the world as we knew it. This book has tried to confirm that simple fact.

References

Introduction

1 For a criticism of the idea of Atlantic history, see J. H. Elliott, *History in the Making* (London and New Haven, CT, 2012), pp. 203–08.

1 Africa and Africans

1 For the details of Jacques Francis, see Gustav Ungerer, *The Mediterranean Apprenticeship of British Slavery* (Madrid, 2008); 'Recovering a Black African's Voice in an English Lawsuit', *Medieval and Renaissance Drama in England*, 17 (2005).
2 Natalie Zemon Davis, *Trickster Travels: In Search of Leo Africanus, A Sixteenth-century Muslim between Two Worlds* (London, 2007), p. 4.
3 Philip Curtin, *The Image of Africa* (Madison, WI, 1964), pp. 10–11.
4 G. V. Scammell, *The First Imperial Age: European Overseas Expansion, c. 1400–1715* (London, 1992), pp. 54–6.
5 J. H. Parry, *The Discovery of the Sea* (London, 1974), pp. 24–6.
6 Ibid., chap. 6.
7 Ibid., p. 42.
8 E.G.R. Taylor, *The Haven-finding Art: A History of Navigation from Odysseus to Captain Cook* (London, 1956), pp. 156–61; C. R. Boxer, *The Portuguese Seaborne Empire* (London, 1969), pp. 27–8.
9 David E. Waters, *The Art of Navigation in England in Elizabethan and Early Stuart Times* (London, 1958), pp. 11–15.
10 J. H. Parry, *The European Reconnaissance* (New York, 1968), pp. 323–7.
11 Boxer, *The Portuguese Seaborne Empire*, pp. 27–8.
12 Peter Russell, *Prince Henry 'The Navigator': A Life* (New Haven, CT, 2001), p. 297.
13 My italics. *The Journal of a Slave Trader (John Newton, 1750–1754)*, ed. Bernard Martin and Mark Spurrell (London, 1962), 13, 16 and 19 October 1750, pp. 10–11.

14 Hugh Thomas, *The Slave Trade: The History of the Atlantic Slave Trade, 1440–1870* (London, 1997), pp. 64–7.

15 Boxer, *The Portuguese Seaborne Empire*, pp. 20–23.

16 Annemarie Jordan, 'Images of Empire: Slaves in the Lisbon Household and Court of Catherine of Austria', in *Black Africans in Renaissance Europe*, ed. T. F. Earle and K.J.P. Lowe (Cambridge, 2005), chap. 7.

17 See 'Northern Africa in a Wider World', in Philip Curtin, Steven Feierman, Leonard Thompson and Jan Vansina, *African History* (Harlow, 1978), chap. 2.

18 John Iliffe, *Africans: The History of a Continent* (Cambridge, 1995), p. 42.

19 Fernand Braudel, *The Mediterranean and the Mediterranean World in the Age of Philip II* (Berkeley, CA and London, 1992), vol. I, pp. 466–8.

20 Ibid., p. 469.

21 David Abulafia, *The Discovery of Mankind: Atlantic Encounters in the Age of Columbus* (New Haven, CT, 2008), pp. 65–8.

22 Boxer, *The Portuguese Seaborne Empire*, p. 24.

23 Elizabeth Donnan, *Documents Illustrative of the History of the Slave Trade to America* (Washington, DC, 1965), vol. I: *1441–1700*, p. 3.

24 Donnan, *Documents Illustrative*, p. 32, n. 26.

25 James Walvin, *Atlas of Slavery* (London, 2006), p. 23.

26 Curtin et al., *African History*, p. 108.

27 John Reader, *Africa: A Biography of a Continent* (London, 1998), p. 284.

28 Iliffe, *Africans*, pp. 129–30.

29 Sidney Mintz, *Sweetness and Power: The Place of Sugar in Modern History* (London, 1985).

30 Robert Harmes, *The Diligent: A Voyage through the Worlds of the Slave Trade* (Oxford, 2002), p. 286.

31 Walvin, *Atlas of Slavery*, chap. 6; David Eltis and David Richardson, *Atlas of the Transatlantic Slave Trade* (New Haven, CT, 2010), p. 7.

2 Slave Trading on the Coast

1 David Abulafia, *The Discovery of Mankind: Atlantic Encounters in the Age of Columbus* (New Haven, CT, 2008), pp. 92–3.

2 William St Clair, *The Grand Slave Emporium: Cape Coast Castle and the British Slave Trade* (London 2006), pp. 11–12.

3 Quoted in William D. Phillips, Jr, *Slavery from Roman Times to the Early Transatlantic Slave Trade* (Manchester, 1985), p. 139.

4 Emma Christopher, *A Merciless Place: The Lost Story of Britain's Convict Disaster in Africa* (Oxford, 2010), p. 101.

5 J. H. Parry, *The Discovery of the Sea* (London, 1974), chap. 6.

6 For the development of Elmina, see A. W. Lawrence, *Fortified Trade-posts: The English in West Africa, 1645–1822* (London, 1969), pp. 97–107.

7 K. G. Davies, *The Royal African Company* (New York, 1970), p. 7.

8 Lawrence, *Fortified Trade-posts*, chap. 2.

9 'Bunce Island', Embarkation Ports, in *The Trans-Atlantic Slave Trade Database*. Hereafter, TSTD. See www.slavevoyages.org.

10 St Clair, *The Grand Slave Emporium*.

11 James Walvin, *The Zong: A Massacre, the Law and the End of Slavery* (New Haven, CT, 2011), pp. 80–81; 'Anomabu', Embarkation Ports, TSTD.

12 James Walvin, *Atlas of Slavery* (London, 2006), Map 23, p. 40; St Clair, *The Grand Slave Emporium*, p. 1.

13 Christopher, *A Merciless Place*, pp. 98–9.

14 Joseph Miller, *Way of Death: Merchant Capitalism and the Angolan Slave Trade, 1730–1830* (Madison, WI, 1988), pp. 16–17 and chap. 9.

15 Miller, *Way of Death*, pp. 390–91.

16 Robin Law, *Ouidah: The Social History of a West African Slaving 'Port', 1727–1892* (London, 2004), chap. 4.

17 Embarkation Ports, TSTD.

18 Embarkation Ports, TSTD.

19 'Lagos', Embarkation Ports, TSTD.

3 Ships, Cargoes and Sailors

1 'Introduction', in *Extending the Frontiers: Essays on the New Trans-Atlantic Slave Trade Database*, ed. David Eltis and David Richardson (New Haven, CT, 2008).

2 Antonio de Almeida Mendes, 'A Reassessment of the Slave Trade to the Spanish Americas', in *Extending the Frontiers*, ed. Eltis and Richardson, chap. 2.

3 David Eltis and David Richardson, *Atlas of the Transatlantic Slave Trade* (New Haven, CT, 2010), Table 2, p. 23.

4 Alexandre Vieira Riberio, 'The Transatlantic Slave Trade to Bahia', in *Extending the Frontiers*, ed. Eltis and Richardson, chap. 4.

5 Jelmer Vos, David Eltis and David Richardson, 'The Dutch in the Atlantic World', in *Extending the Frontiers*, ed. Eltis and Richardson, chap. 8.

6 Nuala Zahedieh, *The Capital and the Colonies: London and the Atlantic Economy, 1660–1700* (Cambridge, 2010), p. 212.

7 Eltis and Richardson, *Atlas*, Map 18, p. 32.

8 Ibid., Table 3, p. 30.

9 For an important discussion, see Marcus Wood, *Blind Memory: Visual Representations of Slavery in England and America, 1780–1865* (Manchester, 2000), pp. 25–9.

10 Dolben's Act of 1788 restricted the numbers of slaves carried to five slaves for every 3 tons up to 200 tons and one slave per ton above that figure. Marcus Rediker, *The Slave Ship: A Human History* (London 2007), p. 337.

11 *The Brookes*, 'List of Voyages, 1780–1799', in *The Trans-Atlantic Slave Trade Database*. Hereafter TSTD. See www.slavevoyages.org.

12 M. K. Stammers, '"Guineamen": Some Technical Aspects of Slave Ships', in *TransAtlantic Slaver: Against Human Dignity*, ed. Anthony Tibbles (London 1994), pp. 35–40.

13 Stammers, '"Guineamen"', p. 39.

14 James Walvin, *The Zong: A Massacre, the Law and the End of Slavery* (New Haven, CT, 2011), pp. 23–4.

15 Johannes Postma, *The Dutch in the Atlantic Slave Trade, 1600–1815* (Cambridge, 1990), chap. 6.

16 Stammers, '"*Guineamen*"', p. 40.

17 The *Parr*, 'Voyage Number 83006', 1798, TSTD.

18 Herbert S. Klein, *The Atlantic Slave Trade* (Cambridge, 1999), pp. 134–5.

19 Ibid., pp. 132–4.

20 Postma, *The Dutch in the Atlantic Slave Trade*, p. 144.

21 Eltis and Richardson, *Atlas*, Map 117, p. 169.

22 Ibid., Map 116, p. 167.

23 Ibid., Map 118, p. 170.

24 Ibid., Map 117, p. 169.

25 Ibid., Map 122, p. 179.

26 Ibid., Maps 127–30, pp. 184–7.

27 Walvin, *The Zong*, 2011, chap. 10.

28 Eltis and Richardson, *Atlas*, Maps 129–30, pp. 186–7.

29 Thomas Clarkson, *An Essay on the Impolicy of the Slave Trade . . .* (London, 1788), p. 53.

30 Walvin, *The Zong*, p. 88, n. 26; N.A.M. Rodger, *The Command of the Sea: A Naval History of Britain* (London, 2004), Appendix VI.

31 Eltis and Richardson, *Atlas*, p. 37.

32 Ibid., Map 37, p. 65.

33 Rediker, *The Slave Ship*, pp. 225–7.

34 Ibid., chap. 8; Emma Christopher, *Slave Ship Sailors and Their Captive Cargoes, 1730–1807* (Cambridge, 2006), pp. 54–5.

35 W. Jeffrey Bolster, *Black Jacks: African-American Seamen in the Age of Sail* (Cambridge, MA, 1997).

36 Vincent Carretta, *Equiano the African: The Biography of a Self-made*

Man (Athens, GA, 2005); Christopher, *Slave Ship Sailors*, pp. 55–6.

37 Klein, *The Atlantic Slave Trade*, pp. 85–6.

38 Rediker, *The Slave Ship*, pp. 224–5.

39 Klein, *The Atlantic Slave Trade*, p. 83.

40 Linda A. Newson and Susie Minchin, *From Capture to Sale: The Portuguese Slave Trade to Spanish America in the Early Seventeenth Century* (Leiden, 2007), Appendices A, B, C.

41 Nuala Zahedieh, *The Capital and the Colonies*, pp. 247–8.

42 Zahedieh, *The Capital and the Colonies*, Table 6.2, p. 249.

43 Klein, *The Atlantic Slave Trade*, pp. 86–9; Eltis and Richardson, *Atlas*, Maps 38–41, pp. 66–70.

44 Melinda Elder, 'The Liverpool Slave Trade, Lancaster and its Environs', and Jane Longmore, 'Cemented by the Blood of a Negro? The Impact of the Slave Trade on Eighteenth-century Liverpool', in *Liverpool and Transatlantic Slavery*, ed. David Richardson, Suzanne Schwarz and Anthony Tibbles (Liverpool, 2007), chap. 8.

4 The Sea

1 *The Journal of a Slave Trader (John Newton, 1750–1754)*, ed. Bernard Martin and Mark Spurrell (London, 1962), pp. 3–62; The *Argyle*, 'Voyage Number 90350', 1781, *The Trans-Atlantic Slave Trade Database*. Hereafter, TSTD. See www.slavevoyages.org.

2 Johannes Postma, *The Dutch in the Atlantic Slave Trade, 1600–1815* (Cambridge, 1990), pp. 159–60.

3 Postma, *The Dutch in the Atlantic Slave Trade*, pp. 160–62; Herbert S. Klein, *The Atlantic Slave Trade* (Cambridge, 1999), pp. 91–2.

4 Postma, *The Dutch in the Atlantic Slave Trade*, pp. 161–2.

5 James Walvin, *The Zong: A Massacre, the Law and the End of Slavery* (New Haven, CT, 2011).

6 All from *The Journal of a Slave Trader (J. Newton)*, pp. 26–46.

7 David Eltis and David Richardson, *Atlas of the Transatlantic Slave Trade* (New Haven, CT, 2010), pp. 159–60.

8 Quoted in Walvin, *The Zong*, p. 93.

9 Eltis and Richardson, *Atlas*, p. 160.

10 Ibid., Map 117, p. 167.

11 Ibid., Map 118, p. 170.

12 Ibid., Map 122, p. 179.

13 Ibid., Maps 123, 129, 139, pp. 180–87. See also Walvin, *The Zong*, chap. 10.

14 *The Journal of a Slave Trader (J. Newton)*, Thursday 1 November 1750, Thursday 14 December 1752, pp. 14, 72.

15 Edward Long, *The History of Jamaica* (London, 1774), vol. III, p. 899.

16 Alfred W. Crosby, *Ecological Imperialism: The Biological Expansion of Europe, 900–1900* (Cambridge, 1986), pp. 190–92.

17 N.A.M. Rodger, *The Command of the Sea: A Naval History of Britain* (London, 2004), p. 402; *The Journal of a Slave Trader (John Newton)*, Wednesday 15 May 1751, p. 52.

18 Quoted in Marcus Rediker, *The Slave Ship: A Human History* (London 2007), p. 69.

19 Walvin, *The Zong*.

20 Thomas Fowell Buxton, *The African Slave Trade* (London, 1839), p. 143.

21 Postma, *The Dutch in the Atlantic Slave Trade*, p. 164.

22 Buxton, *The African Slave Trade*, pp. 138–43.

23 'Piracy' in *Glossary*, TSTD.

5 Mutinies and Revolts

1 John Newton, *Thoughts upon The African Slave Trade* (London, 1788), p. 10.

2 Carl Bernhard Wadstrom, *An Essay on Colonisation . . .* (London, 1794), pp. 85–6.

3 Emma Christopher, *Slave Ship Sailors and Their Captive Cargoes, 1730–1807* (Cambridge, 2006), p. 183.

4 Thomas Clarkson, *The History of the Rise, Progress, and Accomplishment of the Abolition of the African Slave Trade by the British Parliament* (London, 1808), vol. II, p. 377.

5 Eric Robert Taylor, *If We Must Die: Shipboard Insurrections in the Era of the Atlantic Slave Trade* (Baton Rouge, LA, 2006), p. 9. See also the *Scipio*, 'Voyage 90227', 1749, *The Trans-Atlantic Slave Trade Database*. Hereafter, TSTD. See www.slavevoyages.org.

6 Winston McGowan, 'African Resistance to the Atlantic Slave Trade in West Africa', *Slavery and Abolition*, XI/1 (May 1990).

7 Richard Rathbone, 'Some Thoughts on Resistance to Enslavement in Africa', in *Out of the House of Bondage*, ed. Gad Heuman (London, 1986), pp. 14–15.

8 Quoted in Marcus Rediker, *The Slave Ship: A Human History* (London 2007), p. 18.

9 Ibid., pp. 288–91.

10 David Eltis and David Richardson, *Atlas of the Transatlantic Slave Trade* (New Haven, CT, 2010), Maps 131–2, pp. 189–90.

11 John Atkins, *A Voyage to Guinea, Brazil and the West Indies* (London, 1737), p. 115.

12 Taylor, *If We Must Die*, p. 133.

13 Joseph Miller, *Way of Death: Merchant Capitalism and the Angolan*

Slave Trade, 1730–1830 (Madison, WI, 1988), p. 410.

14 Johannes Postma, *The Dutch in the Atlantic Slave Trade, 1600–1815* (Cambridge, 1990), pp. 165–8.

15 Rediker, *The Slave Ship*, p. 294.

16 Alexander Falconbridge, *An Account of the Slave Trade on the Coast of Africa* (London, 1788), p. 54.

17 Rediker, *The Slave Ship*, pp. 294–5.

18 Ibid., pp. 293–6.

19 Taylor, *If We Must Die*, pp. 58–9.

20 James Walvin, *Black Ivory: A History of British Slavery* (Oxford, 2001), p. 30.

21 *The Journal of a Slave Trader (John Newton, 1750–1754)*, ed. Bernard Martin and Mark Spurrell (London, 1962), 11 December 1752, p. 71.

22 Ibid., 28 May 1751, p. 55.

23 Taylor, *If We Must Die*, pp. 45, 205.

24 Ibid., p. 47.

25 Ibid., pp. 47–8.

26 Ibid., pp. 49–50.

27 William Snelgrave, *A New Account of Some Parts of Guinea and the Slave Trade* (London 1734), pp. 189–90.

28 Taylor, *If We Must Die*, pp. 95–6.

29 Ibid., pp. 101–03.

30 Snelgrave, *A New Account*, pp. 183–4.

31 Quoted in Taylor, *If We Must Die*, p. 112.

32 Quoted in Robert Harmes, *The Diligent: A Voyage through the Worlds of the Slave Trade* (Oxford, 2002), p. 272.

33 Taylor, *If We Must Die*, p. 114.

34 James Walvin, *The Zong: A Massacre, the Law and the End of Slavery* (New Haven, CT, 2011), pp. 111–12.

35 Ibid. pp. 112–15.

36 John Wesket, *A Complete Digest of the Theory, Laws and Practice of Insurance* (London 1781), p. 525.

37 Harmes, *The Diligent*, pp. 83–4.

38 Taylor, *If We Must Die*, pp. 104–05.

39 Ibid., pp. 128–9.

6 Landfall

1 *The Journal of a Slave Trader (John Newton, 1750–1754)*, ed. Bernard Martin and Mark Spurrell (London, 1962), 23–4 May 1753, p. 80.

2 Alexander Falconbridge, *An Account of the Slave Trade on the Coast of Africa* (London, 1788), pp. 43–4.

3 Richard Ligon, *A True and Exact History of the Island of Barbadoes*

(1673), p. 46.

4 David Eltis and David Richardson, *Atlas of the Transatlantic Slave Trade* (New Haven, CT, 2010), Table 7, p. 204.

5 J. H. Elliott, *Empire of the Atlantic World: Britain and Spain in America 1492–1830* (London, 2006), pp. 100–01.

6 Eltis and Richardson, *Atlas*, Table 6, pp. 201–03.

7 Ibid., Map 155, p. 235.

8 Ibid., Table 6, p. 201.

9 Ibid., Table 6, p. 202.

10 Ibid., Table 6, p. 203.

11 Ibid., Table 6, p. 200.

12 Gregory E. O'Malley, 'Slave Trading Entrepôts and their Hinterlands', in *Ambiguous Anniversary: The Bicentennial of the International Slave Trade Bans*, ed. David T. Gleeson and Simon Lewis (Columbia, SC, 2012).

13 Ibid., pp. 105, 112.

14 Ibid., p. 116.

15 Eltis and Richardson, *Atlas*, Maps 141–4, pp. 212–16.

16 David Eltis and Paul Lachance, 'The Demographic Decline of Caribbean Slave Populations', in *Extending the Frontiers: Essays on the New Transatlantic Slave Trade Database*, ed. David Eltis and David Richardson (New Haven, CT, 2006), chap. 12, p. 349.

17 Joseph Miller, *Way of Death: Merchant Capitalism and the Angola Slave Trade, 1730–1830* (Madison, WI, 1988), pp. 437–8.

18 Michael Craton and James Walvin, *A Jamaican Plantation: Worthy Park, 1670–1970* (London, 1970), p. 131.

19 Richard Sheridan, *Doctors and Slaves: A Medical and Demographic History of Slavery in the British West Indies 1680–1843* (Cambridge, 1985), p. 132.

20 Vincent Brown, *The Reaper's Garden: Death and Power in the World of Atlantic Slavery* (Cambridge, MA, 2008), pp. 49–50.

21 Slave sale advertisement, Charleston, 1760, in Eltis and Richardson, *Atlas*, p. 217.

22 Slave advertisements, in James Walvin, *The Black Presence: A Documentary History of the Negro in England* (London, 1971), p. 80.

23 Advertisements in *Slavery, Abolition and Emancipation: Black Slaves and the British Empire*, ed. Michael Craton, James Walvin and David Wright (London, 1976), p. 136.

24 Brown, *The Reaper's Garden*, p. 51.

25 Sheridan, *Doctors and Slaves*, p. 134.

26 Miller, *Way of Death*.

7 Resistance

1 On the history of the maroons, see Richard Price, *Rebel Slave Communities in the Americas* (Baltimore, MD, 1996); Michael Craton, *Testing the Chains: Resistance to Slavery in the British West Indies* (Ithaca, NY, 2009); Gad Heuman, ed., *Out of the House of Bondage: Runaways, Resistance and Marronage in Africa and the New World* (London 1986).

2 David Geggus, 'Slave Rebellion during the Age of Revolution', in *Curaçao in the Age of Revolution, 1795–1800*, ed. Wim Klooster and Gert Oostinie (Leiden, 2011), p. 23.

3 James Walvin, *Atlas of Slavery* (London, 2006), chap. 17.

4 Douglas R. Egerton, 'Slave Resistance', in *The Oxford Handbook of Slavery in the Americas*, ed. Robert L. Paquette and Mark M. Smith (Oxford, 2010), chap. 20.

5 Geggus, 'Slave Rebellion', pp. 25, 42, 44.

6 Egerton, 'Slave Resistance', pp. 452–5.

7 Geggus, 'Slave Rebellion', p. 25.

8 Letter, 21 June 1760, in *Du Simitière Papers*, Historical Society of Pennsylvania, PA.

9 Craton, *Testing the Chains*, chap. 10.

10 Ibid., chap. 11, p. 125.

11 Geggus, 'Slave Rebellion', pp. 23, 25.

12 Cassandra Pybus, *Epic Journeys of Freedom* (Boston, MA, 2006); Simon Schama, *Rough Crossings: Britain, the Slaves and the American Revolution* (London, 2005).

13 David Eltis and David Richardson, *Atlas of the Transatlantic Slave Trade* (New Haven, CT, 2010), Table 6, p. 202.

14 There is a rich recent literature on the Haitian revolt, but see in particular David Geggus, *Slavery, War and Revolution* (Oxford, 1982); David Geggus and Norman Fiering, eds, *The World of the Haitian Revolution* (Bloomington, IN, 2009); Laurent Dubois, *A Colony of Citizens: Revolution and Slave Emancipation in the French Caribbean* (Chapel Hill, NC, 2004).

15 Gert Oostinie, 'Slave Resistance, Colour Lines, and the Impact of the French and Haitian Revolutions in Curaçao' in *Curaçao*, ed. Klooster and Oostinie, chap. 1.

16 Craton, *Testing the Chains*, chap. 10.

17 Kit Candlin, *The Last Caribbean Frontier, 1795–1815* (London 2012), chap. 1.

18 The *Código Negro* was drafted by Charles II in 1783–4 and was based on the earlier French *Code Noire* (laws governing slavery) of 1685.

19 Christopher Schmidt-Nowara, 'Emancipation', and Peter Blanchard,

'Spanish South American Mainland', in *Oxford Handbook of Slavery*, ed. Paquette and Smith, chap. 26, pp. 584–5, and chap. 3, pp. 80–84.

20 Michael Craton, *Testing the Chains*, pp. 264–6.

21 Craton, *Testing the Chains*, chap. 21; Emelia da Costa, *Crowns of Glory, Tears of Blood: The Demerara Slave Rebellion of 1823* (Oxford, 1994).

22 Eltis and Richardson, *Atlas*, Table 6, p. 203.

23 Stuart B. Schwartz, *Sugar Plantations in the Formation of Brazilian Society: Bahia, 1550–1835* (Cambridge, 1985), chap. 17.

24 All details from Eltis and Richardson, *Atlas*, Maps 170, 171–3.

25 Robert E. Slenes, 'Brazil', in *Oxford Handbook of Slavery*, ed. Paquette and Smith, chap. 5, p. 123.

26 Schwartz, *Sugar Plantations*, p. 487.

27 Joao Jose Reis, *Slave Rebellion in Brazil* (Baltimore, MD, and London, 1993).

8 Chasing the Slave Ships: Abolition and After

1 *Slavery in Diplomacy: The Foreign Office and the Suppression of the Transatlantic Slave Trade*, Foreign and Commonwealth Office, Historians History Note, No. 17 (London, 2007), p. 12.

2 James Walvin, *The Zong: A Massacre, the Law and the End of Slavery* (New Haven, CT, 2011), chap. 9.

3 Ottobah Cugoano, *Thoughts and Sentiments on the Evil of Slavery* (London, 1787), pp. 111–12.

4 Thomas Clarkson, *The History of the Rise, Progress, and Accomplishment of the Abolition of the African Slave Trade by the British Parliament* (London, 1808), vol. I, p. 207.

5 Maurice Jackson, *Let This Voice Be Heard: Anthony Benezet, Father of Atlantic Abolition* (Philadelphia, PA, 2009), chap. 4: p. 160.

6 Thomas Clarkson, *History of the Rise . . .*, vol. I, chap. XVII.

7 Thomas Clarkson, *An Essay on the Impolicy of the Slave Trade . . .* (London, 1788), p. 52.

8 Stephen D. Behrendt, 'Crew Mortality in the Transatlantic Slave Trade in the Eighteenth Century', *Slavery and Abolition*, XVIII/1 (April 1997).

9 James Walvin, *The Quakers: Money and Morals* (London, 1997); Thomas Clarkson, *Portraiture of Quakerism* (New York, 1806), I, p. i; II, p. 51.

10 For the most recent account of British abolition, see Seymour Drescher, *Abolition: A History of Slavery and Antislavery* (Cambridge, 2009).

11 Anonymous letter, 18 November 1791, in C.O.137/89, TNA.

12 Quoted in Judith Jennings, *The Business of Abolishing the British Slave Trade, 1783–1807* (London, 1997), p. 89.

13 *Declaration of the Objects of the Liverpool Society for Promoting the Abolition of Slavery* (Liverpool, 1823), p. 5.

14 B. W. Higman, *Slave Populations of the British Caribbean, 1807–1834* (Baltimore, MD, 1984).

15 David Eltis and David Richardson, *Atlas of the Transatlantic Slave Trade* (New Haven, CT, 2010), part VI, pp. 271–3.

16 Ibid., pp. 271–2.

17 *Foreign Slave Trade: Abstract of Information* (London, 1821), in American Tracts, 1849 (2001), Beinecke Library.

18 Silvia Scarpa, *Trafficking in Human Beings: Modern Slavery* (Oxford, 2008), p. 43.

19 *Slavery in Diplomacy*, p. 1.

20 Ibid., pp. 6–9.

21 Ibid., p. 10.

22 '31st Congress, 2nd Session [Senate] Executive Document No. 6', Slavery Pamphlets (20), p. 4, Beinecke Library.

23 *A View of the Present State of the African Slave Trade* (Philadelphia, PA, 1824), pp. 55, 58–9; *Extracts from the 18th and 19th Report of the Directors of the African Institution, 1824–1825* (Philadelphia, PA, 1826), p. 22. American Tracts (1826), Beinecke Library.

24 '31st Congress, 2nd Session [Senate] Executive Document No. 6', *'Message of the President of the United States'*, 17/18 December 1850, pp. 3–6, Slavery Pamphlets (20), Beinecke Library.

25 *A View of the Present State of the African Slave Trade* (Philadelphia, PA, 1824), pp. 59–61; *Foreign Slave Trade: Abstract of Information* (London, 1821), p. 37, Slavery Pamphlets (1826), Beinecke Library.

26 *Slavery in Diplomacy*, p. 12.

27 Walvin, *The Zong*, pp. 200–201.

28 *Extracts from the 18th and 19th Reports. . .* p. 33.

29 Details of the *Rodeur* case can be found in *Foreign Slave Trade: An Abstract . . .*, pp. 82–7.

30 *Senate No. 35, Report and Resolves on the Subject of the Foreign Slave Trade*, 7 February 1839, p. 7, Slavery Pamphlets (20); *Extracts from the 18th and 19th Reports . . .*, p. 33.

31 R. R. Madden, *A Letter to W. E. Channing* (Boston, MA, 1839), p. 6.

32 *Senate No. 35, Report and Resolves . . .*, pp. 5–6, Slavery Pamphlets (20).

33 *Extracts from the 18th and 19th Reports . . .*, 1824 (Philadelphia, PA, 1826), p. 22, American Tracts (26).

34 Ibid., pp. 8–9, American Tracts (26).

35 *Foreign Slave Trade: An Abstract of the Information . . .* (London, 1821), p. 14.

36 Ibid., pp. 15–17.

37 *Message from the President of the* U.S., *December 17/18, 1850, 30th Congress, 1st Session [Senate] Executive*, No. 38, pp. 35–40, Slavery Pamphlets (20), Beinecke Library.

38 *Message from the President of the U.S., 30th Congress, 1st Session [Senate] Executive*, No. 28, p. 35, Slavery Pamphlets (20), Beinecke Library.

39 Letter, 30 December 1822, *Clarkson Manuscripts* (MY 52), Huntington Library.

40 Eltis and Richardson, *Atlas*, Maps 187–8, p. 287.

41 *Slavery in Diplomacy*, p. 17.

42 Eltis and Richardson, *Atlas*, p. 272.

43 *Slavery in Diplomacy*, p. 19.

44 Ibid., pp. 19–20.

45 Eltis and Richardson, *Atlas*, p. 273.

46 Ibid., p. 274.

47 *The 13th Annual Report of the British and Foreign Anti-Slavery Society* (London, 1852), pp. 5–6, 12, Slavery Pamphlets (53), Beinecke Library.

48 Madden, *A Letter to W. E. Channing*, p. 5.

49 Richard Huzzey, *Freedom Burning: Anti-slavery and Empire in Victorian Britain* (Ithaca, NY, 2012), pp. 56–7.

50 *Slavery in Diplomacy*, pp. 20–21.

51 *Diplomacy in History*, pp. 26–7.

52 Robin Law, 'Abolition and Imperialism', in *Abolitionism and Imperialism in Britain, Africa, and the Atlantic*, ed. Derek R. Peterson (Cambridge, 2010), p. 150; Huzzey, *Freedom Burning*, chap. 6.

53 Law, 'Abolition and Imperialism', pp. 153–5, 159–64.

54 Ibid., pp. 166–8.

55 Seymour Drescher, 'Emperors of the World', in *Abolition and Imperialism*, ed. Derek R. Peterson, chap. 5, pp. 140–41.

56 Memorandum by W. H. Wylde, Foreign Office, 10 July 1866, F.O. 84/1270, in *Slavery in Diplomacy*, pp. 159–62.

57 *Slavery in Diplomacy*, p. v; Eltis and Richardson, *Atlas*, pp. 272–3.

58 Eltis and Richardson, *Atlas*, Map 186, pp. 284–5.

59 Ibid., p. 272.

60 *Message from the President of the U.S.*, p. 35, Slavery Pamphlets, (20), Beinecke Library.

61 Drescher, 'Emperors of the World', p. 146.

9 The Durable Institution: Slavery after Abolition

1 Kit Candlin, *The Last Caribbean Frontier, 1795–1815* (Cambridge, 2012).

2 David Eltis and David Richardson, *Atlas of the Transatlantic Slave Trade* (New Haven, CT, 2010), Table 6, p. 201.

3 Ibid., Map 144, p. 216.

4 Quoted in James Walvin, *A Short History of Slavery* (London, 2007), p. 192.

5 Nicholas Draper, *The Price of Emancipation: Slave-ownership, Compensation and British Society at the End of Slavery* (Cambridge, 2010).

6 James Walvin, *Atlas of Slavery* (London, 2006), chap. 16.

7 Eric Foner, *Give Me Liberty! An American History* (New York, 2005), p. 317.

8 Walvin, *Atlas of Slavery*, pp. 112–13.

9 James Walvin, *The Slave Trade* (London, 2011), p. 78.

10 Foner, *Give Me Liberty!*, p. 411.

11 Larry E. Tise, *Proslavery: A History of the Defense of Slavery in America, 1701–1840* (Athens, GA, 1987).

12 Eltis and Richardson, *Atlas*, Maps 44 and 45, pp. 73, 75.

13 Matt Childs and Manuel Barcia, 'Cuba', *The Oxford Handbook of Slavery in the Americas* (Oxford, 2010), ed. Robert L. Pacquette and Mark M. Smith, chap. 4.

14 Eltis and Richardson, *Atlas*, Map 150, pp. 228–9.

15 Ibid., Map 151, pp. 230–38.

16 Seymour Drescher, *Abolition: A History of Slavery and Antislavery* (Cambridge, 2009), pp. 283–4.

17 David Eltis, *Economic Growth and the Ending of the Transatlantic Slave Trade* (Oxford, 1987), p. 263, Table c2.

18 Drescher, *Abolition*, p. 285.

19 Childs and Barcia, 'Cuba', pp. 102–6.

20 Data from *The Trans-Atlantic Slave Trade Database*. Hereafter, TSTD. See www.slavevoyages.org.

21 William Hawthorne, *From Africa to Brazil: Culture, Identity and the Atlantic Slave Trade, 1600–1830* (Cambridge, 2010).

22 Eltis and Richardson, *Atlas*, Maps 38–40, pp. 66–9.

23 Ibid., Maps 48–50, pp. 80–83.

24 Ibid., Map 50, p. 83.

25 Table, 'Average Middle Passage Days', TSTD.

26 Eltis and Richardson, *Atlas*, Map 173, p. 261.

27 Adrian Desmond and James Moore, *Darwin's Sacred Cause: Race, Slavery and the Quest for Human Origins* (London, 2009), chap. 4.

28 Eltis, *Economic Growth*, Appendix F., pp. 284–6.

29 Ibid., pp. 195–6.
30 Steven Topik, *The World Coffee Market in the Eighteenth And Nineteenth Centuries: From Colonial To National Regimes*, Working Paper No. 04/04, Department of History, University of California, Irvine, May 2004.
31 Drescher, *Abolition*, pp. 350–54.
32 Ibid., pp. 356–71.

10 Then and Now: Slavery and the Modern World

1 For the cultural ties between Angola and Brazil, see Roquinaldo Ferreira, *Cross-cultural Exchange in the Atlantic World* (Cambridge, 2012).
2 Philip D. Morgan, 'The Poor: Slaves in Early America', in David Eltis, Frank D. Lewis and Kenneth L. Sokoloff, *Slavery in the Development of the Americas* (Cambridge, 2004).
3 Silvia Scarpa, *Trafficking in Human Beings: Modern Slavery* (Oxford, 2008), p. 44.
4 Michael N. Barnett, *Empire of Humanity: A History of Humanitarianism* (Ithaca, NY, 2011).
5 Scarpa, *Trafficking*, pp. 48–60.
6 Anne Applebaum, *The Gulag: A History of the Soviet Camps* (London, 2003).
7 James Walvin, *Atlas of Slavery* (London, 2006), Maps 85–6, pp. 133–4.
8 Applebaum, *Gulag*, pp. 515–16.
9 Seymour Drescher, *Abolition: A History of Slavery and Antislavery* (Cambridge, 2009), p. 424.
10 Lizzie Collingham, *The Taste of War: World War Two and the Battle for Food* (London, 2012), p. 41.
11 Drescher, *Abolition*, p. 431.
12 Walvin, *Atlas of Slavery*, p. 132.
13 Ian Kershaw, *The End: Hitler's Germany, 1944–1945* (London, 2012).
14 Tony Judt, *Postwar: A History of Europe Since 1945* (London, 2007), p. 53.
15 Scarpa, *Trafficking*, pp. 43–6.
16 Collingham, *The Taste of War*, p. 7.
17 Max Hastings, *All Hell Let Loose: The World at War, 1939–1945* (London, 2012), p. 496.
18 'What We Do', *Anti-Slavery International*, www.antislavery.org/English.
19 Scarpa, *Trafficking*, pp. 50–55, 68–73.
20 BBC News, 18 October 2012, www.bbc.co.uk/news.
21 'How an Ancient Evil Survives: A Special Report', *Newsweek* (4 May 1992), front cover, pp. 8–15.

22 Andrew Cockburn, '21st Century Slaves', *National Geographic* (September 2003), pp. 2–29.

23 BBC News, www.bbc.co.uk/news.

24 Melissa Hogenboom, 'A Tipping Print in the Fight Against Slavery', www.bbc.co.uk/Magazine

25 Gethin Chamberlain, 'India Targets the Traffickers who Sell Children into Slavery', BBC News, 18 October 2012, www.bbc.co.uk/news.

26 Scarpa, *Trafficking*, p. 81.

27 For a broader discussion about 2007 and its context, see the essays in 'Remembering Slave Trade Abolitions: Reflections on 2007 in International Perspectives', *Slavery and Abolition*, ed. Diana Paton and Jane Webster, XXX/2 (June 2009).

28 James Walvin, 'The Slave Trade, Abolition and Public Memory', *Transactions of the Royal Historical Society*, XIX Sixth Series, 2009, pp. 139–40.

29 Drescher, *Abolition*, p. 415.

30 *Bicentenary of the Abolition of the Slave Trade Act, 1807–2007* (HM Government, London, 2007).

31 Hansard, House of Commons Debate, 20 March 2007, column 77, www.publications. Parliament.uk.

32 Council of Europe Convention on Action against Trafficking in Human Beings (CETS) No. 197, www.conventions.coe.int. See also British Home Office, press release, 1 December 2008, *Reaching Out: An Action Plan on Social Inclusion*, Cabinet Office, September 2006.

33 Stephen Farrell, Melanie Unwin and James Walvin, eds, *The British Slave Trade: Abolition, Parliament and People*, Edinburgh University Press for The Parliamentary History Yearbook Trust (2007).

34 James Walvin, 'The Slave Trade, Abolition and Public Memory', *Transactions of the Royal Historical Society*, Sixth Series, XIX (Cambridge, 2009).

35 Among the many pamphlets published by local authorities see Kirklees Council, *The Abolition of the Slave Trade* (2007); City of Westminster, *Abolition of the Slave Trade: Events to Mark the Bicentenary of the 1807 Act of Parliament*, (2007); Birmingham City Council, *Connecting Histories* (2007).

36 'Abolition of the Slave Trade', www.royalmail.com, accessed 2007.

37 See www.bbc.co.uk/history/british/abolition, accessed 2013.

38 *In God's Name: The Role of the Church in the Transatlantic Slave Trade*, City Hall, London, August 2007.

39 John Charlton, *Hidden Chains: The Slavery Business and North East England, 1600–1865* (Newcastle, 2008).

40 'National Curriculum Links', www.understandingslavery.com, accessed 2013.

Acknowledgements

This book draws on my work on slavery over a number of years, but it has evolved directly from more recent research and public history. First, there was the bicentenary in 2007 of the abolition of the British slave trade in 1807. It was a year marked, in Britain, by a remarkable series of commemorations. The very public debate, conducted in an amazing variety of venues from crowded village halls to the Palace of Westminster, had a profound effect on the way I think about the subject I had worked on for years. In the course of 2007 I gave 89 different talks on the subject, at venues ranging from small village schools to major cultural institutions on both sides of the Atlantic. For the first time since my teens I kept a journal of my year, in the hope that, later, I might be able to capture the sense and feeling for what took place in 2007. There were times when those of us who had worked on the subject for years had to pinch ourselves: where had this massive, widespread interest in one small corner of the scholarship of slavery come from?

The commemorations of 2007 prompted a number of serious questions about British history, about slavery and the slave trade and, inevitably perhaps, about national identity in modern Britain. In the process, it became apparent that the study of Atlantic slavery had shifted from its formerly marginal position and now occupied a central role in the way historians, and a wider interested public, think about the British past. Forty years ago, when viewed from Britain, slavery had seemed distant and exotic – out of sight and generally out of mind (though it never felt that way when viewed from Africa or the Americas, of course). Today, in twenty-first-century Britain, few would challenge the view that slavery was a seminal experience in the shaping of the Western world.

My experiences that year, and my engagement with large numbers of people in what became, in effect, a rolling debate across the year, forced me to reconsider some of the issues I had long taken for granted. It was not so much that 2007 changed my mind about the slave trade, but that I came to think about it in a different light. In part, then, this book is a by-product of the events of that year.

Second, I have been very fortunate to spend extended periods between 2008 and 2012 at Yale University; what follows is very much a Yale book. I owe a number of personal and professional debts to friends and colleagues at Yale: first, for offering me access to that university's wonderful facilities, and second, for their friendship and support. The book was shaped by two study periods at Yale, initially as a Fellow in the Gilder Lehrman Center. There, Melissa McGrath, Dana Shaffer and Tom Thurston made my time comfortable and productive. David Blight, then and since, has proved himself not only a friend but a tower of intellectual generosity and support. I was able to trawl the treasures of Yale's Beinecke Library thanks to a library Fellowship. I am immensely grateful to the Librarian, Edwin Schroeder, and to his staff on the issue desk who helped me promptly and with remarkable good nature. My time at Yale was also greatly helped by the hospitality afforded at Calhoun College and by the welcome and assistance of Amy Hungerford, the acting Master. Others at Yale helped and encouraged in their own distinctive ways. Caryl Phillips and Hazel Carby, friends and supportive colleagues, encouraged and supported me throughout.

As will become clear from my footnotes, I am, like any other student of the slave trade, deeply indebted to the scholars, especially to David Eltis and David Richardson, who created the *Trans-Atlantic Slave Trade Database*. Similarly, the *Atlas of the Transatlantic Slave Trade* (Yale University Press, 2010) by Eltis and Richardson is a treasure trove which I have used with great profit.

Ben Hayes at Reaktion Books has proved an ideal editor to work with, and my agent Charles Walker was, as always, encouraging and supportive throughout. Jenny Walvin, more than anyone else, has made this book possible.

Finally, I have been greatly influenced by being a trustee of Anti-Slavery International. I am especially indebted to Andrew Clark, who was Chairman for most of that period, and to Aidan McQuade, the Director, for the congenial atmosphere they created at Anti-Slavery International but also, more important, for the patience and friendship they extended to me. More generally, their staff and associates at Thomas Clarkson House in Stockwell, and in many corners of the globe, work tirelessly in a continuing struggle against the varieties of slavery which continue to infest societies around the world. I dedicate this book to the people who make up Anti-Slavery International, both as a token of appreciation and a tribute to them, individually and collectively, for their work.

Photo Acknowledgements

The author and publishers wish to express their thanks to the below sources of illustrative material and/or permission to reproduce it. (Some locations uncredited in the captions for reasons of brevity are also given below.)

Beinecke Rare Book and Manuscript Library, Yale University, New Haven, Connecticut: pp. 8, 31, 42–3, 44, 46, 47, 50–51, 64, 85, 109, 142, 145, 156, 164; Library of Congress, Washington, DC (Prints and Photographs Division): pp. 61, 76, 102 (Rare Book and Special Collections Division), 116, 124, 131, 133, 214; Musées Royaux des Beaux-Arts de Belgique, Brussels: p. 25; from *Atlas of the Transatlantic Slave Trade* by David Eltis and David Richardson, © Yale University Press, New Haven, 2010: pp. 6–7.

Index